Warfare in Independent Africa

This book surveys the history of armed conflict in Africa in the period since decolonization and independence. The number of post-independence conflicts in Africa has been considerable, and this book introduces readers to a comprehensive analysis of their causes and character. Tracing the evolution of warfare from anti-colonial and anti-apartheid campaigns to complex conflicts in which factionalized armies, militias, and rebel groups fight with each other and prey on non-combatants, it allows the readers a new perspective to understand violence on the continent. The book is written to appeal not only to students of history and African politics, but also to experts in the policy community, the military, and humanitarian agencies.

William Reno is Associate Professor of Political Science at Northwestern University. He is the author of *Corruption and State Politics in Sierra Leone* (Cambridge, 1995) and *Warlord Politics and African States* (1998) and numerous other academic and policy publications about conflict in Africa. Professor Reno's research focuses on the politics of conflict in Africa.

D0145459

New Approaches to African History

Series Editor
Martin Klein, *University of Toronto*

Editorial Advisors
William Beinart, *University of Oxford*
Mamadou Diouf, *Columbia University*
William Freund, *University of KwaZulu-Natal*
Sandra E. Greene, *Cornell University*
Ray Kea, *University of California, Riverside*
David Newbury, *Smith College*

New Approaches to African History is designed to introduce students to current findings and new ideas in African history. Although each book treats a particular case and is able to stand alone, the format allows the studies to be used as modules in general courses on African history and world history. The cases represent a wide range of topics. Each volume summarizes the state of knowledge on a particular subject for a student who is new to the field. However, the aim is not simply to present views of the literature; it is also to introduce debates on historiographical or substantive issues and may argue for a particular point of view. The aim of the series is to stimulate debate and to challenge students and general readers. The series is not committed to any particular school of thought.

Other Books in the Series:

1. *Africa Since 1940*, by Frederick Cooper
2. *Muslim Societies in African History*, by David Robinson
3. *Reversing Sail: A History of the African Diaspora*, by Michael Gomez
4. *The African City: A History*, by William Freund

Warfare in Independent Africa

William Reno
Northwestern University

CAMBRIDGE
UNIVERSITY PRESS

CAMBRIDGE UNIVERSITY PRESS
Cambridge, New York, Melbourne, Madrid, Cape Town,
Singapore, São Paulo, Delhi, Mexico City

Cambridge University Press
32 Avenue of the Americas, New York, NY 10013-2473, USA

www.cambridge.org
Information on this title: www.cambridge.org/9780521615525

First published 2011
Reprinted 2012

A catalog record for this publication is available from the British Library.

Library of Congress Cataloging in Publication Data

Reno, William, 1962–
Warfare in independent Africa / William Reno.
    p.   cm. – (New approaches to African history ; 5)
Includes bibliographical references and index.
ISBN 978-0-521-85045-2 (hardback) – ISBN 978-0-521-61552-5 (paperback)
1. Africa – History, Military – 20th century. 2. Africa – History – 1960–
3. Violence – Africa – History – 20th century. I. Title.
DT30.5.R447   2011
355.0096 – dc22   2011001943

ISBN 978-0-521-85045-2 Hardback
ISBN 978-0-521-61552-5 Paperback

Contents

Maps

Figures

Acknowledgments

This book is the product of a chain of unexpected circumstances. In 1989, I moved to West Africa to conduct field research for what I thought would be a dissertation on the politics of economic reform. In hindsight, I arrived just in time to experience the start of a series of West African wars. This was a most unwelcome development. Yet this disruption led to field work, a dissertation, and a larger research agenda focused on the study of warfare in sub-Saharan Africa. I am indebted to Crawford Young and Michael Schatzberg for their enthusiastic support as I abandoned my initial focus late in my graduate career and shifted to this absorbing topic, and to Christopher Clapham, whose work and advice guided me in the right direction as I grappled with the intellectual challenges of this research venture.

Field research into the politics of violence eventually took me farther east and onward to the Horn of Africa as West Africa's wars began to wind down. Not surprisingly, the conduct of research in this kind of environment is not easily separated from the nonacademic aspects of war. There are no simple spectators in this kind of work. With the mundane process of research come the sudden rude anxieties that hit in the midst of chaos, or more typically in nighttime hours long after, or the impatient irritation at smooth-tongued spokespersons for the UN, various governments, and NGOs who never seem to act as effectively as one might wish. Then there are the desperate insults to one's soul that are integral to warfare.

Through these encounters with conflicts over the past two decades it has been through the networks of friends, hosts, brokers, and honest protectors who have provided me with insights, suggestions, and criticisms that I have been able to keep focused on research for this book and for my other projects. I cannot imagine what research in the field would have been like without the guidance and companionship of these often sharp-minded people who opened their doors to me. I have benefited from their experience and wisdom, and the protection of those who have extended their hospitality. They and others have opened doors and directed me to others with whom I needed to speak. This short book does little justice to the emotion, intelligence, and fervor with which they spoke of their ideas, beliefs, and hopes for the future. One way for the guest to repay the host is through commitment to the promise of anonymity.

I am grateful to the many people who listened to my arguments, invited me to present my research, read my work, offered advice, and pressed me to refine my ideas. There are too many to list, so I single out a few. They include Ana Arjona, Christine Cheng, LaRay Denzer, Georgi Derluguian, Danny Hoffman, Nelson Kasfir, Stathis Kalyvas, Zachariah Mampilly, Ken Menkhaus, J-P Peltier, Jeff Rice, Øystein Rolandsen, Klaus Schlichte, Tom Sheperd, Jon Temin, and Christoph Zürcher.

I am fortunate to have benefited from intelligent and insightful students in my Politics of Violence seminars. Their criticisms and suggestions forced me to hone and focus my argument. Several of these students accompanied me in the field, including to Sierra Leone, Uganda, Sudan, and Somalia. Authorities in their own rights, their companionship and intellectual stimulation have been vital to these enterprises. Among them are Chris Day, Miklos Gosztonyi, Patrick Johnston, Kendra Koivu, Claire Metelits, and Lee Seymour. A special thanks also goes to the Dispute Resolution Research Center at the Kellogg School of Management at Northwestern University for its generous support of this collaborative research. In an age when travel to conflict zones has become more fraught and many scholars have had to draw away from direct contact with their subjects of research, the faith and confidence of this institution have been invaluable to educating the next generation of experts with the language skills, experience, and expertise to conduct field research and build meaningful relations with overseas colleagues whose lives are directly affected by ongoing conflicts.

I am very grateful to work several steps away from The Melville J. Heskovits Library of African Studies, the largest separate Africana collection on the globe. This institution is the jewel in the crown of African Studies at Northwestern University, and it has played a critical role in facilitating my research for this book. For superb assistance, I am especially grateful to David Easterbrook, Patricia Ogedengbe, and Esmeralda Kale. I thank Alisa Anderson for her tireless and intelligent assistance with research.

This book would not exist but for the sage advice of Martin Klein, the series editor for the New Approaches to African History series at Cambridge University Press. I cannot convey how grateful I am to him for having suffered my interminable delays, yet remaining faithful to this project. My thanks also go to Eric Crahan for his editorial guidance at the Press and to Ott Sanderson for her expertise and generous assistance with graphic design. Finally, I thank Barbara Walthall and Laura Wilmot, who have provided so many sensible and sound editorial suggestions. So many have assisted, but it is with the author that the final responsibility lies for the production of the work and for the views and analyses within.

Abbreviations

AAPSO	Afro-Asian People's Solidarity Organisation
ACOA	American Committee on Africa
ADF	Allied Democratic Forces (Uganda)
ADFL	Alliance des Forces Démocratiques pour la Libération du Congo (Alliance of Democratic Forces for the Liberation of Congo)
AFL	Armed Forces of Liberia
AFRC	Armed Forces Revolutionary [later, Ruling] Council (Sierra Leone)
ALF	Afar Liberation Front (Ethiopia)
ANC	African National Congress (South Africa)
AU	African Union
CANU	Caprivi African National Union
CCB	Civil Cooperation Bureau (South Africa)
CDF	Civil Defense Forces (Sierra Leone)
CIO	Central Intelligence Organisation (Rhodesia)
CNL	Conseil national de libération (National Liberation Council [Congo])
CODESRIA	Council for the Development of Social Science Research in Africa
CONCP	Conferência das Organizações Nacionalistas das Colonias Portuguesas (Conference of the Nationalist Organizations of the Portuguese Colonies)
CYL	City Youth League (Southern Rhodesia / Zimbabwe)
ECOMOG	Economic Community of West African States Monitoring Force

EDU	Ethiopian Democratic Union
ELF	Eritrean Liberation Front
ELM	Eritrean Liberation Movement
EPLF	Eritrean People's Liberation Front
ERA	Eritrean Relief Association
ERD	Emergency Relief Desk
FAO	Food and Agriculture Organization
FAPC	Forces Armées pour le Congo (Armed Forces for Congo)
FARP	Forças Armadas Revolucionãrias de Povo (Revolutionary Armed Forces of the People [Guinea-Bissau])
FDLR	Forces Démocratiques de la Libération du Rwanda (Democratic Liberation Forces of Rwanda)
FESCI	Fédération estudiantine et scolaire de Côte d'Ivoire (Federation of Students and Scholars of Ivory Coast)
FLCS	Front de Libération de la Côte des Somalis (Front for the Liberation of the Somali Coast [Djibouti])
FLEC	Front pour la Libération de l'Enclave de Cabinda (Front for the Liberation of the Cabinda Enclave [Angola])
FLGO	Forces de Libération du Grand Ouest (Front for the Liberation of the Grand West [Côte d'Ivoire])
FLING	Frente para a Libertação e Independência da Guiné Portuguesa (Front for the Liberation of Portuguese Guinea)
FNDIC	Federated Niger Delta Ijaw Communities
FNLA	Frente Nacional de Libertação de Angola (National Front for the Liberation of Angola)
FNLA-GRAE	Frente Nacional de Libertação de Angola – Govêrno Revolucionário de Angola no Exílo (National Front for the Liberation of Angola – Revolutionary Government of Angola in Exile)
FPI	Front populaire ivoirien (Ivorian Popular Front)
FRELIMO	Frente de Libertação de Moçambique (Front for the Liberation of Mozambique)
FROLIZI	Front for the Liberation of Zimbabwe
FRONASA	Front for National Salvation (Uganda)
FUL	Frente Unida de Libertacão (United Front for Liberation [Guinea-Bissau])

GRAE	Govêrno Revolucionário de Angola no Exílio (Revolutionary Government of Angola in Exile)
ICJ	International Court of Justice
ICRC	International Committee of the Red Cross
IMF	International Monetary Fund
INPFL	Independent National Patriotic Front of Liberia
IYC	Ijaw Youth Council (Nigeria)
JEM	Justice and Equality Movement (Sudan)
KANU	Kenya African National Union
LDF	Lofa Defense Force
LGA	Local Government Area (Nigeria)
LLA	Lesotho Liberation Army
LPC	Liberia Peace Council
LRA	Lord's Resistance Army (Uganda)
LURD	Liberians United for Reconciliation and Democracy
MANU	Mozambique African National Union
MEND	Movement for the Emancipation of the Niger Delta
MISER	Makerere Institute of Social and Economic Research
MJP	Mouvement pour la justice et la paix (Movement for Justice and Peace [Côte d'Ivoire])
MK	Umkhonto we Sizwe (Spear of the Nation [South Africa])
MLC	Mouvement de Libération Congolais (Movement for the Liberation of Congo)
MLEC	Mouvement de Libération de l'Enclave de Cabinda (Liberation Movement for the Cabinda Enclave [Angola])
MNR	Mozambique National Resistance
MODEL	Movement for Democracy in Liberia
MOJA	Movement for Justice in Africa (Liberia)
MONUC	Mission de l'ONU en RD Congo (United Nations Organization Mission in the Democratic Republic of the Congo)
MOSOP	Movement for the Survival of the Ogoni People (Nigeria)
MPIGO	Mouvement populaire ivoirien du Grand Ouest (Ivorian Popular Movement of the Great West [Côte d'Ivoire])
MPLA	Movimento Popular de Libertação de Angola (People's Movement for the Liberation of Angola)

NDPVF	Niger Delta People's Volunteer Force (Nigeria)
NDVS	Niger Delta Vigilante Service (Nigeria)
NFDLF	Northern Frontier District Liberation Front (Kenya)
NGO	nongovernmental organization
NPFL	National Patriotic Front of Liberia
NPRAG	National Patriotic Reconstruction Assembly Government
NRA	National Resistance Army (Uganda)
NRM	National Resistance Movement (Uganda)
OAU	Organization of African Unity
OLF	Oromo Liberation Front (Ethiopia)
OPC	Oodua People's Congress (Nigeria)
OPO	Ovambo People's Organisation (Namibia)
ORA	Oromo Relief Association (Ethiopia)
OYM	Oodua Youth Movement (Nigeria)
PAC	Pan-African Congress (South Africa)
PAFMECSA	Pan-African Movement of East, Central, and Southern Africa
PAIGC	Partido Africano da Independência da Guiné e Cabo Verde (African Party for the Independence of Guinea and Cape Verde)
PAL	Progressive Alliance of Liberia
PDP	People's Democratic Party (Nigeria)
PF	Patriotic Front (Rhodesia / Zimbabwe)
PLAN	People's Liberation Army of Namibia
PUSIC	Parti de l'unité et la sauvegarde de l'intégrité du Congo (Party for Unity and Safeguarding of the Integrity of Congo)
RANU	Rwandan Alliance for National Unity
RCD	Rassemblement Congolais pour la Démocratie (Rally for Congolese Democracy [Congo])
RCD-ML	RCD-Mouvement de Libération (RCD-Movement for Liberation [Congo])
RDL	Rassemblement pour la démocratie et des libertés (Rally for Democracy and Liberty [Chad])
RENAMO	Resistência Nacional Moçambicana (Mozambican National Resistance)
REST	Relief Society of Tigray
RPA	Rwandan Patriotic Army
RPF	Rwandan Patriotic Front

RUF	Revolutionary United Front (Sierra Leone)
SACP	South African Communist Party
SADF	South African Defence Force
SAP	South African Police
SASO	South African Students' Organisation
SDM	Somali Democratic Movement
SIDA	Swedish International Development Authority
SLA	Sudan Liberation Army
SNA	Somali National Alliance
SNF	Somali National Front
SNM	Somali National Movement
SPLA	Sudan People's Liberation Army
SPM	Somali Patriotic Movement
SRRA	Sudan Relief and Rehabilitation Association
SSDF	Somali Salvation Democratic Front
SSIM	Southern Sudan Independence Movement
STAR	Sudan Transitional Assistance Rehabilitation
SWAPO	South West Africa People's Liberation Organisation (Namibia)
SYL	SWAPO Youth League (Namibia)
TLF	Tigray Liberation Front
TNO	Tigray National Organization (Ethiopia)
TPD	Tous pour la Paix et le Développement (All for Peace and Development [Congo])
TPLF	Tigrayan People's Liberation Front (Ethiopia)
UDENAMO	União Democrática Nacional de Moçambique (National Democratic Union of Mozambique)
UDF	United Democratic Front (South Africa)
UDI	Unilateral Declaration of Independence (Rhodesia / Zimbabwe)
UFM	Uganda Freedom Movement
ULAA	Union of Liberian Associations in America
ULIMO	United Liberation Movement for Democracy (Liberia)
UNAVEM	United Nations Angola Verification Mission
UNHCR	United Nations High Commission for Refugees
UNICEF	United Nations Children's Fund
UNITA	União Nacional para a Independência Total de Angola (National Union for the Total Independence of Angola)

UNITAF	Unified Task Force (UN-Somalia)
UNOSOM	United Nations Operation in Somalia
UPA	União das Populações de Angola (Union of Angolan Peoples)
UPC	Union des Patriotes Congolais (Union of Congolese Patriots)
UPDF	Ugandan People's Defense Force
UPNA	Union of Peoples of Northern Angola
USAID	United States Agency for International Development
USARF	University Students' African Revolutionary Front (University of Dar es Salaam)
USC	United Somali Congress
WFP	World Food Program
WHO	World Health Organization
WSLF	Western Somali Liberation Front
ZANLA	Zimbabwe African National Liberation Army
ZANU	Zimbabwe African National Union
ZAPU	Zimbabwe African People's Union
ZIPA	Zimbabwe People's Army
ZIPRA	Zimbabwe People's Revolutionary Army

CHAPTER 1

Evolving Warfare

Warfare in Africa has undergone considerable change. In 1972, supporters of an anti-colonial liberation struggle in Guinea-Bissau reported that a United Nations (UN) delegation spent seven days in rebel-held territory to learn about the administration that rebels had built to provide services to people there. To the rebels' supporters, this was "the only government responsible to the people it has ever had."[1] A person suddenly transported from that "liberated zone" three and a half decades forward through time would be in for a shock. UN officials in West Africa reported that in Guinea-Bissau it was hard to distinguish between state security forces and armed drug traffickers; they were allegedly in league with one another and showed little concern for the welfare of the wider population.[2] This time traveler might hear of factionalized fighting in Liberia and Sierra Leone during the 1990s. Young fighters there did not seem to be very different from those who participated in anti-colonial struggles. But the aims of their leaders seemed to be far more parochial: to grab power in the existing political system instead of creating a new one, or to defend a particular ethnic community. Congo, Somalia, Nigeria's Delta region, and many other places suffered from what seemed to be an excess of rebel groups who were fighting one another as much as governments and who largely

---

[1] American Committee on Africa, "State of the Liberation Struggle in Africa," mimeo, New York, 1 June 1972, 2.

[2] United Nations Security Council, *Report of the Secretary-General on the United Nations Office in West Africa* (New York: United Nations, 30 June 2008), 4.

displayed a dearth of interest in providing people with an alternative vision of politics or even in administering them in "liberated zones."

Conflict in much of Africa has shifted from a focus on battles over which side should control and administer the non-combatant population to situations in which governing non-combatants is often less relevant as a central strategy of war fighting. The other great shift concerns how rebels and government forces fight. Colonial governments tried to exploit superior resources and bureaucratic effectiveness to beat back bands of rebels. Rebels had to compensate for their weaknesses through mobilizing and disciplining fighters around a cause and through attempting to gain local acceptance. With popular support or even just tolerance, rebels could out-govern the state. Later, most government forces and rebels would reflect each other in their high degrees of fragmentation, use of similar tactics against each other, low levels of interest in instilling a common sense of purpose among recruits, and seeming disregard for the welfare of non-combatants.

This book explores these and other aspects of the evolving strategies and behavior of armed groups that have fought in Africa since the start of decolonization. From the early 1960s the majority of wars in Africa have involved armed groups that are not part of national armies, or what in this book are called rebels. Although rebels have launched numerous attacks across international borders, declared wars between the armies of states remain scarce in Africa. A contemporary political map of Africa shows only minor changes in boundaries compared to a map from 1890, but such geographical stability masks the considerable internal challenges faced by Africa's states. Thus an analysis of the evolution of warfare in independent Africa must focus on rebels who challenge states from within and who try to fight to power by taking control of a capital city. As shown by the preceding example from Guinea-Bissau and by numerous examples in the following pages, how this is done has undergone considerable changes.

Why call these armed groups rebels? Labels reflect the changing contexts of warfare in Africa as well as the development of different ways of fighting. In the 1950s, colonial administrators called those who fought for independence "terrorists," whereas most Africans saw them as nationalist heroes wresting power from alien occupiers. The Federal Government of Nigeria in the late 1960s regarded the leaders of the breakaway Eastern Region as "ethnic separatists" fighting for an independent state of Biafra. Well into the 1970s, Portuguese colonial rulers in Guinea-Bissau, Cape Verde, Angola, and Mozambique faced "communist insurgents" that many local people viewed as "freedom fighters" dedicated to ending colonial rule. Some people lived in their "liberated zones," where these fighters administered and implemented their political programs. During the 1980s several armed groups organized "states-within-states" in areas that they dominated in defiance of authoritarian regimes. The Ugandan National Resistance Army (NRA) and the Eritrean People's Liberation Front (EPLF) swept into capitals with large armies in 1986 and 1991, respectively. Small predatory bands of fighters who crossed the border from Côte d'Ivoire in late 1989 to become the National Patriotic Front of Liberia (NPFL) joined with the Revolutionary United Front (RUF) in Sierra Leone to become "warlords." Opponents of such fighters proudly called themselves "vigilantes" and "civil defense forces." Whatever these armed groups are called, they share the feature of challenging the authority of Africa's state regimes over the last half century, and for that purpose they will be called "rebels" in this book.

This book examines the history of armed conflicts in Africa to explain how and why the groups that fought in them have evolved. The analysis here is that the behavior and organization of rebels and state forces reflect changes in the wider political context in which they fight. The very fact that states – instead of empires or networks of small, autonomous polities as in centuries past – form the blueprint for politics on the African continent indelibly shapes warfare. Thus most rebels fight to take control of states. In this regard, they reflect the political order against which they fight. The more articulate among them offer political programs that they believe will make better states. Some capture territory and set up "liberated zones" where they organize administrations aimed to show local people an alternative vision of the government that the rebels intend to establish after winning their struggle. More recently, an increasing proportion of rebel leaders have had careers as key members of the political systems and regimes that they seek to overthrow. This connection imparts to rebels a distinctive set of goals and strategies and shapes how they recruit and discipline their fighters and how they treat non-combatant populations.

Not every rebel group behaves in the dominant fashion of its time, and the deviation of some groups from these patterns reveals important information. Some rebels owe a great deal to the style, ideas, and initiatives of particular leaders. It is hard to imagine what the Lord's Resistance Army (LRA) in Uganda would be like without the distinctive ideas of Joseph Kony. Kony's goal to create a government based on his interpretation of the Ten Commandments is unique among major armed groups. Liberia's Charles Taylor played an integral role in the day-to-day management of the NPFL during the 1990s, using first satellite telephones and then mobile telephone networks to keep in constant contact with his associates. In mid-2005, the depth of popular mourning in southern Sudan after the death of "Doctor John" Garang in a helicopter crash revealed the extent to which the grass roots associated the Sudan People's Liberation Army (SPLA) with the personality of that charismatic leader.

Categories of Rebels

Although every rebel group and every conflict in Africa exhibit particular characteristics, broad differences in the general context shape the environment in which rebels make choices. For example, after the collapse of the Soviet Union in the early 1990s, it was not realistic to present a Marxist-Leninist political program and expect diplomatic or material support from Moscow. Rebel leaders of the time found it politic to adopt labels like Liberia Peace Council (LPC) or Liberians United for Reconciliation and Democracy (LURD), regardless of their actual behavior or motivations or those of their fighters. Although the term "liberation" has not disappeared entirely from the nomenclature of contemporary rebels, as in the case of the Congo's Mouvement de Libération Congolais (MLC), others like LURD have adopted names that suggest that they are prodemocracy groups or community-based nongovernmental organizations (NGOs). Since the late 1990s some rebels in Nigeria – the Niger Delta People's Volunteer Force (NDPVF) and its rival, the Niger Delta Vigilante Service (NDVS) – have taken names that evoke community self-defense amid societal violence, official corruption, and regime incompetence.

Over the decades the emergence of different kinds of rebel leaders has reflected large-scale shifts in the character of African societies and the changing role of state administrations. For example, in the 1950s, university education in sub-Saharan Africa served a tiny segment of the population. With a few exceptions, such as Sierra Leone's Fourah Bay College, Uganda's Makerere College, and several South African universities, nearly all institutions of higher education were founded after the Second World War. Although Africans were generally interested in politics before independence, those who enjoyed the social space to discuss and formulate programs for change and devise concrete plans to make this happen were most likely to be found among the extremely small numbers of university students studying outside the continent. These students directed the discussions of the indigenous nationalist intelligentsia in a more militant vein. Eduardo Mondlane, the leader of Mozambique's anti-colonial Frente de Libertação de Moçambique (FRELIMO) from 1962 until his death in a parcel bomb blast in 1969, received his bachelor's degree at Oberlin College in Ohio (1953) and his doctorate in sociology from Chicago's Northwestern University (1960). Upon graduation, he had two options: a post in the colonial government service of Mozambique, which had instituted a limited policy of co-opting skilled Africans, or a lectureship at Syracuse University.[3] He rejected the first position and served briefly in the second because he chose instead to lead a major liberation struggle.

This background shaped the first generation of armed groups in this survey and the subjects of the next chapter, the **anti-colonial rebels** who accompanied the end of intransigent European colonial empires in Africa. Mondlane's counterpart in the colony of Portuguese Guinea, Amilcar Cabral, founded nationalist student groups while studying agronomy in Lisbon. By 1962, he led the Partido Africano da Independência da Guiné e Cabo Verde (PAIGC), having first served a stint as a colonial administrator attached to the agriculture and forestry service. Like Mondlane, he developed his political ideas and plans for action in metropolitan student and professional groups in Lisbon that were interested in anti-colonial politics. Other African students in Lisbon during the 1950s were Agostinho Neto, who became the leader of the Movimento Popular de Libertação de Angola (MPLA) and Angola's first president, and Marcelino dos Santos, a key figure in Mozambique's FRELIMO. International congresses of anti-colonial activists from other parts of the world facilitated sharing of ideas and strategies. Attendance lists and programs included a global community of activists who conversed in European languages with other intellectuals, primarily from Europe, whose anti-imperialist critiques were grounded in socialist-inspired state-building ideas.

Massive increases in state support for higher education in the 1960s, especially in the social sciences, created new venues for young people to discuss ideas and political action. State policies to promote higher

---

[3] Gueorgui Derluguian, "Social Decomposition and Armed Violence in Postcolonial Mozambique," *Review* 13:4 (1990): 439–62.

education at public universities resulted in the growth of the indigenous intelligentsia. For example, the student body at the University
College of Ibadan (Nigeria), founded in 1948, grew from about 1,000
in 1958 to 8,500 in 1976. Similar increases occurred at other institutions like Makerere University (Uganda) and the University of Dar es
Salaam (Tanzania). Social science research occupied a special place in
the nationalist intellectual worldview.[4] It brought together large numbers of students sharing a strong sense of national pride and revulsion
at the continuation of colonial control in parts of Africa and, for the first
time on a large scale, anger at the scourge of apartheid in South Africa.
By the late 1960s, the eruption of armed struggle against Portuguese
colonial rule in southern and West Africa energized scholarly activists.

The expansion of secondary and university education also shaped
the organization of **majority rule rebels** in the white minority–ruled
southern African states that included Zimbabwe (then known as Rhodesia), South Africa, and Namibia. These rebels, the subjects of Chapter
3, saw themselves as closely linked to their anti-colonial brethren, and
on occasion they gave aid and advice to one another. Like their anti-
colonial colleagues, they saw world politics as a resource that could
be used to leverage their struggles against regimes that turned out to
be much more militarily formidable than those faced by earlier anti-
colonial struggles.

The University of Dar es Salaam stands out during this period. Yoweri Museveni, a young student from Uganda, discussed strategies and
tactics of revolutionary struggle there before going on to help form
the NRA and fight his way into power in 1986. Among his lecturers
was the Guyanese historian and theorist Walter Rodney, a key figure in Pan-Africanist political thought, who taught there from 1968,
after his expulsion from Jamaica and a short stay in Cuba. In 1968
Museveni and six other students visited liberated zones in northern
Mozambique to report back to the University Students' African Revolutionary Front (USARF) that he and his classmates had founded the
year before. His student essays reflect the influence of Rodney's idea
that African development was only possible through a radical break with
the international capitalist system and the cooperation of revolutionaries across Africa's inherited colonial borders.[5] The ideas of Martinique-
born Franz Fanon also played an important role in Museveni's formal

[4] Ebrima Sall, *The Social Sciences in Africa: Trends, Issues, Capacities and Constraints* (New
York: Social Science Research Council, 2003).
[5] Yoweri Museveni, *Sowing the Mustard Seed* (London: Macmillan, 1997), 26–27.

education.[6] Fanon wrote that true revolution in Africa could come only from among marginalized peasants. They alone, he believed, were free of compromise with the structures of global imperialism that corrupted urban working classes and professionals.[7]

Museveni's trip to liberated zones in northern Mozambique brought him into direct contact with members of FRELIMO who had established a guerrilla base among peasants in rural Mozambique. While there, Museveni and other young Ugandans observed how FRELIMO administered their liberated zone, disciplined fighters, and advanced their political program against what they saw as the main problem of divisive tendencies of local ethnic chauvinists. This trip and Museveni's USARF activities brought together in Dar es Salaam what soon became an international community of liberation fighters. John Garang, the future head of the SPLA in southern Sudan, belonged to the USARF. Aware of the impact of the rise of educational opportunity on the African continent, he turned down admission to a doctoral program at the University of California at Berkeley after receiving his bachelor's degree in economics at Grinnell College (Iowa) in 1969. Instead he attended the University of Dar es Salaam on a Thomas J. Watson Fellowship from the United States before joining the Anya Anya insurgency in Sudan in 1970.

Museveni put this practical experience to use when he and a few others founded the Front for National Salvation (FRONASA) in 1973 to liberate Uganda from the authoritarian rule of Idi Amin. Unlike Mondlane or Cabral, Museveni was not fighting against a colonial power occupying his homeland but against an oppressive internal tyranny. Having learned the theoretical and practical arts of insurgency, he considered the practical challenge facing his armed group in preparing to invade the now-independent Uganda and install a government that would implement the revolutionary ideas studied in school and discussed informally with international contacts and in study groups. This third category of armed group, the vanguard of the **reform rebels** who emerged on the scene in the 1980s (the subject of Chapter 4), was intimately familiar with the debates and challenges that affected the first wave of anti-colonial liberation struggles. They were reformers of states in their recognition that independence alone was not enough to build

---

[6] Yoweri Museveni, "Fanon's Theory on Violence: Its Verification in Liberated Mozambique," in Nathan Shamuyarira (ed.), *Essays on the Liberation of Southern Africa* (Dar es Salaam: Tanzania Publishing House, 1971), 1–24.

[7] Franz Fanon, *The Wretched of the Earth* (New York: Grove Press, 1963).

strong African countries. Most redoubled the efforts of the anti-colonial rebels to create genuine liberated zones and paid explicit attention to how they would transfer this experience to transform their states. They saw this as the key to liberation from a generation of despotic and corrupt state leaders.

In East Africa, the ideas and experiences of FRELIMO were passed directly through Museveni to a new generation of rebel leaders via the struggle of FRONASA. These included Fred Rwigyema, the first leader of the Rwandan Patriotic Army (RPA), among the most militarily formidable and organized insurgent forces to fight in Africa in recent decades. Although Rwigyema was killed in 1990, the RPA went on to drive out a regime that had perpetrated genocide in 1994. Previously he had served as the acting commander of Museveni's NRA. By 1985, Paul Kagame, Rwigyema's successor and president of Rwanda from 2000, played an important role in the NRA. Although no convincing evidence exists of physical contact between these key RPA commanders and Mondlane, after 1994 Rwandan government publications claimed that there had been. They stressed the continuity and connections of liberation struggles from the anti-colonial nationalists to this third category of liberation in a bid to take over the mantle of legitimacy associated with the earlier rebels.

Elsewhere in Africa, universities and student organizations played crucial roles in reform rebel struggles. In the late 1960s militants were an important element in the student body at Haile Selassie I University (now Addis Ababa University). Through expanded educational opportunities, students from the isolated province of Tigray encountered each other in the capital. There they found like-minded youth who joined in discussions about their grievances against Ethiopia's regime and plans for political action. Like Dar es Salaam students, they framed their critiques in terms of problems of an international imperialist global economy. Their analysis of the Ethiopian political situation fit well in this Marxist framework, because it had an emperor whose customs and habits of government could be branded feudalistic. In the early 1970s the Tigrayan Students' Association was formed, which included the founding members of the Tigrayan National Organization, which transformed into the Tigrayan People's Liberation Front (TPLF).[8] Like the USARF student group in Tanzania, this association included

---

[8] Aregawi Berhe, "Origins of the Tigray People's Liberation Front," *African Affairs* 103 (2004): 575–76.

student activists involved in radical university politics. Most notable among them were the future leaders of the EPLF, a connection that facilitated coordination in their mutual struggle against Ethiopia's imperial regime and EPLF's rivals in the 1980s and early 1990s.[9]

Economic troubles and declining state support for higher education in the 1980s, however, changed the relationship of universities to rebels. Shrinking budgets for higher education, especially in the social sciences, followed World Bank and International Monetary Fund (IMF) insistence that governments devote a greater percentage of expenditures toward primary and secondary education in practical skills.[10] These shifts in the basic structure of higher education shrank the social spaces that earlier activists utilized as they became revolutionaries and rebels. New independent research centers were best situated to adapt to the pressures from global creditors, national governments, and university administrations to focus on income-generating activities. Groups of scholars like the Makerere Institute of Social and Economic Research (MISER) at Makerere University became adept at bidding on foreign aid contracts and grant-supported research for Ugandan policy makers. Others, like the United Nations–supported Council for the Development of Social Science Research in Africa (CODESRIA), have had a significant impact on academic networking but never became centers of activism. Most of CODESRIA's associates from the 1980s onward had to struggle with shrinking government budgets for research, low pay, and deteriorating facilities. Moreover, the appearance of corporate training centers and the growth of private universities in the 1990s fragmented the academic scene even further.

The recession in higher education directly affected the numbers of students with whom activists could share ideas. In 2001–02, the department of political science at the University of Sierra Leone had only one doctoral candidate, who also doubled as a junior lecturer. Its department of economics produced no doctorates that year. Popular perceptions of breakdown and growing political violence on campuses served as added incentives to families that could afford to send their sons and daughters abroad for their educations. Programs in the Ford and Rockefeller foundations assisted others to study outside of Africa.

[9] John Young, "The Tigray and Eritrean Peoples Liberation Fronts: A History of Tensions and Pragmatism," *Journal of Modern African Studies* 34:1 (1996): 105–20.

[10] Joel Samoff and Bidemi Carrol, *From Manpower Planning to the Knowledge Era: World Bank Policies on Higher Education in Africa* (Paris: UNESCO Forum Secretariat, 2003), 1–2.

Although overseas universities are venues for political discussion and organizing, it is hard – but as we will see in the following, not impossible – to begin building a rebel group on an American or European campus. It is reasonable to expect, however, that this demographic shift in education and the general pursuit of opportunity had an impact on the sources of political activism that would eventually evolve into rebel groups.

The fact that about 40 percent of Africans pursuing doctoral degrees in the United States between 1986 and 1996 chose to remain after completion of their degrees further shrank the pool of potential organizers.[11] This did not mean that they were uninvolved; for the members of group came to play important roles from abroad with their financial contributions and provision of support communities for some armed groups. Immigration statistics reflect this trend. In the early 1990s, census figures indicated that more than 26 percent of adult African immigrants to the United Kingdom held academic qualifications higher than "A" or college levels, compared with 13.4 percent of white adults.[12] The 1990 US census showed that 57.1 percent of the more than 360,000 African-born adults who lived in the United States had completed some form of university education. By then Africans constituted the most highly qualified group of immigrants, outstripping the qualifications of immigrants from affluent countries, including those from Europe (18 percent with college degrees) and Japan (35 percent).[13] By 2000, 83 percent of the 109,000 Nigerian adults who had moved to the United States after 1990 had a university education.[14] Although no one can say for certain what would have become of these vigorous, enterprising, and skilled Africans had they stayed home, one wonders whether the would-be liberation fighter of former years instead became a doctor or a financial analyst or an engineer in New York or London.

Back home in many countries, citizens experienced growing personal insecurity, greater economic hardship, and declining government capacities to deliver basic services. During the 1980s, presidents, who

[11] Mark Pires, Ronald Kassimir, and Mesky Brhane, *Investing in Return: Rates of Return of African PhDs Trained in North America* (New York: Social Science Research Council, 1999), 10–11.

[12] Theodore Cross, "Black Africans Now Most Highly Educated Group in British Society," *Journal of Blacks in Higher Education* 3 (Spring 1994): 92.

[13] "African-Born U.S. Residents Have Achieved the Highest Levels of Educational Attainment," *Journal of Blacks in Higher Education* 4 (Summer 1994): 10–11.

[14] Devish Kapur and John McHale, *Give Us Your Best and Brightest* (Washington, DC: Center for Global Development, 2005), 17.

presided over severe declines in state revenues and weakened administrations, developed new political strategies to weather these challenges.
Because popular expectations outstripped their capacities to deliver
benefits and some foreign governments attached stringent conditions
to aid after the end of the Cold War, the political elite had to find less
expensive ways to assert their authority. Unable to deliver adequate
social services to citizens, some simply used their control over national
governments as a façade behind which to conclude deals with foreign
businesses. They then distributed places in joint ventures and other
business arrangements in exchange for the support of local strongmen.
Not surprisingly, the president's ethnic kinsmen also found opportunities in these commercial deals. In return, they played key roles in enforcing the president's authority, using their share of private profits and the
corrupt appropriation of state assets to field their own militias against
the president's critics and perceived opponents. These ventures also
could extend to clandestine economies, relying on the president's willingness to manipulate his country's laws to target political outsiders
and grant selective exemption from investigation and prosecution to
allies.

Once these presidents faced a significant political or financial crisis,
their associates had to make a decision. Either they could rely on their
president to continue to favor them and grant them access to wealth and
capacity to protect themselves or they could use their militias and business deals to launch their own bid to become president. Thus there arose
a fourth category of rebels, the **warlord rebels**, who are the subjects
of Chapter 5. The argument here is that warlord rebels are particular
to a certain kind of authoritarian regime politics and are an expression
of an expansion of political competition that previously existed in these
regimes. Like earlier rebel leaders, the new warlords possessed backgrounds in higher education and previous political experience. Their
primary social assets were their positions in the prewar political networks of the regimes that they later helped to destroy. For example,
General Mohammed Farah Aidid went from serving as President Siad
Barre's minister of defense, and thus being responsible for organizing
overseas arms shipments for his boss, to head of the United Somali
Congress (USC), whose militia controlled much of Mogadishu from
1991 up to his death in 1996. In the early 1980s, Charles Taylor, head
of the NPFL, served as chief of a procurement agency for his future
foe, President Samuel Doe (1980–90). His rivals included Alhaji G.
V. Kromah, a former information minister, who became head of the

United Liberation Movement for Democracy in Liberia (ULIMO), and George Boley, a former secretary to the president, who led the LPC.

These and other warlord rebel leaders had similar educational qualifications to some of the first liberation rebel leaders. Boley, for example, earned his doctorate in education at the University of Akron (Ohio). Taylor graduated with a bachelor's degree in economics in 1977 from Bentley College (Boston), where he joined and then became the chairman of the Union of Liberian Associations in the United States. Of the major faction leaders, only Kromah completed his schooling in Liberia, receiving a bachelor in law from the University of Liberia in 1976. For this group, higher education became a way of qualifying for high state office, which they could then use to build personal commercial and political connections while serving their president. These positions did not translate into significant venues for sharing ideas and developing political programs to attract followers to a vision of a reformed or radicalized future regime. Instead, these networks of connections gave future warlord rebel leaders the means to prevail over ideologues who, under other circumstances, might have become leaders of liberation struggles, but in these circumstances were pushed aside, killed, or chased away in favor of warlord rebel leaders who had previous access to commercial and diaspora connections that later provided them with resources to mobilize fighters.

Ordinary citizens bear the brunt of stagnant or declining economies in the midst of weakened state administrations, political instability, and the insecurity that these bring. Some of these people, especially those with little formal education, fight for warlord leaders. Although some scholars and journalists claim that these people fight for personal enrichment through whatever loot they can seize, this happens in all wars.[15] Museveni, for example, wrote in his memoirs of the challenges of disciplining uneducated urban youth and preventing them from looting and harassing local people.[16] The difference in warlord rebels lies in the degree to which the interests and organization of the marginalized youth shape group behavior. This absence of coordinated fighting, failure to build durable administrative structures in areas that they control, and the relative lack of importance of formal hierarchies of command for

---

[15] See especially Paul Collier and Anke Hoeffler, "Greed and Grievance," World Bank research paper #21, Oct 2001.

[16] Museveni, *Sowing the Mustard Seed*, 85–90.

organizing actual fighting are compatible with warlord leaders' objectives. Like leaders of anti-colonial and state-building rebels, warlord leaders aim to overthrow an incumbent regime and take control of the state. Unlike those earlier rebels, warlord leaders see the control and expansion of informal networks of clandestine commerce and political violence at the outset as the main priority. They do this in the course of their quest to claim the power that their old boss used to assert authority. Because armed youth groups and localized militias were already integral elements of this strategy before widespread fighting broke out, they come to play important roles as armed muscle behind the political aspirations of their leaders.

This is not to say that young fighters are duped into fighting for corrupt politicians. Field researchers have found that fighters in these armed groups articulate grievances that, under different circumstances, would make them good candidates for anti-colonial and state-building rebel groups as well as for warlords. But in the context of collapsing state institutions and growing insecurity, they must choose how to respond to their difficult socioeconomic situations. Some join rebels so that they can acquire a gun to protect themselves and provide for their families. They integrate into the rebel groups that they recognize are responsible for many of the troubles in their society, yet believe that this represents their best short-term option, given that no government will help to protect them. Some have no choice, particularly in instances in which children are kidnapped and forced to join their captors in battle. A few discover that they excel at this kind of fighting and may conclude that this is a wise career choice. The opportunity to command other people and participate in their warlord patron's political plans outweighs the risks of combat.

Not all marginalized youth fight for warlords. Some address personal insecurity and scarcity through joining local self-defense forces. These are organized by local communities, usually using existing social institutions like market and religious organizations to mobilize and discipline young fighters. Their main objective is to protect themselves from the corruption of the state and the predators around them, instead of capturing the states like their warlord counterparts. Take, for example, groups like the Oodua People's Congress (OPC), formed in the late 1990s in western Nigeria to resist the harsh dictatorship of General Sani Abacha, who had seized power in a coup in 1994 after an aborted multiparty election. These are **parochial rebels**, the subjects of Chapter 6, who fight to protect circumscribed communities. Usually they appear during times when and in places where politicians are evolving into warlords as state institutions and security are breaking down. Unlike their warlord counterparts, however, these fighters face different local and regional constraints in their behavior and organization. Their leaders realize that they cannot gain access to the resources they need to arm their followers unless they heed the interests and values of local communities. For example, Nigeria's OPC leaders had to negotiate with customary heads of market associations. If OPC members mistreated their patrons, these people could withhold the resources that OPC leaders needed to arm and run their group.

Parochial rebels are more likely to develop political programs and try to administer areas under their control in comparison to their warlord counterparts. This is partly because they face obligations to heed the interests of their community backers. This situation creates opportunities for members with well-developed political ideas and administrative expertise that open avenues for upward mobility and prestige within the marginalized rebel group. Their political ideas and notions about how to administer populations typically differ from the political programs and liberated zones of earlier armed group categories. The latter tended to take cues from international ideas about anti-colonialism, global support for self-determination, and perhaps, socialist critiques of capitalism and the operation of the world economy. Parochial armed groups, however, are more likely to articulate distinct local ideas about politics and administration. This can include support for ethnic chauvinism. In the 1990s, the Lofa Defense Force (LDF) appeared in northwestern Liberia to protect local Kissi and Lorma ethnic communities from ULIMO predations. The specific ethnic institutions exclusive to these communities simultaneously became instruments for mobilizing fighters and shaping their ideas and actions.

The circumscribed political ideas and practices of parochial rebels further hinder the efforts of ideologues, the would-be heirs to anti-colonial and other rebels who successfully advanced broad narratives around which people mobilized to fight. Some of these ideologues in more recent times might offer ideas that are attractive to individuals, such as a vision of global militant jihad to liberate Muslims from the oppression of corrupt secular states and to roll back the negative global influences on their cultures. Others might articulate narratives that Africans suffer because the French government supports hopelessly corrupt governments and provides weapons to their puppets that are then used to kill Africans. Or ideologues could argue that America sustains repressive dictators so that it can rob the continent of its underground wealth. These are ideas that are current in some quarters, but a key argument in this book is that the politics leading to the emergence of warlord and parochial rebels overwhelms and undermines the efforts of ideologues to translate their broad ideas into the processes of recruitment and fighter discipline that they need to pursue their vision of armed rebellion. Ultimately, this development is a consequence of the strategies of control on the part of a distinctive type of authoritarian regime in sub-Saharan Africa over the past several decades.

The boundaries between these categories, especially in the last two decades, have become blurred. In the 1960s and 1970s, rebels tested themselves against regimes that in many cases had a greater capability to control their own state territories than they would in the 1980s and 1990s. Their leaders overwhelmingly came from among the country's educational elite, and few defected from the regimes that they fought. Warlord leaders, however, brought to warfare the networks and resources acquired through their positions in high office. These resources combined with the growing insecurity and economic desperation of their collapsing states, give these leaders new tools for co-opting what began as marginalized rebels. Some marginalized rebels recognize this danger. A member of the Bakassi Boys, a Nigerian vigilante group, complained that "politicians are interfering with everything, lobbying this group against that group" when some of his group accepted a local governor's offer to deputize them as the Abia State Vigilante Force to fight his political opponents in return for a share of any loot that they could acquire in the service of the governor's interests.[17] This blurring of boundaries reflects the changing character of African states, especially the serious weakening of the administrative capacities of a significant number of them. This development, along with changes in Africa's position in the international system, plays a fundamental role in the evolution of warfare in independent Africa. It is to these major developments that we turn to understand how and why these distinct categories of rebels emerged.

The Centrality of States in the Stakes of Warfare in Africa

After 1950 most conflicts in Africa reflect a political environment in which rebels fight to capture the capital city of their country and install themselves as the new government. This has been true from

[17] Anayochukwu Agbo, "Bakassi v MASSOB in Abia State," *Tell*, 26 Nov 2001, 63.

the first anti-colonial liberation struggles to contemporary warlords. Even parochial rebels who provide protection to narrowly circumscribed communities rarely question the existence of the states in which they find themselves. Some Mayi Mayi militias manage the defense and other affairs of local ethnic communities in eastern Congo almost as if they were a kind of government, but they do not use this authority to argue that they should be recognized as a new country or should join a neighboring state.[18] The great majority of warlords fight to capture the capital city or at least to get included in a post-conflict government. Existing states clearly hold great attraction for rebels, play a key role in their definitions of goals, and shape their strategies. The reasons why armed groups are so accepting of existing states and their boundaries shed light on the distinctive nature of Africa's states.

Nationalist politics after the Second World War took place in the context of a growing global recognition that each colony deserved national independence. The right to independence found expression in international law when United Nations (UN) Resolution 1514 was passed in 1960, ninety votes to none, with nine abstentions. It called on colonial rulers to transfer "all powers to the peoples of those territories, without any conditions or reservations." This declaration gave international diplomatic and political weight to the view held by many nationalists that colonial rule was a crime. It ensured that anti-colonial, and eventually majority rule, rebels would be regarded as fighting "on the right side" of their conflicts and could thus claim the mantle of true representation of their peoples' aspirations for independence. The resolution admonished that "inadequacy of political, economic, social, or educational preparedness should never serve as a pretext for delaying independence," thus ensuring that there would be no minimum standard for independence except prior identity as a colony. Even tiny Gambia, with a population of less than a quarter of a million in 1960, could not be denied its right to independence.

After 1960 countries that still held colonies in Africa had to respond to this call. Thus Portuguese officials tried to claim that their colonies were really overseas provinces, integral parts of the Portuguese nation. French and British officials found it easier to adjust, because by 1960 they had already determined to dismantle their colonial empires in Africa. South African–born journalist Colin Legum recognized the

---

[18] Koen Vlassenroot and Timothy Raeymaekers, *The Formation of Centres of Profit, Power and Protection: Conflict and Social Transformation in Eastern DR Congo* (Copenhagen: University of Copenhagen, Centre for African Studies, 2005).

growing force of armed nationalist opposition to colonial rule in light of France's record in the 1950s:

> Britain handed over power not because the Africans were ripe, or not ripe, for independence; but because it suited Britain's best interests to do so. A point had been reached where not to hand over power in Africa would have landed Britain in the same pickle as France.... The ghastly war in Indo-China was followed by the seven-year war in Algeria. France, which clung to power too long drained the country materially and physically, destroyed democratic government in the Republic, committed the French Army to one disastrous campaign after another for almost 14 years, and in the end they had to abandon the field just the same.[19]

The idea of national self-determination was too powerful a force to resist. An important factor was that contemporary anti-colonial rebels had access to light weapons much like those used by European armies. Moreover, fighters had the support of local communities that would shelter and protect them if European armies continued in their efforts to perpetuate colonial rule.

Rebels had to confine their goals to the liberation of individual colonies and not to the creation of new countries or the revival of ones that existed before the colonial era. The charter of the Organization of African Unity (OAU), formed in 1963, reinforced the pledge of its member states to "respect the borders existing on the achievement of national independence."[20] Anti-colonial rebels who tried to do otherwise would jeopardize their positions, even if they defeated colonial forces on the ground. Efforts to liberate communities on both sides of a border to make one country would draw condemnation from diplomats around the world. Governments in newly independent states feared that such a precedent could lead to the breakup and absorption of their own state into another or legitimate the efforts of groups to split off to form their own country. Policy makers were in positions to deny militarily successful rebels the prerogatives that came with the status of sovereignty. Without diplomatic recognition, such rebels would experience great difficulty getting aid from abroad, would be ineligible for loans from the IMF or World Bank, would be denied a seat in the UN, and would likely face rival rebels who would receive aid from abroad under the condition that they accept existing borders.

---

[19] Colin Legum, "Pan-Africanism, the Communists and the West," *African Affairs* 63:252 (July 1964): 187.
[20] OAU Charter Article 3 (3).

   This international context pushed anti-colonial rebels to limit their fights for self-determination to the independence of colonies. The exceptions to this rule illustrate the dangers of defying this norm. In July 1967 Nigeria's eastern region began fighting to break free of a military government dominated by northern ethnic groups. The new state was named the Republic of Biafra. A spokesman justified this decision in terms of "unworkable colonial boundaries" that denied justice to "people within them who want nothing more than self-determination."[21] At times during the 1967–70 civil war, Biafra's army proved to be almost as militarily capable as Nigeria's, but this was not enough to convince most other governments to recognize Biafra's independence. Only Zambia, Tanzania, Gabon, and Côte d'Ivoire extended diplomatic recognition to Biafra, a flagrant contravention of African norms endorsing old colonial boundaries.[22] Armed groups in the province of Katanga fought to establish their own country soon after Congo's independence in 1960. That effort met with considerable international intervention on the side of the Congolese state. Both Katanga and Biafra were treated simply as rebellious provinces of globally recognized states. This put the armed forces of both rebellions, regardless of their military capabilities, in a considerably less advantageous position vis-à-vis anti-colonial and majority rule rebels, even ones that could not prevail against the police and armed forces of minor colonial powers like Portugal or against those of the approximately quarter million white Rhodesians in what is now Zimbabwe. Thus the sovereignty of Africa's states depended on the recognition of other states and not simply the ability to exercise supreme power in a particular territory. This aspect of the politics of contemporary Africa (and the rest of the world) stands in stark contrast to practice before the Second World War, when states accepted the results of conquest and addressed the collapse of old states through official recognition that their sovereignty had passed on to another state.

   Eritrea successfully claimed a seat in the UN General Assembly in 1993, a sign of global recognition of its independence. Its success underlined the limits that the global idea of statehood imposes on rebels. At first, Eritrea's split from Ethiopia made it seem like Biafra, a renegade province of an existing state. The EPLF gained international recognition of Eritrea's independence only after it joined with another rebel

[21] Kenneth Dike, "Biafra Explains Its Case," *New York Times*, 28 April 1969, A4.
[22] Crawford Young, "Comparative Claims to Political Sovereignty: Biafra, Katanga, Eritrea," in Donald Rothchild and Victor Olorunsola (eds.), *State Versus Ethnic Claims: African Policy Dilemmas* (Boulder, CO: Westview, 1983), 199–232.

group, the TPLF, to invade Ethiopia's capital. Together they overthrew the old regime and became Ethiopia's new rulers. Then the EPLF petitioned for the right to secede. The decision of other governments to accept Eritrea's de facto independence hinged on the consent of the new Ethiopian government. This situation conformed to the rules of the Badinter Arbitration Commission, a European Community effort to mediate in the Yugoslavia conflict. As Yugoslavia collapsed between 1991 and 1992, French lawyer Robert Badiner's commission oversaw the creation of new countries out of Yugoslavia's six republics. It reinforced the principle that secession was allowed only with mutual consent of all sovereign states directly affected and only so long as the previous internal administrative borders would become the new international boundaries, a principle that guided the dissolution of the Soviet Union in 1991 and Czechoslovakia in 1993. It was the EPLF's good fortune to lay claim to a territory that had been a separate Italian colony before it was joined to Ethiopia after the Second World War. Combined with the consent of the government of Ethiopia (of which the EPLF now was a part), the rebel group could present its struggle as a final step in the liberation of Africa's colonies, turning an old administrative boundary into an international border, just as was done in Yugoslavia.

The experience of the self-declared Republic of Somaliland highlights the limits facing rebels who wish to create new states. Although the Somali National Movement (SNM) drove other armies out of northern Somalia in the early 1990s and set up an administration, and although it prints its own money, polices local communities, and even organizes multiparty elections that unseated an incumbent president, decades later it still lacks international recognition as a state. Like Eritrea, Somaliland was a separate (in this case British) colony until its 1960 unification with the former Italian colony in southern Somalia. Moreover, Somaliland officials are careful to confine their territorial claims to the limits of the old colonial borders. But the SNM did not capture Somalia's capital, Mogadishu; make itself the government; and then grant its own wish for northern independence. The idea of privileging existing states in Africa is so strong, in fact, that Somalia retains a seat in the African Union (AU) and in the UN General Assembly, even though it has not had an effective central government since early 1991.

The strength of this idea means that most rebels who capture capitals are able to convince foreign officials to recognize them as a new government. They succeed in claiming the status of sovereignty, even if they make little actual effort to rule. The warlord Charles Taylor fought his way to Liberia's capital and then convinced UN monitors to accept the results of a 1997 election in which his NPFL intimidated voters to make him president of the country. But he remained so engrossed in his personal business dealings that by 2001 he personally controlled an income that was much greater than the internal revenues of the Liberian government. In such cases, the sovereignty of the state becomes a façade behind which the successful warlord organizes commercial dealings. The façade is useful, because global recognition gives the warlord the right to issue genuine diplomatic passports to criminals to facilitate their international transactions. Central banks can be used to organize clandestine deals, and laws can be enforced selectively against one's business and political rivals. Moreover, the practice of recognizing only existing states deters rebel leaders like Taylor from pursuing alternative goals. Early in his career, between 1989 and 1991, he appeared to be creating a "Greater Liberia" out of parts of neighboring countries, but he was consistent in his efforts to become the globally recognized president of the Republic of Liberia.

As I will discuss in Chapter 5, capturing a capital no longer leads to automatic recognition as a country's sovereign ruler. RUF leaders in Sierra Leone were genuinely shocked when they learned that British and American diplomats continued to recognize an exiled government after the RUF captured the capital in May 1997.[23] They were driven out of the capital in February 1998 by a multinational intervention force. The insistence among international human rights groups and foreign governments that rebels must abide by basic human rights standards, coupled with the belief that overthrowing democratically elected governments disqualifies rebels for recognition, shows signs of reshaping the calculations of some rebels. Ironically, these measures, which international lawyers and activists promote as enhancements of the security of existing states, may convince some rebels that they would not gain outside acceptance even if they captured a state. It is possible that these new norms could cede the field to rebels who articulate radically different visions of the future and who do not care so much about what the rest of the world thinks. Some rebels in Nigeria's predominantly Muslim north, for example, have begun to voice complaints about the existing state system itself, complaining of inconvenient borders that

---

[23] Interview with junta leader Johnny Paul Koroma, Freetown, Sierra Leone, 7 May 2001.

divide religious and ethnic communities and of the oppressive nature of Western-style states. But as noted earlier, the persistence of a distinctive type of authoritarian politics in some African states, along with the kinds of political violence that are a part of its systems of control and that emerge among the warlord and parochial rebels that it spawns, continues to undermine and suppress more radical rebel alternatives.

The sanctity of African states also plays a key role in limiting the incidence of interstate wars. Even parties to Africa's few interstate wars have claimed to fight for the principle of preserving existing borders. In 1985, conflicting interpretations of the true colonial borders caused a five-day war between Mali and Burkina Faso over a contested territory known as the Agacher Strip. The following year, the International Court of Justice (ICJ) ruled on the dispute, using colonial survey maps to define the border. Tanzania's attack on Idi Amin's government in Uganda in 1978–79 followed his decision to occupy the Kagera Salient. Amin claimed antigovernment rebels used it as a refuge from which to attack his regime. He also wanted to weaken Julius Nyerere, whom he suspected of allowing Ugandan rebels to have a base in Tanzania. Tanzanian forces took care to recognize their mutual border even after they invaded Uganda in a counterattack, fighting to install a friendlier regime, not to absorb Ugandan territory into their own.

Libya's military intervention in Chad tested the principle of respecting former colonial borders. Starting in 1973, President Muammar Qaddafi's government aided rebels in Chad. At the same time, Libyan soldiers started to occupy parts of northern Chad, laying claim to the 100,000-square-kilometer Aouzou Strip, while Qaddafi pressured the faction that he was backing to accept a political union with Libya. Only after obtaining French military aid did Chad's army expel the Libyans. In 1988, both governments agreed to abide by the OAU principle of accepting the old colonial border. They still disagreed about where that border lay, but instead of resorting to war, they referred their case to the ICJ in the Netherlands for arbitration. The ICJ ruled in Chad's favor in 1994, citing a 1955 French treaty with Libya's government that demarcated the border.

The Horn of East Africa has also seen contention over international borders. The border war between Eritrea and Ethiopia that began in 1999 resulted in well more than 100,000 casualties on both sides. Both sides, however, claimed that they were fighting about the true location of the colonial border, not to change it. The Somali invasion of Ethiopia in 1977–78 stands as a rare case of unabashed irredentism. Somalia's

independence constitution declared a mission to unify ethnic Somalis in an expanded Pan-Somali state. The country's five-pointed star
recalls "lost Somali" communities in Kenya, Ethiopia, and Djibouti. In
1964, Somalia's government first tested its claims through inciting ethnic Somali communities to demand unification with Somalia. A more
concerted effort began in 1977, when Somalia sent Western Somali
Liberation Front (WSLF) guerrillas to probe Ethiopian defenses, taking advantage of the turmoil produced by Ethiopia's 1974 revolution.
In April 1978 the Somali army invaded, but Ethiopia's army routed the
invaders with Soviet aid and advice and reestablished the old imperial
border.

These and other interstate conflicts in sub-Saharan Africa (see
Table 1) underline the consistent influence of three core principles
shaping the nature of conflict, regardless of the evolution in the ways
that states and rebels fight. First, only existing borders are legitimate
in the eyes of governments, regional organizations like the OAU (now
African Union), and the international community beyond Africa. This
is true even in the frequent instances when regimes reach across borders to make alliances with rebel groups as proxies, as will be seen in
Chapters 5 and 6. This is a kind of interstate war, but it does not involve
the clash of national armies (unlike in most of the examples in Table 1),
and there is practically no hint that any of the parties to conflict pro-
pose to change an existing international border. Second, the consent of
all affected parties is required to make new borders, as occurred during Eritrea's independence in 1993. Third, efforts to change borders
by force are considered illegitimate and will be met with international
efforts to reverse them. The 1991 multinational invasion of Iraq after
its occupation of Kuwait invoked this principle. In practical terms, this
means that the rest of the world accepts secessionists who want to divide
a country more readily than it does irredentists who want to unify parts
of different countries. As in Ethiopia, this acceptance usually follows
a negotiated settlement of a conflict and the mutual recognition that
dividing a country would be the best way to preserve peace.

Rebel leaders recognize the incentives and obstacles that these principles present. Rebels who fight to create an entirely new country or
revive a pre-colonial state will face stiff opposition. They will find few
overseas friends and are likely to suffer significant constraints on their
access to resources, especially compared to their opponents. Separatist
rebels face better prospects, although the Somaliland case shows that
this is a difficult path too. Thus rebels recognized the value of claiming to

Table 1 *The Rare Instances of Classic Interstate War in Sub-Saharan Africa*

Date(s)	Countries Involved	Event	International Action
1958	Egypt and Sudan	Egypt occupied territory on the Red Sea coast that Sudan claimed.	The Arab League pressured Egypt to withdraw. Egypt accepted Sudan's claim.
1964	Ghana and Upper Volta (now Burkina Faso)	Ghana occupied a village that Upper Volta claimed.	Ghana withdrew under OAU pressure.
1964	Somalia, Ethiopia, and Kenya	Somalia incited rebels in Ethiopia and Kenya to seek unification with Somalia.	The OAU mediated the conflict, and Somalia temporarily ceased to press its claims.
1973–87	Libya and Chad	Libya engaged in a creeping occupation of the Aouzou Strip and then pressured Chad's government to accept Libyan plans to unify the two countries.	France aided Chad's army in driving out Libya's army in 1987 after OAU mediation failed. Libyans accepted ICJ arbitration in 1990 and complied with a 1994 ruling in Chad's favor.
1975 and 1985	Mali and Burkina Faso	Mali occupied territory in both incidents. In 1985, both countries launched cross-border attacks.	In 1975, the OAU mediated, and Mali withdrew. Both countries accepted ICJ arbitration in 1985, which led to partition of the disputed area.
1978–79	Uganda and Tanzania	Uganda's army occupied the Kagera Salient. The Tanzanian army drove them out and overthrew Uganda's regime.	The successful Tanzanian invasion reaffirmed the original boundary.
1999–2000	Eritrea and Ethiopia	The two countries fought over a disputed border that resulted in more than 100,000 casualties.	A peace agreement in December 2000 led to the creation of the peacekeeping UN Mission in Ethiopia and Eritrea and the Eritrea-Ethiopia Boundary Commission to demarcate a mutually agreed border.

Source: Robert Jackson and Mark Zacher, "The Territorial Covenant: International Society and the Stabilization of Boundaries," Working Paper No. 15 (Vancouver, BC: Institute of International Relations, University of British Columbia, July 1997).

represent the entire country. The names adopted by major rebel groups
in Angola's liberation struggle revealed this awareness: the National
Union for the Total Independence of Angola (UNITA), the National
Front for the Liberation of Angola (FNLA), and the People's Movement for the Liberation of Angola (MPLA). This was true even though
local support and leaderships of all three of these groups overwhelmingly reflected the different ethnic constituencies of each. Regardless,
each aimed to seize control of the existing state, a result that foreigners
were much more likely to accept and support with political and material
assistance.

This is not to say that African governments never send their armies
into the territories of neighboring states. But when they do so, these
general principles make it attractive to them to seek out local armed
groups as proxies. Moreover, when national armies cross international
borders in Africa, they typically claim that they are restoring order
and explicitly reject any hint that they are making territorial claims.
Widespread reluctance of governments to challenge the legitimacy of
existing borders plays an important role in shaping the character of
warfare. The collapse of central government authority in Congo in the
1990s, for example, opened that country's territory to the influence
of neighboring governments. Five states – Uganda, Rwanda, Angola,
Namibia, and Zimbabwe – sent soldiers to support the local rebels that
each state favored. Some even created new rebel groups to extend their
influence. But in the 1996 Rwandan invasion of eastern Congo, when
several army officers stated that Rwanda sought to annex parts of Congo
occupied by ethnic kinsmen, their words met with swift condemnation
from their capital, followed by repeated clarifications to international
organizations. Control over existing states remains the prize for which
the great majority of rebels (and their foreign backers in cases like
Congo) have fought and continue to fight. The nature of international
support for rebels reinforces this state focus of African warfare. For
the past half century, such external support has emerged as an important element of an explanation for why warfare in sub-Saharan Africa
has evolved from anti-colonial liberation insurgencies to contemporary
warlords and parochial rebels.

The International Relations of Rebels

Soon after the OAU's establishment in Ethiopia in May 1963, its thirty-
two charter member states hastened to transform the remaining African

colonies into independent states. These members created the Coordinating Committee for the Liberation of Africa, commonly referred to as the Liberation Committee, to recognize "legitimate sole representatives" of oppressed peoples in regions where colonial rulers were not making preparations to depart. The committee focused on the Portuguese colonies – Mozambique, Angola, and Guinea – and the white minority–ruled territories of Southern Rhodesia (henceforth Rhodesia), South Africa, and Namibia, soliciting contributions from member states to finance liberation struggles. Official recognition offered the seal of legitimacy to particular liberation rebels, because internal and external states and organizations took the committee's cues concerning which group to support. In 1963, for example, it recognized Holden Roberto of the FNLA as the "legitimate leader of Angola," despite the earlier establishment of the MPLA and its status as the first to arrive on the field of battle against the Portuguese. The preference for FNLA lasted barely a year, for after the committee paid a field visit to the MPLA in 1964, it accepted the MPLA as a legitimate movement and gave it preferential aid after 1966.[24] Although OAU member states differed over whether to insist that competing rebel groups merge into a single anti-colonial rebel group or form a united coalition, the preferred rebels became the reference point against which other rebels were measured. The committee also influenced the UN Decolonization Committee, which sent missions to visit rebels and make recommendations to the UN General Assembly concerning diplomatic support and aid.[25]

This process rewarded articulate and diplomatically savvy rebel leaders, especially those steeped in the political debates of their university days and familiar with the languages, values, and lifestyles of the global Westernized elite among whom these rebels sought support. Through the Liberation Committee, they ensured that their struggle remained on the OAU agenda, and through the efforts of African diplomats, they retained the attention of the UN and the global audience. Such recognition encouraged other states to host their headquarters and give refuge to their fighters. In return, anti-colonial rebels had to present a reasonably unified façade to the committee, causing their leaders to focus on managing factional struggles to suppress rival claimants to the

---

[24] Fernando Andresen Guimarães, *The Origins of the Angolan Civil War* (New York: St. Martin's Press, 2001), 65–66.

[25] Emmanuel Dube, "Relations between Liberation Movements and the OAU," in N. M. Shamuyarira (ed.), *Essays on the Liberation of Southern Africa* (Dar es Salaam: Tanzania Publishing House, 1975), 25–68.

status of standard bearers of the anti-colonial struggle. Majority rule rebels fighting against white minority regimes in southern Africa, such as the South West Africa People's Liberation Organization (SWAPO), exhibited the overt strains over tactics and strategies that developed between exile leaderships, driven to secure external support for their cause, and local leaders who faced the practical challenges and risks associated with direct confrontation with the security forces of oppressive regimes.[26] Tensions between exile leaderships were more likely to stress a modern, secular nation-state project along the lines of European models, whether liberal or socialist, while local commanders dealt with the realities of local ideas about legitimate authority and the cultures of those among whom these commanders fought.

Considerable rebel effort went into deciding what kind of image to present to the rest of the world in the context of Cold War rivalries. Potential patrons scrutinized the personalities who made up the rebel leadership. Americans looked for evidence that anti-colonial rebels were willing to sideline radical leaders, while Soviet officials sought reliable socialists. This Cold War dynamic, although important to rebel efforts to secure outside support, aggravated factional struggles as rival rebel leaders sought their own foreign patrons. Factionalism also developed out of the tendency of rebel groups to retain separate organizational identities among followers, even after they merged into "official" anti-colonial rebel groups to obtain material and political benefits.

Overseas ideas also inspired rebel leaders and fighters. Marxism-Leninism appealed greatly to anti-colonial, majority rule, and state-building rebels. Not only did it offer the prospect of material assistance from countries such as Cuba, which began providing military training to the MPLA in 1965, but it also provided a useful framework for combining the nation-state idea with the struggle against oppression under the command of a unified rebel organization. This was true even among rebel groups, like the EPLF and TPLF, that fought against a government that received considerable military assistance from the Soviet Union. In those groups, a secular nation-state-building ideology helped to minimize religious and regional divides that threatened military and political cohesion. This ideology also glossed over differences in the ethnic and social identities of rebel leaderships (such as *mestiços* in Angola and Guinea and university-educated exiles from Rhodesia and South

---

[26] This theme is developed in Colin Leys and John Saul, *Namibia's Liberation Struggle: The Two-Edged Sword* (London: James Currey, 1995).

Africa) when their identities diverged from that of the majority of the population.[27] This is not to say that rebel leaders were personally cynical in their ideological pronouncements, although UNITA's Jonas Savimbi moved fairly readily from a Maoist perspective to an anticommunist stance once US support appeared attainable. Overseas student experience, ties with radical thinkers, and the practical exigencies of waging a successful military campaign influenced rebel ideology and tactics. Organizations such as the Conferência das Organizações Nacionalistas das Colonias Portuguesas (CONCP) brought insurgent leaders in the Portuguese colonies into regular contact with radical intellectuals and the Portuguese Communist Party for exchanges of practical advice and political debate; this sort of interchange helped to socialize rebel leaders to a particular set of goals and tactics.

The disappearance of socialist programs among armed groups in the 1990s reflected the 1980s political reforms in the Soviet bloc and the rapid adoption of market reforms in China and Vietnam that decimated the ranks of potential external sponsors of secular nationalist rebels. Rebels like the southern Sudan's SPLA courted American Christian groups and missionary societies after they lost the support of the Marxist Ethiopian leader when the socialist EPLF and TPLF ousted him from power, even as they retained elements of a centralized Marxist-Leninist party structure that they inherited from their experience under their old Soviet-backed patron.

Warlord leaders often turn to overseas business contacts that they made while abroad or while serving in pre-conflict governments. Some look to warlords in neighboring countries with whom they share personal and commercial contacts. Parochial rebels usually rely on support from communities and their diasporas that is circumscribed by ethnic or other social criteria, which limits their shared interests and hence cooperation with other rebels. Some, such as Sierra Leone's Civil Defense Forces (CDF), were able to attract support from overseas members of their ethnic community in the mid-1990s. Most find that humanitarian assistance can easily be converted to their purposes. This does not mean that these tendencies in rebel groups were absent before the 1990s, but that the incentives and opportunities available to rebels have changed. Consequently internal priorities shift, different skills become more highly prized, and individuals from different kinds of backgrounds rise to prominence.

[27] David and Marina Ottaway, *Afrocommunism* (New York: Africana, 1981), 101.

Even though most warlord rebels and parochial rebels do not challenge the existence of contemporary African states, hindsight suggests
that the socialist orientation of many earlier rebels provided them with
considerable incentives to accept the continued existence of Africa's
states on the colonial territorial pattern. Most of the influential global
political ideas of the second half of the twentieth century – communism,
liberalism, modernization – and even less influential ideas like North
Korea's Juche Path of self-sufficiency or the Libyan leader Qaddafi's
Third Way focused on how to make existing states work more effectively
through building a secular multiethnic national community to support
this project. The collapse of some of these models and growing suspicions of those that survive left the political field open to the spread of
more diverse ideas. Even so, the idea that politics should be organized in
states rather than empires, global religious communities, or some other
alternative, along with the difficulties of getting the rest of the world
to recognize such alternatives, continues to shape most rebel groups in
Africa. The mutual recognition of existing states on the part of regimes
and the rebels who challenge them has emerged as one of the strongest
global norms across all phases in the history of African warfare.
Whether alternatives to this norm have become more likely or would be
sustainable will be discussed further in Chapter 6. It is to the engine of
this change, the evolving nature of African states, that we now turn.

African States and the Changing Behavior of Rebels

Rebels contend not only with global society's idea of the state, but
also with the capabilities of actual states. Are regimes that run states
strong enough or clever enough to withstand assaults from rebels?
White minority–ruled Rhodesia and South Africa possessed some of
the world's more effective militaries, a remarkable feat given the unpopularity of their regimes among the majority of the population. In South
Africa, the African National Congress (ANC) concluded that public anger about South Africa's repressive measures would enable it to
establish liberated zones from which it could indoctrinate and organize the population to carry out a popular military assault against the
apartheid regime. Moreover, by the 1960s, international condemnation of the apartheid system led the ANC to believe that it would
obtain widespread outside support. But even though the ANC formed
Umkhonto we Sizwe (Spear of the Nation) in 1961 to fight a guerrilla

war, by the mid-1960s, most of the ANC leadership had been captured or forced into exile. Such setbacks left the ANC with little choice but to increase its reliance on outsiders for support. The ANC's political affiliations and strategies reflected its reliance on external support. Toward the end of the 1960s, the bulk of its military aid and a significant amount of other support may have derived from the Soviet Union and allied countries, some of which was funneled through the OAU's Liberation Committee.[28] Outside ties helped the ANC preserve its international visibility and legitimacy, but its inability to operate effectively in South Africa left the field open to other groups. The 1976 Soweto Uprising demonstrated the extent to which community leaders and local youth took on the burdens of fighting the apartheid regime and devised their own strategies. The growth of activism, which spread to government-organized labor unions and community associations, forced the ANC to recognize the interests and ideas of other groups. It effectively incorporated the new groups and infiltrated some government bodies, a move that by 1994 enabled it to force the white-majority government to hold South Africa's first democratic elections and to hand over power to the black majority.

In minority-ruled Rhodesia, the ability of the Zimbabwe African People's Union (ZAPU) and the Zimbabwe African National Union (ZANU) to occupy parts of the country in the 1970s allowed majority rule rebels the opportunity to create their own liberated zones. In 1978 the government could field only 14,000 white conscripts, through a draft extending to men up to the age of sixty, against a similar number of trained and armed rebels.[29] By the following year, Rhodesian forces faced more formidable conventional rebel forces armed with heavy weapons, including some "borrowed" from the newly liberated Mozambique's government. Because both of these majority rule rebel groups possessed considerable capabilities, they could fend off foreign pressures to form a single united "official" rebel group and could even devote some of their resources to fighting each other for primacy and to seeking out their own patrons.

Charles Tilly's formulation that making war against capable opponents forces rebels to develop their organizational capabilities fits neatly

---

[28] Sheridan Johns, "Obstacles to Guerrilla Warfare – A South African Case Study," *Journal of Modern African Studies* 11:2 (1973): 278–79.

[29] Anthony Clayton, *Frontiersmen: Warfare in Africa since 1950* (London: University College of London Press, 1999), 66–68.

with the experiences of many anti-colonial, majority rule, and state-reform rebels. Provided they did not become overwhelmingly dependent on outside aid, leaders of these rebel groups had to build the extractive tools of administration to collect taxes in their liberated zones and ensure the compliance and support of local people through courts and effective policing. In short, they had to create a state-within-a-state.[30] Those who were bereft of outside aid, or who rejected reliance on it, like the state-building EPLF, gained practical experience and built extensive social bases to which they could turn once in power. Although this did not guarantee that they would become effective rulers of states, combined with the expectation on the part of the Liberation Committee and other international bodies, this promoted the fortunes of the more bureaucratically proficient among the rebels.

Warlords and parochial rebels also reflect the characters of the states that they fight. Both fight states that have become quite weak in terms of their bureaucratic capabilities. As fighting became widespread in Liberia and Sierra Leone in the early 1990s, government revenues in both states had sunk to less than 10 percent of annual domestic outputs, about the equivalent of seventeenth-century English claims on subjects. A substantial body of scholarship points to the lure of easily looted resources such as diamonds or gold as a critical variable in shaping the behavior of warlords and marginal rebels.[31] But the dominance of easily looted resources and the behavior of warlords and parochial rebels reflect the particular nature of the states in which warlord and rebels fight. This is because, since independence, many regimes in Africa have faced considerable threats from groups within their own countries. Two and a half years after becoming independent in 1961, Tanzania's government faced a military mutiny. Three years after independence, Togo's president was killed in a successful coup. The year 1966 saw two coups in Nigeria, two in Burundi, and one each in the Central African Republic, Upper Volta (Burkina Faso), Uganda, and Ghana. Patrick McGowan estimated that from Sudan's independence in 1956 to the mid-1970s, there was a 60 percent chance that a sub-Saharan African president would be forced out of office through

[30] Charles Tilly, "War Making and State Making as Organized Crime," in Peter Evans, Dietrich Rueschemeyer, and Theda Skocpol (eds.), *Bringing the State Back In* (New York: Cambridge University Press, 1985), 169–91.

[31] A classic statement is found in Paul Collier and Anke Hoeffler, "Greed and Grievance in Civil War," World Bank Working Paper (Washington, DC: World Bank, Oct 2001).

coercive means, which included being killed in the process.[32] Consequently, many rulers created multiple security services, as much to watch potentially dangerous rivals in their own ranks as to protect the regime against enemies from outside of their political establishment. Presidents turned to ethnic kinsmen and family members whom they felt would be reliably loyal. Sprawling patronage networks bought off opponents, giving them a reason to curry the favor of the president and inform on one another. Although patronage politics provides short-term stability, it undermines the long-term capacity of the state to generate revenues and control corruption. This makes regimes less legitimate in the eyes of many citizens, which argues for more intense focus on patronage and creating yet more security services.

Increasing corruption, the predations of undisciplined security forces, and the political instability of unpopular regimes combined to undermine economic performance. Sometimes these conditions led to the collapse of entire economic sectors as businesses and entrepreneurs sent their money abroad instead of investing in the country. As economies declined, natural resources grew in importance as sources of revenues, particularly in relative terms. As the productive sectors of economies shrank, regimes that were denied tax revenues seized opportunities to exploit natural resources, especially diamonds, timber, and other easily transported goods, and used them as alternative avenues of patronage. Their political allies and clients became deeply entrenched in these activities, usually in conjunction with foreign partners. To the extent that presidents manipulated laws to allow some clients to pursue business deals in smuggling and other clandestine opportunities, less favored groups suffered economic disadvantage. These regime strategies also crowded into the businesses and other activities that hard-pressed communities customarily used to evade state control.

Ordinarily, these avenues of evasion, which instead were absorbed into the patronage networks of many African regimes, could offer social networks for liberation rebels to build support and extract resources. Eric Wolf explains that such areas of social activity that are normally beyond the domains of state control favor emerging rebel leaders who learn best how to leverage their access to a global field of political ideas, material support, and commercial networks to recruit and mobilize these insulated communities around a single narrative of rebellion.

---

[32] Patrick McGowan, "African Military Coups d'État, 1956–2001: Frequency, Trends and Distribution," *Journal of Modern African Studies* 41:3 (2003): 355.

These "fields of leverage," removed from the direct influence of state power, have played central roles in the history of rebellions, linking the everyday grievances and interests of fighters to the grand narratives that the leaders of rebellions convince participants are the real reasons why they fight.[33] But when regime kingpins occupy these would-be fields of leverage, the ideologically driven leaders of rebellion are denied their customary venues for recruiting and organizing unified forces of opposition. Even when the survival of the patron's regime comes into question, these resources are likely to finance the quest of a high-placed rival – a warlord – to become the next president and are kept beyond the reach of ideologically driven rebels.

Bureaucratically weak states in which regime authority is based on patronage in clandestine markets and other rackets turn out to be strong in an important way that decisively shapes the nature of armed groups. That is, they are able to prevent alternative political groups from organizing by denying them the social space and resources that they need to sustain their fighters, even when these states lack the bureaucratic capacity to control territory or police remote communities. This is partly because this kind of political authority normalizes the use of youth militias and other violent gangs as a central part of the patronage-based political system. These gangs often begin as youth wings but evolve into the personal militias of politicians as regimes lose the capacity to pay them directly. Patrons allow key political supporters to maintain these groups, partly to defend positions of privilege in illicit markets and against local critics when they are not being used directly in support of the regime. Although attention in studies of conflict often focuses on national armies and rebel groups, this element of authoritarian regimes (including regimes that tolerate regular elections) plays a critical part in shaping local politics. The youth militias and gangs disrupt and occupy the fields of leverage in which the ideologues that were prominent in anti-colonial and other rebellions would normally organize and acquire resources. Moreover, when these regimes collapse, those most able to mobilize resources for warfare are the politicians and businessmen who are closest to this militarized style of politics. Although this type of authoritarian politics often turns out to be deficient in shaping events at the local level and thus is vulnerable to challenge from its own strongmen, it is very effective at obstructing the organizational

---

[33] Eric Wolf, *Peasant Wars of the Twentieth Century* (New York: Harper & Row, 1969), esp. 288–91.

efforts of political outsiders and ideological critics. It is ironic that these bureaucratically crippled states do a better job of suppressing organized broad-based rebellion than did the formidable bureaucratic colonial and apartheid states. Thus one finds a shocking absence of this kind of rebellion across the continent, despite intense political debate at individual and group levels, considerable ideological content in music, and a host of other influences. In this regard, these authoritarian states discovered that it is better to send alley cats to catch rats than to send tanks for such tasks. And as shown in later chapters, this form of politics imparts patterns of rebel violence that are rarely population-centric in the sense of being used to gain the support of non-combatants and instead focus on capturing and controlling the resources of patronage.

The histories of conflicts in Liberia and Sierra Leone demonstrate this conformity of regime and rebel uses of violence, as new groups struggle to control resources that were the basis of patronage in the old regimes. For example, the articulate ideologue Elmer Johnson, a former US marine and partner of Charles Taylor, toured areas of Liberia that the NPFL controlled, and in the image of anti-colonial and majority rule rebel leaders, he delivered the popular message that the NPFL intended to drive out corrupt leaders through a multiethnic coalition. Johnson's message posed a threat to Taylor; if Johnson were to become more popular than Taylor, Johnson's political activities would impede Taylor's ability to control local resources. By 1990, there was no OAU Liberation Committee to which Johnson could appeal or convince that he best represented the aspirations of Liberian people. Meanwhile, Taylor deployed his control over business deals in stolen timber and other goods to buy guns and field more fighters. Eventually Johnson and other ideologues like him were killed, allegedly at Taylor's behest.

Parochial rebels most often emerge in sectors of the economy that presidential patronage networks had a hard time controlling and that already had local experience in fending off violent threats. Communities that were politically less favored often had to rely on communal networks to protect themselves from the regime's predations. Nigeria's OPC vigilantes, for example, grew out of Yoruba ethnic associations that defended the western region's political and business elites from the predations of the dictator Sani Abacha. Young men from urban streets, much like those who elsewhere fight for warlords, instead received their guns and training from customary religious and commercial authorities rather than from renegade members of the dictator Abacha's predatory patronage network. In these circumstances marginality turns into autonomy and more social pressure on these rebels to build liberated zones, albeit ones that reflect the particular values of those communities rather than the more universal notions of anti-imperialism or national liberation that animated earlier rebels. In addition, their defensive battle against corrupt regimes and, when state administrations collapse, against predatory factions that emerge out of old capital-based political cliques often means that these rebels define goals in terms of community defense rather than the control of the state.

Armed Groups and the Importance of Political Context

The impact that changes in international influences and in African state politics had on rebel behavior does not change the fact that the individuals who make up rebel groups (and the armies and militias of states) usually exhibit a broad range of motives for fighting, at least when they first join conflicts. These motives are consistent in their appearances in conflict after conflict, but this analysis focuses on the more important processes that shape how fighters end up fighting and how they get socialized into privileging some motives over others in their personal justifications for fighting. As James Scott explained, almost all rebel groups contain two influential elements: the leadership, which usually comes from whoever serves as that society's elite, and the followers, who come from among the ordinary people on the street. Their ideas about what they are fighting for are varied and motivate them in different ways.[34] Rebels therefore evolve and develop in ways that reflect how these leaders establish links with followers and how they collect and then manage resources – their fields of leverage. In the 1960s, the harshness of surviving colonial and white minority regimes shaped how rebels devised strategy and tactics along with then-contemporary ideas about the legitimacy of liberation politics, avenues of external assistance, and the constraints of norms of state sovereignty. The advent of politicized university students on the continent, their organizations, and the relative autonomy that these regimes allowed (compared to patronage-based ones later) also supplied social space for ideologically motivated and centrally organized rebels who mobilized people under their control.

---

[34] James Scott, "Revolution in the Revolution: Peasants and Commissars," *Theory and Society* 7:1 & 2 (Jan 1979): 97–134.

Anti-colonial, majority rule, and state-building insurgencies also had to suppress and struggle against the same predatory impulses that – in the context of warlords and patronage politics in general – are useful skills for asserting leadership when the aim is to attract followers. Across these different circumstances, followers still voice all manner of personal objectives in fighting. This researcher has spent enough time with rebels to recognize the huge diversity and sometimes banal and unexpected reasons that people fight. Some, like the West Side Boys in late 1990s Sierra Leone, were very concerned about striking a good image as a "West Side posse" as epitomized by the American West Coast rap star Tupac Shakur. Their interpretation of the violence of 1990s American rap music fit the objectives of renegade segments of the country's army and of a rebel leader who sought to control the country's diamonds in the context of that country's collapsing patronage-based political system. Earlier, in 1973, the state-building Ugandan rebel leader Museveni complained of the same kinds of followers:

> We recruited 54 boys.... Unfortunately these boys had not been well selected. They had mostly been working in towns like Nairobi and had a *kiyaaye* (*lumpen proletariat*) culture.... We even arrested a few of them and put them in jail.... Sometimes it is necessary to take strong action against indiscipline. It is better to combine discipline with administrative action.[35]

Museveni operated in a field of leverage in which he could control resources, but in a sociopolitical context that forced him to take into account local community interests if he wanted to continue controlling them. Very likely, this context favored someone like Museveni, an ideologue who perhaps was more inclined to see this behavior as inappropriate, instead of a warlord like Charles Taylor, an escapee of a US federal penitentiary, where he found himself on charges of embezzling approximately one million dollars in the course of his work on behalf of the Liberian president (whom he later sought to overthrow).

Such changes in context may explain why places like eastern Nigeria, the site of a hierarchical, reasonably effective separatist army in the 1960s, was a hotbed of competing warlords and parochial rebels forty years later. Likewise, southern Sudan's SPLA suffered continuous factional splits in the 1980s and early 1990s and then developed a remarkable coordination and discipline by the late 1990s. This is not to say that deeply rooted relationships are irrelevant. Some observers

---

[35] Museveni, *Sowing the Mustard Seed*, 85, 90.

note, for instance, that warlords and parochial rebels tend to be found in the parts of Africa that had the most decentralized pre-colonial political authorities, such as Sierra Leone, Liberia, and southeastern Nigeria. Societies with significant pre-colonial experiences with state bureaucracies – Eritrea, Ethiopia, Rwanda, and southern Uganda – produce more hierarchically organized armed groups.[36] Although these deep influences are important, changing fields of leverage count for a lot, and thus it is this theme that features in the analysis of the evolution of warfare in independent Africa in the chapters that follow.

[36] Christopher Clapham, *Africa and the International System: The Politics of State Survival* (New York: Cambridge University Press, 1996), 30.

CHAPTER 2

Anti-Colonial Rebels

Between 1961 and 1974 the anti-colonial rebels considered in this chapter fought in the Portuguese colonies of Guinea, Mozambique, and Angola. Majority rule rebels who fought the white minority–dominated governments in other parts of southern Africa are the subject of the next chapter. These two categories of rebels share many features. Nowhere did armed groups win a decisive military victory, although the Partido Africano da Independência da Guiné e Cabo Verde (PAICG) came closest, capturing about 80 percent of Portuguese Guinea by the time Guinea (Bissau) declared unilateral independence in 1973. White minority rule in Rhodesia ended with rebels in control of about a third of the country's territory. Right up to the end of the South African apartheid regime, the ANC had difficulty coordinating action inside the country. International diplomatic and material support for rebels reflected the global condemnation of colonialism. Also facing the intensification of international political isolation and ever-tightening economic sanctions, the white minority regimes recognized that the apartheid system was no longer tenable and held democratic elections that ultimately led to a black majority government in 1994. Thus international support for these rebels and pressure on the governments of target states played decisive roles in shaping the path for rebel victories.

The quid pro quo for international support was that anti-colonial rebels and those who fought against white minority governments had to commit to preserve existing international boundaries. In a rare Cold War consensus, the United States and the Soviet Union agreed that African colonies should become independent only within the boundaries that they inherited. Rebel hopes of receiving aid from the OAU Liberation Committee required unambiguous commitment to this territorial principle. Ethnic appeals to communities inhabiting both sides of a border threatened stability in states that were already independent, for it would create a precedent that people in other countries might split off to join another state, or that rebels might extend their mission of liberation to include communities across international borders.

Ethnic chauvinism and cross-border commercial opportunities would distract and undermine ideologically minded rebel agendas in the future, but during the period 1961–74, political programs were central to the recruitment and discipline of rebel fighters. The diverse interests of peasants and unemployed urban youth, who later played key roles in the armed groups of parochial rebels, were subsumed under the goals of anti-colonial liberation. The grand visions of liberation clashed with the personal ambitions of individual leaders and fighters, leading to serious factional in-fighting, which colonial and white minority governments exploited. Yet internal unity – the domination of a single narrative to explain why the rebels fought – remained a critical ingredient for attracting foreign diplomatic and material support, because most foreign states and organizations, at least up to the 1970s, would formally support only one rebel group in each conflict. Internationally organized peace negotiations in the 1960s and 1970s usually accepted the principle that there was only one legitimate rebel group in each conflict, a contrast to the 1990s trend that favored peace settlements involving coalition governments that incorporated wide arrays of rebel groups. As we will see in later chapters, this practice aided the fragmentation of rebel groups in later wars. But when only one rebel group could attain broad international support, rebels had to convince outsiders and oppressed populations that they were true liberators and that no rivals could challenge their claim. This strategy worked well when, as in Guinea and Mozambique, a single rebel group could dominate the field of diplomatic and military battle, but it was not able to prevent a stalemate in Angola by the 1970s, as opposing rebel groups became proxies for contending state backers.

Virtually all anti-colonial rebels espoused some form of nationalism, often in tandem with socialist ideology. This made sense for leaders who had to organize ethnically diverse groups of fighters if they were to win outside support and prevail over rivals. Promises of social justice offered the best prospect of achieving internal unity among university graduates, urban workers, and illiterate peasants. Socialism was ideally suited to providing a common narrative to which people with diverse grievances could subscribe. Struggles against the "capitalist imperialism" of colonial and white minority rule created the basis for secular, centralized, and disciplined popular movements that appealed to people who experienced everyday life immersed in clan, lineage, ethnic, and religious communities. This narrative of unity and renewal accommodated those for whom socialism at a personal level meant an end to taxation, the promise of easy living, freedom from being bossed about by a local big man, and even the abolition of the state. Thus the promise of independence could be understood in multiple, even contradictory ways during the armed struggle. Given good leadership, this ideological tool helped anti-colonial rebels to mobilize and discipline fighters whose personal ideas and motives later became important elements of warlord and parochial rebel insurgencies.

Socialism gave anti-colonial rebel leaders a global discourse and networks through which to share information and mobilize overseas supporters. It provided leaders with a future plan of action that envisioned a key role for the state, whether their followers wanted this or not. Their socialist focus on industrial development through centralized state planning was not so different from the goals of the regimes that they wanted to overthrow. For example, Portuguese plans to tackle the problems of underdevelopment in their colonies spoke to state-building concerns that the urban elite leaders of many anti-colonial rebellions shared. Moreover, the anti-colonial message offered the promise of upward mobility through removing foreign officials of the state and replacing them with successful rebel leaders. Thus socialism attracted radical intellectuals, their foreign backers, rural peasants, urban workers, and the unemployed through addressing the diverse goals of all these social groups. The results of rebel victory were a great shock to this coalition, as many who fought did not expect to get the centralized, overbearing state preferred by the elites. The international collapse of socialist states in the 1980s, which removed material and ideological support for these rebels and their governments, added to this crisis and greatly affected governance in the newly independent former colonies.

Socialism's ideological appeal during this period was especially important for understanding the dilemmas of contemporary rebels in Africa. Millenarian visionaries, the seemingly unfocused violence of urban unemployed youth, and the predations of enterprising looters were generally incorporated into the socialist milieu in ways that substantially modified or repressed supporters' original motivations within the unity and discipline of centrally organized insurgencies. International jihadist narratives and networks might offer a comparable contemporary philosophy for joining the diverse ideas, social worlds, and motivations of people who fight or could be motivated to fight against their rulers. But most Islamic revolutionaries insist on a rigid cultural and ideological conformity, compared to their socialist predecessors. A much more formidable obstacle to mobilization around this and other broad political narratives appears in the particular nature of recent authoritarian regimes, an issue that will occupy a central place in the arguments in Chapters 5 and 6.

Anti-colonial rebel success required showing outsiders a credible capability to control territory and administer communities. This meant that the first wave of anti-colonial rebel leaders had to convince local people to support them over rival rebel groups. The most effective way of doing this was to set up liberated zones that rebels controlled and administered as best they could. This imperative fit the guerrilla warfare strategy of the Chinese revolutionary leader Mao Zedong, laid out in his famous work, *On Guerrilla Warfare*. First, rebels establish bases along the border or in some inhospitable place that state security forces would find difficult to control. From there, rebels engage in acts of sabotage and hit-and-run attacks to show their presence to local people, among whom they begin political indoctrination. Once expanded bases are established, rebels start to administer liberated zones. They no longer need to use the tactics of irregular guerrilla warfare to fight the national army, because they can use their liberated zone refuge to build their own army to fight against the state's military.[1]

Foreign delegations and sympathetic academics visited liberated zones and wrote reports and essays praising the forward-looking rebels; they showed how the rebels out-governed the repressive and backward colonial state. They contributed to the argument that the rebels really were a state-in-waiting, devoted to the interests of the population (even if the reality was that these rebels used heavy doses of coercion and intimidation to keep non-combatants in line), and that they deserved global political recognition and support. When liberated zones were established, especially in Portuguese Guinea and Mozambique, and to lesser degrees in Rhodesia and Angola, they indeed became bases from which to involve local people directly in the liberation struggle, capture

---

[1] Mao Tse-tung (trans. Samuel Griffith), *On Guerrilla Warfare* (New York: Praeger, 1961).

arms from government garrisons, and bolster propaganda campaigns with concrete advances on the ground. Liberated zones also became places where rebels could eliminate their rivals through assassination or exile. This was not always easily done. In Angola, rebel leaders suffered serious factional splits that forced opposing rebel groups to devise different strategies and redouble campaigns for foreign support as the international supporters began to become more divided among themselves into the 1970s and later. It is the strategies of the anti-colonial liberation rebels that I now discuss in detail.

Differences in capabilities and strategies reflected the skills and networks of rebel leaders and the capabilities of their enemies. In Mozambique, until his death in 1969, Eduardo Mondlane maintained a high degree of discipline among the diverse groups that made up FRELIMO. Amilcar Cabral's pre-conflict experience in Guinea in the 1950s as an agronomist and his busy travel schedule helped him to develop a strong working accommodation among foreign diplomats, urban intellectuals, and peasants who were otherwise socially distant from one another. The improvisational skills of these leaders contributed to these accommodations, although factionalism would come to plague Angola's liberation struggle. These and other successes also reflected the nature of their enemies and the context in which backers gave assistance, all of which played a decisive role in shaping rebels' liberation struggles in each conflict.

Unity and Pragmatism in Portuguese Guinea

The anti-colonial struggle against Portuguese rule provides an excellent basis for comparing the challenges faced and the strategies adopted by anti-colonial rebels. Armed struggle began in Angola in 1961, in Guinea (later Guinea-Bissau) in 1963, and in Mozambique in 1964. By April 1974, the PAIGC controlled most of Guinea but had not completely defeated Portugal's army. Liberation came only after the military coup that month in Portugal, itself a consequence of the pressures on domestic politics produced by fighting African colonial wars. Similarly, the politics of liberation in Mozambique and Angola were integrally linked to the demise of authoritarian Portuguese politics.

By the time of the 1974 coup in Portugal, the French and British had just about completed the liquidation of their colonial empires. Whereas British officials bent before the pressures of nationalism in the 1950s

and devised new ways to co-opt local activists into transition governments, the Portuguese dictator Antonio de Oliveira Salazar had opted
for even tighter colonial state control. "The Overseas Territories of
Portugal shall be known as 'provinces,'" the national constitution read,
as "an integral part of the Portuguese State"[2]; it envisioned merging
Africans into Portuguese culture and civic life as *assimilados*. In practice, these were usually mixed-race *mestiços* who lived in cities. Salazar's
policy actually spread nationalist sentiment more rapidly among individuals in this small group, who made up less than one percent of
the non-European populations in the Portuguese colonies. *Assimilados*
among the founders of Angola's Movimento Popular de Libertação de
Angola (MPLA) and Guinea's PAIGC, for example, had already developed a strong intellectual focus. As students in Portuguese universities
in the 1950s, they had discussed ideas and enjoyed exposure to European critics of colonial rule. Overseas education, combined with later
participation in armed struggle, imparted a high degree of ideological
focus among this small, tight-knit group of liberation rebels, linking
them to contemporary political debates in Europe and helping them
to formulate political strategies for armed struggle. The irony of this
kind of intensification of state control – once called modernization –
was that it created all sorts of social spaces, such as university classrooms, technocrats' offices, and so forth, that were very difficult for the
bureaucratic authoritarian colonial regime to control. In effect, the state
was getting better at fighting a bureaucratic form of regular warfare at
the same time that it was (unintentionally) creating the kinds of fields
of leverage that bureaucracies did not reach and that were ideal for
future guerrilla war fighters to organize themselves, recruit followers,
and propagate their nationalist ideas.

At the start of armed struggle in Angola in February 1961, it was
not yet evident that Portugal would fight to keep its colonies. That year
the UN General Assembly condemned Portugal's policies, beginning
the international isolation of Salazar's government. At about the same
time, the US government voted to support a UN measure to force the
Portuguese to submit information about their overseas "provinces"
to the UN Decolonization Committee. Later international opposition
led to the establishment of the UN Special Committee on Territories
under Portuguese Administration, a base for regular denunciations of

---

[2] Articles 134 and 135 of the Portuguese Constitution in 1957, in Ronald Chilcote,
Emerging Nationalism in Portuguese Africa: Documents (Stanford, CA: Hoover Institution
Press, 1972), 18.

Portuguese policies. Portugal's refusal to accept the principle of decolonization became an obstacle to joining the European Economic Community (later the European Union), just as the benefits of association with that organization were becoming more widely known.

Some Portuguese military officers supported ending colonialism in favor of closer ties to the rapidly developing postwar western European economy; they preferred to focus instead on modernizing the military. Dissatisfaction with Portugal's growing isolation contributed to a failed coup attempt on 13 April 1961. Salazar responded by appointing loyal officers to higher ranks and blocking the promotions of reformers. In the aftermath of India's invasion of Goa, a Portuguese colonial enclave, in December 1961, Salazar found an effective means of controlling his critics among the officers. Portuguese resistance collapsed after a few days, and Portugal's military failure on the Indian coast gave Salazar the opportunity to blame reformist officers for the country's defeat. His message was clear: If officers did not defend the colonies heroically in the coming wars, they would be punished. Thus Salazar not only politicized promotion in the military ranks; he also attached the defense of the colonies to the survival of his regime.

Nationalists in Portuguese colonies quickly realized that liberation would not follow the relatively peaceful path to independence of the British and French colonies.[3] The violent Portuguese response to the 1959 dockworkers' strike in the capital of Portuguese Guinea forced Guinea's nationalist intellectuals to recognize that they would have to use more militant means in their fight for liberation. Cabral led a cohesive and unified rebellion against the colonial administration. Cabral had to overcome the dangers of factionalism in the PAIGC and difficulties in organizing followers that plagued rebel groups in other Portuguese colonies and white minority–ruled countries. At the outset, he had to contend with the rival Frente para a Libertação e Independência da Guiné Portugesa (FLING), which received modest support from the government of neighboring Senegal. From 1960, the PAIGC leadership found refuge in the neighboring Republic of Guinea, the former French colony that became independent in 1958 under the radical President Sekou Touré.

---

[3] Those liberations from colonialism did experience nationalist violence, especially in Cameroon, Kenya, and Congo. See, for example, Richard Joseph, *Radical Nationalism in Cameroon* (Oxford: Clarendon Press, 1977); and Wunyabari Maloba, *Mau Mau and Kenya: An Analysis of a Peasant Revolt* (Bloomington: Indiana University Press, 1998).

Cabral's choice of refuge was crucial. Unlike Senegal's President Léopold Senghor, who insisted that FLING adopt a moderate program, Touré shared Cabral's socialist rhetoric and permitted the PAICG to set up the Pilot School training camp and use the Republic of Guinea to receive military aid from African and Soviet sources. The Pilot School gave Cabral the means to organize and control the recruitment and training of commissars, or political agents within the rebel group who would enforce the organization's political purpose and would root out critics and those – shades of warlord rebels of the future – who would misbehave and play to the short-term personal interests and desires among PAICG's rank and filers. Unlike Senghor, who allowed dissident intellectuals and PAIGC members to settle in Senegal, Touré used his authoritarian control in the Republic of Guinea to repress critics of the PAIGC. After Cabral's visit in 1966 to the Tricontinental Conference of Socialist Insurgent Groups in Havana, the PAICG benefited from Cuban military advisors, who were also welcome in the Republic of Guinea. Although Cabral was a very skilled political and military thinker, his good fortune in finding refuge with an ideologically compatible neighbor who dealt with him as the sole and rightful leader of the rebellion helped him to control insurgents, eliminate rivals, and present his PAIGC as the only viable recipient of foreign assistance able to confront the Portuguese colonial forces.[4]

By 1963, Cabral was ready to lead the PAIGC in battle inside Portuguese Guinea. The insurgent army, the Forças Armadas Revolucionárias de Povo (FARP), opened two fronts, forcing the Portuguese to disperse soldiers over a wide area. This allowed Cabral to establish liberated zones from which to confront colonial forces. The PAIGC guarded against rival groups by winning over the local population through providing social services and involving them in the liberation struggle, a strategy that raised the standard of effectiveness that any competitor would have to meet. Portugal's military attacked these liberated zones from the air with bombs and napalm raids, but they failed to cut PAIGC routes back into the Republic of Guinea. By the mid-1960s, FARP's 5,000 fighters had achieved great success against the opposing force of 40,000 Portuguese soldiers and their local recruits, thus giving the

---

[4] Several scholars stress Cabral's leadership skills: Basil Davidson, *The Liberation of Guiné: Aspects of an African Revolution* (Harmondsworth: Penguin, 1968); Gérard Chaliand, *Armed Struggle in Africa: With the Guerrillas in "Portuguese" Guinea* (New York: Monthly Review Press, 1969); and Patrick Chabal, *Amilcar Cabral: Revolutionary Leadership and People's War* (New York: Cambridge University Press, 1983).

PAIGC access to Portuguese Guinea's rural economy. As a result of attacks on foreign plantations and their control over borders and trade routes, the PAIGC added trade in agricultural goods to their source of income with which to buy weapons and other supplies and to administer their liberated zones.[5] By 1968, the PAIGC had acquired Soviet anti-aircraft guns, which it used against air attacks and artillery to destroy Portuguese garrisons.

The PAIGC successes reflected a classic application of Mao's strategy of setting up liberated zones and then mobilizing local people to fight for control of more area, culminating in an outright military confrontation against the enemy.[6] "We decided," said Cabral, "that we should never struggle from outside. . . . We adopted a strategy that we might call centrifugal: we started in the center and moved toward the periphery of our country."[7] Nonetheless, the availability of a neighboring country's territory as a refuge, that neighbor's intolerance of rival rebels, the internal capacity to reinforce the unity of the PAIGC, and the global connections to acquire sophisticated weapons were crucial elements of this strategy. This success made the PAIGC especially appealing to overseas supporters who shared their anti-colonial agenda. It discouraged rival groups from forming, for FARP dominated fighting on the ground and the PAIGC controlled liberated zones inside Portuguese Guinea. By contrast, neither the African National Congress (ANC) in South Africa nor the rebels in Angola could effectively develop such a strategy. The ANC was never able to set up liberated zones inside South Africa, whereas Angolan rebels suffered factional splits in their own ranks. Both organizations showed how the absence of one condition – a hegemonic rebel group with strong backing from a neighboring state – could compromise attainment of the others and undermine the whole rebel enterprise.

In the course of the liberation of Guinea, Cabral's fighters did suffer significant military setbacks at the hands of the Portuguese, who used counterinsurgency strategies that would be deployed by other white minority regimes. But the arrival in Portuguese Guinea of General António Ribeiro de Spinola in March 1968 marked a turning point in colonial policy. Recognizing the importance of PAIGC's mobilization of people in liberated zones, Spinola sought to do much the same

[5] Mustafa Dhada, "The Liberation War in Guinea-Bissau Reconsidered," *Journal of Military History* 62 (July 1998): 572. Dhada's analysis informs the following discussion of Portuguese strategy.

[6] Mao, *On Guerrilla Warfare*.

[7] Amilcar Cabral, "Determined to Resist," *Tricontinental* 8 (Sept 1968): 118.

against the PAIGC. Mimicking some of the irregular warfare strategies of the rebels, he organized Commandos Africanos with highly trained and well paid recruits drawn disproportionately from Fula ethnic communities and then set up a political counterforce, the Frente Unida de Libertacão (FUL). Spinola hoped that FUL would exploit the fact that Cabral and many of his associates were educated, mixed-race *mestiços* from Cape Verde and would become a sort of counter-rebel group. Unlike the anti-colonial narrative, Spinola's plan rested on the mobilization of parochial concerns among recruits. For example, some mainland PAIGC leaders, like Rafael Barbosa, resented what they saw as the ethnic favoritism for mixed-race *mestiços*. After his release from a Portuguese prison, Barbosa's dissatisfaction led him to become the leader of FUL. The colonial government also distributed goods, experimented with local government reforms to strengthen the authority of local chiefs who might influence young men to fight on the side of the colonial government, and promoted agricultural development projects in areas that FUL operated as rival "liberated zones."

Spinola adroitly exploited social divisions within the PAIGC. Portuguese security forces released political prisoners, some of whom joined the FARP as paid informers or on threat of blackmail. They recruited what Cabral called "the really *déclassé* people, the permanent layabouts, the prostitutes and so on." He complained that such persons "have been a great help to the Portuguese police in giving them information; this group has been outrightly against our struggle."[8] Infiltration became so great a problem for the PAIGC that FARP commander Luiz Cabral (Amilcar's half-brother) complained that infiltrators joined FARP to sow rumors about nepotism among leaders. After Portuguese bombing in January 1973 provoked a refugee exodus into the Republic of Guinea, Portuguese agents mingled with these refugees – a political use of refugees that will appear in later conflicts to be discussed in Chapter 4 – to plot against the PAIGC in its rear base. Their infiltration aggravated other factional splits within the PAIGC that led to Cabral's assassination on 20 January 1973 in the Republic of Guinea.

Then, in a turnabout, FARP began using Soviet heat-seeking missiles against Portuguese helicopters and heavy artillery against Portuguese positions. This sowed the seeds of serious future factional splits, but at the time it helped to deal a blow to the colonial army. By

---

[8] Amilcar Cabral, "Brief Analysis of the Social Structure in Guinea," in his *Revolution in Guinea* (New York: Monthly Review Press, 1969), 62.

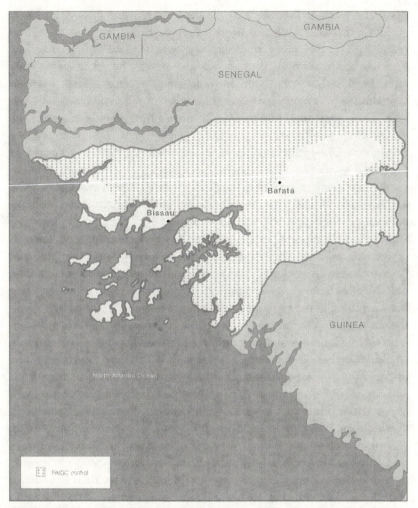

MAP 1. PAIGC Liberated Zone, Guinea-Bissau, September 1973. Based on
Basil Davidson, "Portuguese-Speaking Africa: The Fight for Independence," in
Michael Crowder (ed.), *The Cambridge History of Africa*, vol. 8 (New York:
Cambridge University Press, 1984), 787.

September 1973, PAIGC leaders concluded that they had liberated
enough of the country – about 80 percent – to declare independence unilaterally (Map 1). Substantial documentation of PAIGC's
population-centric efforts was marshaled on the basis of the work
of numerous journalists, filmmakers, and academics who had visited liberated zones. More than seventy-five nations recognized this

declaration, and in November 1973 the Organization of African Unity (OAU) admitted PAIGC-controlled Guinea-Bissau as its forty-second member. The UN General Assembly passed a resolution demanding Portuguese withdrawal. Portuguese withdrawal, however, came only after April 1974, when Spinola himself led a coup against Marcelo Caetano, Salazar's successor. Although the coup denied the FARP and PAIGC outright total military victory, once Spinola was in power, he agreed to a ceasefire and negotiations. In July 1974 he announced that Portugal would grant independence to what by then was known as Guinea-Bissau.

The Portuguese strategy, particularly from 1968, highlighted the danger that multiple grievances and agendas of fighters posed to anti-colonial rebel groups. Spinola's attempts to split the insurgency along ethnic lines exploited Cabral's inability to counter ethnic grievances if he were to maintain colonial boundaries as a condition of outside aid. "For example, in Guinea," wrote Cabral, "there are ethnic groups, the so-called tribes.... We know how great the contradictions were between them in the past, and sometimes a not-so-distant past.... And the Portuguese can and do exploit this to provoke conflicts between our folk."[9] Cabral hoped that fighting for liberation from colonial rule would erase these differences, but the PAIGC's failure to protect many of these people, especially as bombing raids intensified in the 1960s and Spinola's Commandos Africanos began to invade liberated zones, exposed the limits of this strategy. Moreover, Portuguese attacks on liberated zones exploited the everyday concerns of people living there. "Remember always that the people do not fight for ideas, for things that only exist in the heads of individuals," wrote Cabral. "The people fight and they accept the necessary sacrifices. But they do it in order to gain material advantages, to live in peace, and to improve their lives, to experience progress..."[10] Spinola lowered tariffs so as to fill markets with cheaper foreign imports, including food, a policy that strained the PAIGC's resources where they had opened people's stores to attract farmers with promises to pay higher prices.[11] As later chapters will show, authoritarian African regimes would discover all sorts of

[9] Amilcar Cabral (trans. Michael Wolfers), *Unity and Struggle: Speeches and Writings* (London: Heinemann, 1980), 40.

[10] Quote from Thomas Henriksen, "People's War in Angola, Mozambique, and Guinea-Bissau," *Journal of Modern African Studies* 14:3 (1976): 381.

[11] Al J. Venter, *Portugal's War in Guiné-Bissau* (Pasadena, CA: Munger Africana Library, 1973), 39.

nonbureaucratic means to exploit these short-term and parochial interests among followers that were of such concern to Cabral.

Beyond Portuguese threats, Cabral complained of the difficulty of mobilizing people behind an ideological message and militarily disciplined insurgency. He wrote, "In Guinea, the peasants are subjected to a kind of exploitation equivalent to slavery, but even if you try to explain to them that they are being exploited and robbed, it is difficult to convince them . . ."[12] Thus although anti-colonial nationalism remained a powerful force and Portugal's international isolation intensified, Spinola's strategy attracted some support among Africans. As Spinola's counterinsurgency effort exploited social divisions and material concerns to entice people to collaborate, the PAIGC adopted pragmatic responses and tolerated the cultural particularities of peasant communities. In some instances it literally purchased compliance. For example, Cabral said of Fula itinerant traders, among whom Spinola was able to recruit soldiers, that "their fundamental aim is to make bigger and bigger profits." Their trading network, however, could also be turned into a useful tool for surveillance and passing messages for the liberation movement. "All we would have to do was give them some reward, as they usually would not do anything without being paid."[13]

Cabral also contended with the social distance between the top PAIGC leaders, including himself, and rank-and-file fighters in Guinea. As late as 1960, Cabral was one of only fourteen non-European university graduates in Portuguese Guinea's population of about half a million.[14] During his student days in the late 1940s, he engaged in discussions with other colonial intellectuals about African culture, including the poet and a future founder of Angola's MPLA anti-colonial rebel group, Mário Pinto de Andrade. But his social distance from Portuguese rulers turned out to be greater. It was fortuitous for the anti-colonial cause that on Cabral's return to Guinea in 1950, his application for a job in the Portuguese civil service was rejected on racial grounds. Instead he found work as a "grade two agronomist" in the UN Food and Agriculture Organization (FAO). This obstacle to his upward mobility in colonial society forced him into circumstances better suited to recruiting future PAIGC members than to pursuing his

---

[12] Quoted in Patrick Chabal, "The Social and Political Thought of Amilcar Cabral: A Reassessment," *Journal of Modern African Studies* 19:1 (1981): 40.

[13] Cabral, "Brief Analysis," 60.

[14] David Andelman, "Profile: Amilcar Cabral," *Africa Report* 15:4 (May 1970): 18. Information on Cabral's background is found in Chabal's study, *Amilcar Cabral*.

ambitions in a constricted civil service career. His conduct of an FAO agricultural census brought him in contact with local leaders. In 1958, his travels in Angola gave him insights into the dynamic of mobilization in the countryside, especially of the difficulties of organizing peasants to give up their everyday activities, accept new ideas, and take personal risks to fight colonial rule. This sojourn also introduced him to Angolan nationalists beyond his earlier university network.

The early leadership of the PAIGC included salaried state workers. Aristide Periera managed the telephone office in the capital, and Fernando Fortes used his position as head of the post office to help Cabral evade the police. Domingos Ramos, an early regional commander of a liberated zone, was the son of a colonial bureaucrat. Others whose upward mobility was limited under colonial rule and whose skills and connections could earn them higher status in an independent Guinea relocated to PAIGC headquarters in the Republic of Guinea. Among "young people recently arrived from the rural areas," Cabral found that those with some education "gradually [came] to make a comparison between the standard of living of their own families and that of the Portuguese."[15] Francisco Mendes, who became the first prime minister of Guinea-Bissau, left secondary school to travel to the Republic of Guinea to join the PAIGC. Other commanders included rural clerks, artisans, and partially educated young men who were influenced by nationalist teachers in mission schools. During Cabral's career as an agronomist in Portuguese Guinea, he had the opportunity to meet Balanta chiefs, many of whom had rejected Portuguese colonial rule when it threatened to dilute their power. Once these chiefs cast their lot with the PAIGC, young men from their areas joined the liberation struggle in large numbers. Connections to rural chiefs who controlled armed youth were a crucial asset for Cabral for maintaining discipline within the diverse PAIGC.

Cabral's education and diplomatic skills were critical for solidifying PAIGC control of the rebellion. Along with his university connections, his multilingual ability (he spoke English and French as well as Portuguese) enabled him to reach broad audiences. His constant travel for the PAIGC – eighty-eight trips between 1960 and 1974, according to one scholar – took him to diverse venues, including trips to Sweden to attend the Swedish Social Democratic Party meeting (1970), to the United States to testify before the Senate (1970), to the USSR to

---

[15] Cabral, "Brief Analysis," 62.

negotiate military aid (1968), to Cuba to attend a Third World solidarity meeting (1966), to Tanzania to help organize a Pan-African federation of liberation movements (1965), and to Ethiopia to petition the UN and the OAU's Liberation Committee for support (1965).[16]

Cabral's success illustrated the huge importance of skillfully exploiting international opportunities in the 1960s and 1970s offered by the global rejection of colonialism, which later disappeared. Internally, it showed the importance of mobilizing and disciplining the diverse interests and grievances among fighters in the anti-colonial rebellions, a task that the flexible adoption of socialist ideas facilitated. A remarkable feature of this record is the extent to which groups that played dominant roles in later conflicts, such as those Cabral called "the really *déclassé*," or what in future conflicts would appear as a "lumpen proletariat," were incorporated into the pragmatic ideological and military framework of the PAIGC. Cabral also showed the importance of mobilizing skilled and educated middle managers to join the liberation movement, social groups that have played and continue to play central roles in a great number of Africa's wars. Members of this social group, however, would find over time that emigration and work in NGOs offered alternative paths to leading and staffing rebel groups to pursue personal aspirations. This became especially important in the 1980s and 1990s as other conditions hampered the sustenance of ideological and program-driven rebellions.

Pragmatism and Precarious Unity in Mozambique

Frente de Libertação de Moçambique (FRELIMO) in Mozambique found a skilful leader in Eduardo Mondlane and critical backing from a sympathetic neighboring state. Within a year of Tanzanian independence in December 1961, FRELIMO held its first congress in Dar es Salaam. Supported by Tanzanian President Julius Nyerere, Mondlane capitalized on his personal connections to other anti-colonial nationalists, including Cabral, Agostinho Neto, and Mário Pinto de Andrade, then the leader of MPLA in Angola. Together they established the Conferência das Organizações Nacionalistas das Colonias Portuguesas (CONCP) as a forum for the internationally recognized anti-colonial

---

[16] Mustafah Dhada, *Warriors at Work: How Guinea Was Really Set Free* (Denver: University Press of Colorado, 1993), 174–80.

rebels in Portuguese territories. Previously, Mondlane had used his position as a UN research officer on trust territories to hear appeals from anti-colonial activists in Mozambique and to develop personal connections to local community leaders and educated nationalists, much as Cabral had used his UN connection.[17]

Mondlane's rise to leadership over a unified movement was precarious. Marcelino dos Santos, an activist in the Rhodesia-based União Democrática Nacional de Moçambique (UDENAMO), invited Mondlane to join his organization just as it prepared to move to Tanzania in 1961. Recognizing dos Santos's close ties to Kwame Nkrumah, the ardent Pan-Africanist leader of Ghana, Mondlane refused the offer. He knew that Nyerere was suspicious of Nkrumah's bid to influence anti-colonial rebels and of dos Santos's connections to Nkrumah's African Freedom Fighters Conference in Ghana. Mondlane also knew that Nyerere backed the Mozambique African National Union (MANU), which already had strong roots in the Mozambican migrant community in Tanzania. Part of MANU's attraction to Nyerere lay in its inclusion of Tanzanian officials among its members, including the head of Tanzania's ruling party and several ministers of government who had been born in Mozambique.[18] Aware that Nyerere preferred to back only one set of Mozambique anti-colonial rebels, dos Santos realized that the most viable option for getting Tanzanian support was to merge UDENAMO with MANU. As long as UDENAMO remained in white-ruled Rhodesia, it could not expect support from that quarter. As Cabral's association with the Republic of Guinea's Sekou Touré showed, access to the territory and diplomatic support of a friendly regime in a neighboring state was critical to establish liberated zones and gain broader international political and military support.

Mondlane exercised considerable pragmatism in becoming the head of this alliance of organizations. After a June 1962 conference in Dar es Salaam, he succeeded in persuading MANU to merge with his group, a necessity if he was going to get significant outside support, and christened the new coalition FRELIMO. His rise to prominence in the anti-colonial movement revealed a personal commitment to nationalist revolution in Africa. At first it was not apparent that he would even return

---

[17] On Mondlane's connections and background, see Helen Kitchen, "Conversation with Eduardo Mondlane," *Africa Report* 12:8 (Nov 1967): 31–51.
[18] This and the next paragraph draw from João Cabrita, *Mozambique: The Torturous Road to Democracy* (New York: Palgrave Macmillan, 2003), 3–13.

to Africa. He and his American wife, Janet,[19] were not at odds at first with Portugal's minister for colonies, whom they met when Mondlane worked for the UN. He accepted a lectureship in sociology at Syracuse University in New York (where he taught from 1961 to 1963, traveling to Africa during summer break) and was sought to teach at a university in Portugal or at a new institution in Mozambique. He visited Mozambique for the first time in eleven years in 1961, a time when Portuguese repression had intensified and local revolutionary ideas had gained grassroots support. The visit convinced him to commit his career to joining the anti-colonial rebellion and taking up a leadership position in it. Meanwhile, he had developed contacts among Kennedy administration officials in Washington and met with State Department officials to advise them that "the United States should be in a position to encourage Portugal to accept the principle of self-determination . . . set target dates and take steps towards self-government and independence by 1965."[20] Perhaps, like other African intellectuals, Mondlane had hoped that Portugal would leave its African colonies peacefully as the British and French had. With backing from the United States and a strong base in Tanzania, he could capitalize on favorable international developments. If freeing his country from what turned out to be entrenched Portuguese domination – and becoming its first president – was the goal, ideological pragmatism and the services of a powerful state were necessary. Timing was important, because other ambitious people competed for this prize, and they too looked for sponsors.

Mondlane's opportunity came in June 1962, as Mozambique groups convened in Dar es Salaam. A key UDENAMO organizer had left for India to appeal for support for the anti-colonial movement. In his absence, Mondlane explored with UDENAMO members a pragmatic proposition that he could help supporters get scholarships to study in the United States.[21] Even as an undergraduate at Oberlin College in the early 1950s, Mondlane had been sought after as a speaker on Portuguese African issues on campuses and in conferences. He attracted the

---

[19] Janet Mondlane was born Janet Rae Johnson in 1934 and grew up in a small town in Illinois. She met Mondlane in 1951 at a church camp in Geneva, Wisconsin. They were married in 1956, and she went on to receive her MA from the African Studies Program at Boston University.

[20] Quoted in Cabrita, *Mozambique*, 6.

[21] A number of influential groups – including the Ford Foundation, the Institute of International Education, and the African American Institute – as well as universities and the Kennedy administration recognized the importance of American education in establishing links with emergent African elites.

attention of Northwestern University professor Melville J. Herskovits and other people interested in African issues, and he graduated from that institution in 1960 with a doctorate in sociology.[22] He had appeared in public settings with Wayne Fredericks, a former Ford Foundation official who became in 1961 the deputy assistant secretary of state for Africa in the State Department's new Africa Bureau. Fredericks initiated quiet contacts between US government officials and leaders of southern Africa's anti-colonial rebels and would later play a role in US engagement in South Africa while working as a manager for the Ford Motor Company. Mondlane turned these and other influential contacts into political resources to promote his bid for leadership of the unified organization and to help him to secure Tanzanian backing.

The OAU's Liberation Committee was headquartered in Dar es Salaam, where it received Nyerere's strong support. This helped to assure recognition of FRELIMO as Mozambique's official liberation movement. Recognition, aid, and military training for several hundred members gave FRELIMO the means to launch its first major attack on Portuguese positions in Mozambique on 24 September 1964. Nyerere also allowed Mondlane and his wife to establish the Instituto Moçambicano (Mozambique Institute) in Dar es Salaam. There FRELIMO-trained fighters lobbied the OAU Liberation Committee for aid, and aided by Tanzanian authorities, they received arms shipments from Soviet bloc states. The institute gained wide international appeal: The Ford Foundation and then Swedish International Development Authority (SIDA) gave it substantial grants.[23]

Nyerere's patronage protected FRELIMO from challenges from other factions, just as Touré's patronage protected the PAIGC from rivals. Until Malawi's independence in 1964, Tanzania was the only independent African-ruled territory bordering Mozambique. White-ruled Rhodesia and South Africa were not viable bases for anti-Portuguese liberation insurgencies. Moreover, after 1964, Malawi's new president, Hastings Banda, was hostile to what he saw as a dangerously radical liberation movement. Thus Mozambican migrant workers and students in those countries who wanted to fight for liberation saw FRELIMO as their best choice for independence. Not all recruits were

---

[22] Eduardo Mondlane, "Role Conflict, Reference Group and Race," PhD dissertation, Department of Sociology, Northwestern University, 1960.

[23] For details on arms shipments, see Paul Whitacker, "Arms and the Nationalists," *Africa Report* 15:4 (May 1970): 14; non-military aid, Tor Sellström, Sweden and *National Liberation in Southern Africa*, vol. 1 (Uppsala: Nordiska afrikainstitutet, 1999), 449–56.

reconciled to this state of affairs. Some of MANU's ethnic Makonde members complained that FRELIMO's leadership only represented educated *assimilados* and *mestiços* from southern Mozambique and that they sought northern Makonde as foot soldiers in their fight to become the rulers of an independent country but were unwilling to share the rewards of office. Nyerere's interference and police threats to investigate non-citizens facilitated the expulsion of critics, but the armed phase of the anti-colonial rebellion could only be started from the north with the help of a friendly state, and this fact aggravated these ethnic tensions.

FRELIMO rank-and-file suspicions of southern dominance affected leadership decisions. In late 1962, Mondlane sent FRELIMO's secretary for defense and security, Leo Milas, whom he had met earlier in the United States, to mediate in Dar es Salaam. Milas played a central role in expulsions and defections from the movement and emerged as an ambitious figure. But now Mondlane had to shed the image of a remote elitist among FRELIMO's northern Makonde followers, which Milas's actions had helped to promote. In fact, Milas turned out to be a controversial character. Mondlane had suspected his sincerity and hired an agency to investigate his background. It was discovered that Milas was an imposter. He really was Leo Clinton Aldridge, an African American who had learned Portuguese at the University of Southern California.[24] Expelled by FRELIMO in August 1964, he moved to Khartoum, where he published anti-FRELIMO documents under the name of Seifak-Aziz. By 1977 he allegedly played a role in organizing the Mozambique National Resistance (MNR).[25] This organization would become the Resistência Nacional Moçambicana (RENAMO), which rebelled against the FRELIMO-led government of Mozambique in the 1980s.

The Milas affair provides a good illustration of the point that most of Africa's rebel groups through the earlier decades of independence contained people with diverse motivations. In a later time, Milas might have found more opportunities to pursue his personal ambitions in a rebel group, or perhaps to organize his own faction at the expense of the rebel group's overall political program. But in the context of the 1960s anti-colonial rebellions, FRELIMO's leader received considerable backing to address these divisive tendencies. Moreover, Mondlane had to

---

[24] John Marcum, "Three Revolutions," *Africa Report* 12:8 (Nov 1967): 18–19.

[25] Alex Vines, *Renamo Terrorism in Mozambique* (London: James Currey, 1991), 11; Phyllis Johnson and David Martin (eds.), *Destructive Engagement: Southern Africa at War* (Harare: Zimbabwe Publishing House, 1986), 8–9.

present himself as a broadly appealing leader who could demonstrate concrete achievements on the ground in return for external support. At that time, characters with personal skills and ambitions that resembled those of Milas were at a disadvantage.

FRELIMO continued to use its Tanzanian base to mobilize Makonde people who straddled the Tanzania-Mozambique border. In 1966 FRE-LIMO attacked fortified Portuguese positions, after which it held a conference in Niassa province to demonstrate to foreign backers and local supporters that FRELIMO controlled a liberated zone. Compared to the situation in Guinea, these liberated zones were more vulnerable to Portuguese countermeasures. Portuguese authorities succeeded in exploiting ethnic and community conflicts between Makonde and others in northern Mozambique. In addition, they sought support from Muslim brotherhoods in northern regions that were wary of FRELIMO.[26] As in Portuguese Guinea, Portuguese countermeasures included supplying local communities with social services and recruiting local headmen who feared FRELIMO attacks in a sort of counter-population-centric strategy.[27] The colonial administration facilitated the establishment of local militias and the recruitment of local spies.[28] Official regrouping of rural inhabitants in *aldeamentos* (strategic hamlets) limited FRELIMO's contact with local people; by 1970 about 60 percent of the African population of Niassa province and 45 percent of Cabo Delgado lived in these settlements.

Factionalism plagued FRELIMO. Lázaro Nkavandame, one of the founders of MANU and later FRELIMO provincial secretary for Cabo Delgado, left FRELIMO in March 1969 after he complained that northerners bore the brunt of fighting and Portuguese counterattacks while FRELIMO undermined local leaders. He maintained that FRELIMO's support for cooperative agricultural production in its liberated zones undercut the authority of local elders. After independence in 1975 this issue played a large role in the decision of some local elders to support anti-FRELIMO forces. Nkavandame himself was a Makonde traditional leader. His support for the anti-colonial struggle had been

---

[26] Edward Alpers, "Islam in the Service of Colonialism? Portuguese Strategy during the Armed Liberation Struggle in Mozambique," *Lusotropie* 6 (1999): 165–84.

[27] Walter Opello, Jr., "Guerrilla War in Portuguese Africa: An Assessment of the Balance of Force in Mozambique," *Issue* 4:2 (1974): 29–37.

[28] Thomas Henriksen, *Revolution and Counterrevolution: Mozambique's War of Independence 1964–1974* (Westport, CT: Greenwood, 1983) provides the most comprehensive account of the war.

critical in mobilizing local support for FRELIMO and in recruiting fighters. But FRELIMO's plans for administering its liberated zones would free young men from the control of people like him.[29]

Disagreement over the aims and methods of the political program of liberation reflected the wide gulf in social origins and interests between FRELIMO's local commanders and those who spoke to the outside world. Some of the younger generation of organizers, like future president Joaquim Chissano, had studied in Europe. They saw the conflict in Mozambique in broad terms and sought diverse allies, including white Mozambicans. Operating in a world that supported their anti-colonial project at the broad theoretical level, they were less focused on local issues. When commanders like Nkavandame used his contacts with Tanzanian officials, who had ethnic kinsmen in northern Mozambique, to divert aid to FRELIMO to support his own position, he was declared a class enemy. When Mondlane was assassinated in a parcel bomb blast on 3 February 1969, Nkavandame immediately came under suspicion, which he did not diminish when he defected to Portuguese forces on the condition that he would be allowed to lead a local militia.

FRELIMO's socialist vision of Mozambique's economic future, including the collectivization of agriculture, clashed with the aspirations of many Mozambican migrant laborers who had journeyed to Tanzania to earn money to buy land back home but who had joined FRELIMO while abroad. The same problem emerged in other parts of Mozambique in the late 1970s and early 1980s, when more than 100,000 migrant laborers returned from South Africa after their mass expulsion from that country. Their ideas diverged from the radical state-building ideology of FRELIMO's leadership. But the development of cooperative agriculture and FRELIMO-controlled commerce in liberated zones coincided with the declaration in 1967 by FRELIMO's Tanzanian hosts that they favored these policies in their own country. Although these ideas were not necessarily widely popular on either side of the border, this ideological link between the anti-colonial rebels and their Tanzanian patrons was reinforced among future FRELIMO managers who had attended the University of Dar es Salaam.[30]

---

[29] William Finnegan, *A Complicated War: The Harrowing of Mozambique* (Berkeley: University of California Press, 1992), 108.

[30] John Saul was a lecturer in the University of Dar es Salaam department of political science and worked in FRELIMO's office. Lionel Cliffe and John Saul (eds.), *Socialism in Tanzania: An Interdisciplinary Reader*, 2 vols. (Nairobi: East African Publishing House, 1972).

Like Cabral, Mondlane was well aware of and concerned about the dangers of infiltration and factionalism. He explained:

> This is connected with the problem of splinter groups, since [Portuguese agents] may use a member of the main organization to try to spread dissent, so as to bring over a section of the membership. The complexities of motive behind divisive conduct make it the more difficult to guard against: individual neuroses, personal ambitions, real ideological differences are muddled up with the tactics of the enemy secret services.[31]

Mondlane blamed this fractiousness on the self-interested motives of individual FRELIMO members, much as critics of future warlord rebels would blame greed and ambition for the divisive and predatory tendencies in those rebel groups, and ethnic agendas for the narrow visions of parochial rebels. Before Nkavandame's defection, Mondlane had accused him of stealing funds from FRELIMO's people's stores in liberated zones.[32] Further, Mondlane himself faced serious challenges from the Catholic priest Father Mateus Gwenjere, who brought students from his seminary in Beira to fight for FRELIMO. In 1968 Gwenjere's seminarians rioted, complaining that they were being trained as fighters and not as administrators. They feared that a liberated Mozambique would be governed by southerners. One observer thought that Gwenjere really wanted to assume control of the institute.[33]

Mondlane's task of maintaining ideological focus and internal unity was quite difficult. The student leaders, who came from central Mozambique, had discovered that they could receive support from opposition groups in newly independent Zambia, which had attracted the leaders from UDENAMO who had earlier joined FRELIMO in Tanzania. Ghana was another source of financial and moral support, but this possibility ended when Nkrumah was overthrown in 1966. Both the students and Gwenjere found the Makonde-dominated armed fighters receptive to their ideas. Mondlane responded to such opposition by accusing "certain student comrades" of "egotistical tendencies" and threatening them with expulsion.[34] Amid this factional struggle, it was difficult to disentangle personal greed, individual desires for upward

---

[31] Eduardo Mondlane, *The Struggle for Mozambique* (London: Zed, 1969), 132.

[32] "Mozambique: A Chief Surrenders," *Africa Confidential* 1:8 (April 1969): 7–8.

[33] John Saul, "FRELIMO and the Mozambique Revolution," *Monthly Review* 24:10 (1973): 22–52.

[34] Eduardo Mondlane, "FRELIMO White Paper," *African Historical Studies* 2:2 (1969): 321.

mobility, and complaints about ethnic marginalization. Diverse motives were portrayed as ideological indiscipline, although it would be just as easy to regard them as individual, materialist, or status interests in the warlord rebel contexts described in Chapter 5. Moreover, the students, who praised Nkrumah as a "true revolutionary," expressed fears that FRELIMO killed dissidents inside liberated zones.[35] The purge of students and the accusations of executions in the field, however, fit with FRELIMO's need to retain its position as the exclusive armed anti-colonial movement for Mozambique to deny external resources to rivals.

After Mondlane's assassination, Marcelino dos Santos and Samora Machel quickly asserted control over FRELIMO as Portuguese military pressure forced FRELIMO to shift its military strategy toward creating new liberated zones in the center of the country (Map 2). The need to extend fighting meant that FRELIMO had to win over groups that had earlier founded UDENAMO before its merger with FRELIMO in 1962.[36] A risky strategy, it required that FRELIMO operate in areas distant from its Tanzanian refuge and among returned migrant laborers from Rhodesia and South Africa, who were liable to support dissident anti-colonial leaders. To manage the new situation, FRELIMO commanders developed contacts with Zimbabwe African National Union (ZANU) fighters along the border with Rhodesia. ZANU's successes in Rhodesia offered FRELIMO the strong possibility that Mozambique might soon share an 800-kilometer border with an ideologically friendly government. FRELIMO's Marxist-Leninist ideological stance strengthened a modernist vision that papered over ethnic and personal divisions with "a popular and revolutionary culture based on the traditions of our people." It also envisioned closer collaboration with other anti-colonial rebels in Africa.[37]

FRELIMO's military strategy enabled it to control substantial areas of Mozambique after the 1974 coup in Portugal, leading to its recognition as the new government of independent Mozambique on 25 June 1975. FRELIMO's links to ZANU played a role in the new government's decision to sever rail links between Rhodesia and Mozambique's

---

[35] National Union of Mozambican Students, "The Mozambican Revolution Betrayed," *African Historical Studies* 3:1 (1970): 173, 175–76.

[36] Barry Munslow, *Mozambique: The Revolution and Its Origins* (New York: Longman, 1983), 79–86.

[37] FRELIMO, "Statutes and Programme," Meeting of the Central Committee, mimeo, 1970, 7.

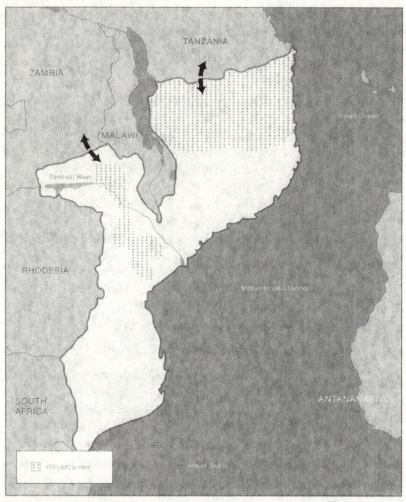

MAP 2. Areas of FRELIMO Control, 1973. Based on Basil Davidson, "Portuguese-Speaking Africa: The Fight for Independence," in Michael Crowder (ed.), *The Cambridge History of Africa*, vol. 8 (New York: Cambridge University Press, 1984), 791.

ports, giving Mozambique decisive leverage with the white minority regime. When, in 1976, the FRELIMO government decided to provide bases to ZANU, the Rhodesian Central Intelligence Organisation (CIO) countered by encouraging a clandestine anti-FRELIMO movement in Mozambique. After 1974, CIO intelligence improved immensely from access to Portuguese police files that contained information about infiltrators into FRELIMO who could be recruited to RENAMO.[38] Meanwhile, local notables and disgruntled villagers, who resented FRELIMO policies and the forced regrouping of villages, provided RENAMO with an internal support base.

The FRELIMO government used cooperative agricultural schemes to separate local people from RENAMO rebels inside fortified centers, much as Portuguese counterinsurgency strategies had done. By the early 1980s, for example, 47 percent of the FRELIMO group villages in Tete province had originated as Portuguese *aldeamentos*, but by then they had become part of the campaigns against "feudalism" that targeted local chiefs.[39] This showed the extent to which rural politics in Mozambique was extremely localized, involving diverse agendas and grievances that had little to do with broad matters of ideology but could still be mobilized in violent campaigns. Chiefs, for example, recognized the threat posed by FRELIMO to their local power, as Nkavandame and other FRELIMO dissidents had anticipated. Chiefs attempted to tighten their customary control over young men, encouraging them to attack FRELIMO officials considered by the youth as bossy outsiders. An anthropologist visiting RENAMO-controlled areas in 1983–84 found that some critics believed that FRELIMO-led cooperative agricultural policies denied local villagers their future status as landowners in favor of cooperative administrators from far-off cities, who had education and connections not available locally.[40] Some of them supported RENAMO in the 1994 elections that followed the 1992 peace agreement. These voters saw RENAMO membership as the vehicle for fast-track advancement for the excluded, especially the unemployed and less educated.[41]

RENAMO collaborated with local spiritual mediums, especially in the most remote areas of the country. Many of these local militias evolved in much the same way as the parochial rebels I discuss in Chapter 6. This development again points to the diverse motivations that characterize every war in Africa. In the context of Mozambique in

---

[38] Ken Flower, *Serving Secretly: An Intelligence Chief on Record, Rhodesia into Zimbabwe, 1964–1981* (London: John Murray, 1987), 145–52.

[39] João Paulo Borges Coelho, "State Resettlement Policies in Postcolonial Rural Mozambique: The Impact of the Communal Village Programme on Tete Province, 1977–1982," *Journal of Southern African Studies* 24:1 (1998): 61–91.

[40] Christian Geffray, *La Cause des Armes au Mozambique: Anthropologie d'une Guerre Civile* (Paris: Karthala, 1990).

[41] Carrie Manning, "Cultivating Opposition in Mozambique: RENAMO as a Political Party," *Journal of Southern African Studies* 24:1 (1998): 174–75.

the 1980s, however, Cold War ideological frameworks and external support for rebels channeled the transformation of local opposition into a
"conservative" reaction to a victorious socialist insurgency. Unlike later
decades, armed dissenters confronted what were still fairly imposing
bureaucratic hierarchies of the state, and not personal political networks
of politicians rooted in clandestine commercial ventures, as would be
true in the failing states of warlord rebellions. In Portuguese Guinea, the
PAIGC successfully absorbed many people who otherwise might have
joined such groups. In contrast FRELIMO defined such individuals
as "bandits" and "primitive" fighters from the countryside, a holdover
from the past.[42] Whatever they were called, such local militias were
always present in the evolution of warfare in Africa. Their appearance
illuminated the problems that FRELIMO encountered in appealing to
Mozambicans beyond its narrow socioethnic base, especially because
socialist policies failed to deliver the modernization that most urban
elites expected or the respite from an intrusive state and domineering
officials that many in rural areas took as the promise of independence.

Thus when local religious mediums mobilized young men to protect communities against what they saw as a predatory and disruptive
state, RENAMO tapped into this social network to get access to already-
armed young men and incorporate them into RENAMO's wider project
of forcing FRELIMO out of power. RENAMO also relied on coercion,
intimidation, and kidnapping of children and committed atrocities to
recruit fighters and guarantee support.[43] Naturally such extreme measures had consequences. In northern areas in 1990–91, the Naprama
movement, led by Manuel António, a peasant in his late twenties, mobilized fighters through religious rituals to oppose RENAMO. Instead of
using an anti-colonial or socialist narrative, he recruited and organized
young fighters with a promise that they could acquire purpose and
wealth through an alternative independent social organization, much as
RENAMO had done earlier.[44] Thus the first real success against REN-
AMO came in areas of Mozambique cut off from FRELIMO control

---

[42] FRELIMO, *Who Are the Armed Bandits?* (Maputo: FRELIMO, 1988).

[43] Robert Gersony, *Summary of Mozambican Refugee Accounts of Principally Conflict
Related Experience in Mozambique* (Washington, DC: US Department of State, 1988);
and William Minter, *The Mozambican National Resistance (Renamo) as Described by Ex-
Participants* (Washington, DC: Georgetown University and African European Institute, 1989).

[44] K. B. Wilson, "Cults of Violence and Counter-Violence in Mozambique," *Journal of
Southern African Studies* 18:3 (1992): 561–81; Gueorgui Derluguian, "Social Decomposition and Armed Violence in Postcolonial Mozambique, *Review* 13:4 (Fall 1990):

where socialist state policies still did not disrupt the social fields of leverage that new rebel organizers needed to convince people to subsume
their diverse personal reasons for fighting into this shared vision.

RENAMO found patrons first in Rhodesia and then, after the end
of the white minority government in 1980, in apartheid South Africa.
South African officials worried about FRELIMO support for the
African National Congress (ANC). After the 1978 electoral victory of
hard-line Prime Minister P. W. Botha, South Africa began aiding REN-
AMO. This strategy rendered Mozambique's government subservient
to South African interests in denying its enemies a friendly base on
South Africa's border. In 1984 RENAMO violence and South African
pressure forced the FRELIMO government to sign the Nkomati
Accord, in which both governments promised to stop giving aid to rival
insurgent movements. As actual South African aid waned, albeit not
until well after 1984, RENAMO gained support from a new source:
right-wing political groups in the United States, where the Reagan Doctrine sought "freedom fighters" against "Marxist" regimes like that in
Mozambique. Hard-line Reagan administration officials saw overthrowing these regimes as a way to roll back Soviet influence; more moderate
officials aimed to force FRELIMO to accept RENAMO in a collation
government.[45] But reform in Gorbachev's Soviet Union and its ultimate
collapse removed a key incentive for right-wing aid to RENAMO.

RENAMO did not fit the mold of anti-colonial rebels. It was neither socialist nor did it offer a modernizing, state-building vision. Its
"international relations" were not focused on gaining outside recognition as the sole "official" liberator of the country: The field of possible
foreign backers was more diverse and was not focused on a common
idea of African liberation. This reflected the changing conditions of the
1980s. During that period the target of the rebels was control of an
independent state surrounded by other independent states. Neighboring countries had administrations willing to support rebels beyond their
borders as an extension of domestic policies and internecine political
rivalries, but not out of devotion to a shared global project of political
change. By this time, Mozambique's domestic politics and its external
relations reflected the breakdown of old assumptions about the unity of
anti-colonial rebels and the idealized post-independence nation-state.
Dissidents within FRELIMO still sought foreign backers on the basis

439–64; and "Mozambique: Renamo under Pressure," *Africa Confidential* 32:18 (13
Sept 1991): 4–5.
[45] On international dimensions, see Alex Vines, *RENAMO Terrorism in Mozambique*.

of claims that they were the true socialists. As the association between socialism and independence weakened in the 1980s (and the disappointing reality of socialist rule sank in), it became easier to recruit rebels on the basis of narrow community interests and an anti-socialist appeal, if that made the organization more acceptable to remaining ideologically driven foreign supporters. Such a shift was not too difficult, because it built on the diverse underlying personal and group interests present at the start of the first anti-colonial rebellions that were of great concern to their leaders.

The fragmentation of rebel solidarity provided new vehicles for enterprising individuals and for excluded elites who thought that incumbent rulers blocked their path of upward mobility. Missing in 1980s Mozambique were the social and commercial connections among anti-FRELIMO leaders that would have come with previous long-term association with the state. RENAMO leaders such as Andre Matsangaissa, a former FRELIMO officer who had been sent to a reeducation camp from which he escaped in 1976, and Afonso Dhlakama, a former Portuguese army recruit–turned–FRELIMO follower who was charged with desertion and theft in 1975, lacked autonomous commercial and political ties to the outside world that would have facilitated the task of creating their own armies. Compared to the former state officials who became warlord rebel leaders in the 1990s, these insurgent leaders were more dependent on foreign backers. When the interests of RENAMO's foreign patrons changed or clashed with the goal of actually attaining power, RENAMO had to build support among a significant segment of civilians within Mozambique if it were to survive. In that sense, RENAMO was not a warlord rebellion as is defined in this book. RENAMO ultimately was forced to build a base of support among non-combatants and to actually try to provide some with benefits, even if this only amounted to an uneven sort of protection. Despite the atrocities attributed to RENAMO in the 1980s, Dhlakama won 33.7 percent of the vote in the 1994 multiparty election that followed a peace agreement. This demonstrated a level of popular support that no warlord rebel has been able to manage in similarly competitive and open election campaigns.

Fragmentation in Angola

In February 1961 fighting broke out in Angola, the first of the three Portuguese colonies to have an emergent anti-colonial rebel movement.

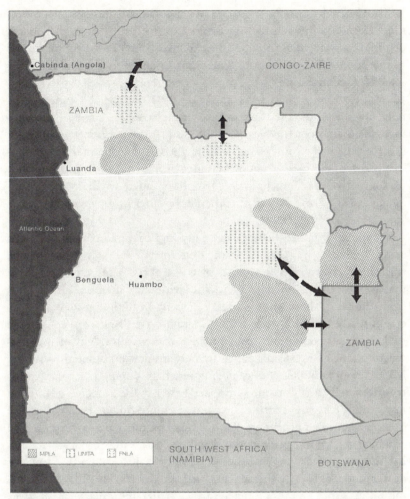

MAP 3. Rebel-Held Areas of Angola, Early 1970s. Based on Basil Davidson, "Portuguese-Speaking Africa: The Fight for Independence," in Michael Crowder (ed.), *The Cambridge History of Africa*, vol. 8 (New York: Cambridge University Press, 1984), 792.

This case turned out to be the most violent and prolonged of the three and exhibited a high degree of fragmentation among the anti-colonial rebels. Its deviation from the ideal of anti-colonial rebel solidarity earns it last place in this chapter but provides us with the benefit of being able to see what had changed so as to produce this outcome. Throughout the years of conflict, the three main rebel factions failed to create a unified organization and were able to hold separate liberated zones (Map 3), complicating the efforts of the UN, OAU, and individual African states to support a single official anti-colonial move-ment. Leaders in each faction could look to future success in battle or diplomacy to turn the tide in their favor, thus reducing incentives to merge into a single group. This fragmentation in part reflected the internal factional politics of Angola's neighboring states. In this light, Cabral was fortunate in 1959 in having the Republic of Guinea as the only obvious choice for a rear base in his struggle. Senegal's unwill-ingness to support the rival FLING and Touré's authoritarianism in the Republic of Guinea assisted the PAIGC in dominating the lib-eration struggle in Portuguese Guinea. Likewise, the initial absence of alternatives to Tanzania as a rear base aided FRELIMO's domi-nance as Mondlane oversaw the merger of other groups with Nyerere's support.

By the end of 1960, Angola already had two independent African states as neighbors. One of them – the former Belgian Congo – was rife with factional divisions of its own and faced a separatist rebellion that broke out within days of its independence in June 1960. Thus from the start, these anti-colonial rebels had multiple potential back-ers. Already the Mouvement de Libération de l'Enclave de Cabinda (MLEC) had sought aid from Fulbert Youlou, president of the just-independent Congo-Brazzaville. Initially Youlou considered using the MLEC to pry Cabinda out of Portuguese hands and add it to his coun-try's territory, a sentiment symbolized by MLEC's choice of French instead of Portuguese for its communiqués and documents. Otherwise Youlou resembled other anti-colonial rebel patrons in encouraging rival rebels to merge into a single "official" group. With Youlou's backing, MLEC became the core of the Front pour la Libération de l'Enclave de Cabinda (FLEC), formed in 1963 in Brazzaville. FLEC's com-muniqués from this conference stressed that the enclave really was a separate protectorate of Portugal, created under a different set of treaties from those that created the colonial regime in Angola proper, and therefore its independence would not violate OAU norms con-cerning the maintenance of existing boundaries.[46] The real signif-icance of FLEC, however, became apparent in light of subsequent Congo-Brazzaville presidential sponsorship of the organization to fur-ther personal and regime goals against domestic and foreign rivals; the enclave's substantial oil reserves aided these aims in no small measure.

---

[46] Chilcote, *Emerging Nationalism*, 127–30.

From the perspective of the early 1960s, Angola (except for Cabinda) seemed to be on course to develop a unified anti-colonial rebellion. Its rebel leaders strove to shed ethnic labels through presenting a nationalist image. The MPLA appeared to have the early advantage. Like PAIGC and FRELIMO, MPLA leaders – among them MPLA founder Mário Pinto de Andrade, Agostinho Neto (first president of Angola), and Jonas Savimbi (leader of União Nacional para a Independência Total de Angola [UNITA]) – had established their political credentials during their student days at the University of Lisbon. Events soon challenged their early advantage. On 4 February 1961, exiled leaders of the MPLA were taken by surprise when several hundred fighters crossed the border from Congo-Zaire to attack Portuguese police stations in Angola. The fighters appeared to believe that they were attacking on behalf of the Union of Peoples of Northern Angola (UPNA). UPNA's predecessor in 1957 had submitted a letter to the UN secretary-general asking for the restoration of the pre-colonial Kongo Kingdom, a vision at odds with the MPLA's socialist and nationalist stance and later OAU practice regarding support for liberation movements.[47]

Although the MPLA initially claimed credit for this attack, UPNA leaders noted their ethnic affiliations with fighters to make convincing claims of credit. This organization had begun to shed its formal ethnic label when it chose Holden Roberto as its head and took the name União das Populações de Angola (UPA) at the 1958 All-African Peoples Conference held in newly independent Ghana. With support from Ghana's President Nkrumah and in an illustration of the centripetal pressures on rebel groups at this time, the group dropped its regionalist program of merging with several smaller groups.[48] It recognized that resurrection of the old Kongo Kingdom elicited little enthusiasm from potential sponsors. After this conference, Roberto embarked on a two-year program of international travel during which he met with UN officials, American solidarity groups in New York, and other potential supporters. The American Committee on Africa (ACOA) sponsored Roberto's travel to visit supporters in the United States and meet with Kennedy administration officials in the Department of State's new Bureau of

---

[47] Fernando Andresen Guimarães, *The Origins of the Angolan Civil War* (New York: St. Martin's Press, 2001), 49.

[48] There were twenty distinct rebel factions between 1955 and 1962. John Marcum, *The Angolan Revolution, Volume I: The Anatomy of an Explosion (1950–1962)* (Cambridge, MA: MIT Press, 1969), 350–51.

FIGURE 1. Female soldier in the Popular Resistance Movement for the Liberation of Angola at AfricaFocus. Credit: The African Studies Program, University of Wisconsin.

African Affairs. This network helped Professor John Marcum, a professor at Nkrumah's alma mater, Lincoln University in Pennsylvania, to visit liberated areas along the border that was to become that of the Frente Nacional de Libertação de Angola (FNLA) in 1962.

Of more immediate importance were Roberto's personal ties to nationalists in Congo-Zaire. He met with Patrice Lumumba at several conferences and meetings before the Congo became independent in 1960. This gave Roberto a secure base in Kinshasa (then known as Leopoldville) to consolidate his political control over Angolan nationalist politics. When President Joseph Kasavubu dismissed Lumumba as prime minister, Roberto lost his patron, and he had to flee to Ghana and then to New York. At this point, Roberto's troubles resembled those faced by other rebel leaders in mastering the personal politics involved in the struggle to become the head of a unified anti-colonial rebellion. When the Congolese government hosted a conference to pressure rebel groups to unify, this became a pressing issue for Roberto. He returned to Kinshasa, where he capitalized on his ethnic and personal connections with the Bakongo ethnic community, which straddled the international border and played a big role in Congo's politics. Still he failed to get Congolese official support, so he withdrew his organization from the proposed united front. As the most influential of the groups, his organization, now called the UPA, became the center of gravity in the exile politics of Angola's liberation.

At this juncture, the UPA, soon to become the FNLA, laid claim to the February 1961 attack and gained diplomatic credit for this event, which now overshadowed an uprising in Lunda the same month led by urban educated members of what a foreign observer recognized as early components of the MPLA.[49] The FNLA's rear base in Congo's Bakongo ethnic community provided the means to organize a second wave of attacks in March. Roberto realized that the Portuguese response to attacks could be devastating and overwhelming, but he apparently hoped to provoke an uprising and use the Portuguese counterattack to provoke anti-colonial violence in Angola similar to the conditions in the Belgian Congo from January 1959 that led the Belgians to quit their colony in June 1960. These multiple local grievances and anti-state actions would reinforce the broader anti-colonial rebel narrative and aid the rebels' political task of recruiting beyond the group's ethnic core. By then, Roberto's friend Cyrille Adoula was prime minister of Congo, giving him the impression of solid backing to establish a UPA rear base there. Indeed the counterattack was vicious, producing numerous atrocities: one scholar estimates that 45,000 Angolans were killed, along with 1,000 Europeans.[50] The inevitable international condemnation of Portuguese colonialism followed, but instead of leaving Africa, an intransigent Portugal chose to stay put and fight.

The second attack helped the UPA to expand its ethnic base. Once it attracted Jonas Savimbi, a key leader from Angola's central highlands, it presented a more convincing nonethnic nationalist image. In 1958 Savimbi had gone to Lisbon on a university scholarship. Here he met Agostinho Neto. Thus, up to this point, Savimbi pursued a collaborative and ideological strategy that was very different from his later strategy, as we will see below. The "merger" with Savimbi in March 1962 created the FNLA and gave Roberto the means to declare in April the Govêrno Revolucionário de Angola no Exílio (GRAE) as a base from which to make a plausible claim of unity and organizational capabilities with which to seek international recognition. Roberto expected a good hearing in Senegal due to his earlier association with President Senghor in Paris, where they both worked for the prominent journal of the

---

[49] Basil Davidson, *In the Eye of the Storm* (Garden City, NY: Doubleday, 1972), 183–86.
[50] Marcum, *The Angolan Revolution*, vol. 1, 150. Following two pages based on Marcum.

Pan-Africanist movement *Présence Africaine*. Roberto also expanded his search for support in Europe and the United States. In 1963 his efforts finally yielded fruit when the OAU recognized the FNLA-GRAE as the legitimate anti-colonial rebel movement for Angola.

Members of the OAU Liberation Committee criticized the MPLA for its fractiousness and considered the FNLA to be a more proficient unifier of rebel forces. Loyal MPLA activists sought protection in the more distant capital of Congo-Brazzaville. At least this freed the MPLA from the personal networks of their FNLA rivals and gave them access to Cabinda, which after all was Angolan territory, despite the position of FLEC separatists. Meanwhile the Congo-Brazzaville president's willingness to support both an anti-colonial rebel group and separatists hinted at naked self-interest and the possibility of future treachery. MPLA leaders benefited from Youlou's demise in August 1963 at the hands of the radical leader Alphonse Massemba-Débat. The new leader's pretensions as a fellow radical Marxist fit well with the Marxist identity of MPLA leaders. Even so, the new leader sponsored another FLEC faction in Angola's Cabinda province. All was not as before, however. The MPLA's new patron gave the organization access to Soviet and Cuban support. This enabled the MPLA to send a delegation to the Tricontinental Conference in Havana, where it, rather than its FNLA rival, was legitimatized as the "official" anti-colonial rebel organization for Angola in the eyes of the socialist world. The MPLA's rising diplomatic fortunes convinced some African governments to give it support, reflecting the beginning of the Liberation Committee's shift in funding away from the FNLA in 1965. By 1968 the MPLA was widely recognized as the dominant anti-colonial rebel organization in Angola.

Signaling FNLA's waning fortunes, Jonas Savimbi abandoned his post as GRAE foreign minister in July 1964. Even worse, the FNLA lost its patrons in Congo-Kinshasa after a coup there in July 1964. Congo's new leader, Moise Tshombe, owed a debt to the Portuguese for supporting his leadership of the Katanga secession and was suspicious of Roberto's political activities among Angolans in Congo. In November 1965 Roberto's personal networks saved him in the nick of time when Joseph Mobutu, a relation by marriage, seized power in Kinshasa. Tshombe's position constituted a problem for all the anti-colonial rebels, however, as his old Katangan gendarmerie – about 2,300 men – fled to Angola, where they became the core of a proxy force to combat

FIGURE 2. MPLA Poster. Artist unknown. Credit: Inkworks Press, Berkeley, California [printer].

rebels and to warn the new Mobutu regime away from unrestrained involvement in Angolan affairs.

To the mid-1960s none of these competing factions actually controlled liberated zones inside Angola. So long as this was the case, factional politics in host countries and personal rivalries within organizations played proportionally greater roles in rebels' fortunes. To the extent that contending rebel leaders really represented ethnic constituencies, including communities that stretched across international borders, these cross-border links often reflected the concerns of rulers in neighboring countries to balance and play contending ethnic interests off one another. This kind of patronage had the effect of intensifying the tendency of onlookers (and recruits) to associate each rebel group with the fortunes of a particular ethnic community, regardless of the ideological nature of the rebel group's official statements. These problems were also internal to Angolan society. The MPLA leadership, in particular, suffered from the same *mestiço*–indigenous African split that bedeviled FRELIMO politics.

Without extensive liberated zones, it was much harder for rebel leaders to overcome such divisions. Lacking control over territory and communities, they found it much harder to sustain political commissars and to get foreign support to discipline (and, if necessary, kill) errant followers and associates. Savimbi, for example, attacked Andrade and Neto as unrepresentative of Angolan society. He branded the MPLA as an elitist organization, noting that "all of these beneficent groups, and those of a political nature, were organized and formed by mulattoes, who were considered by the Angolan masses as instruments of the Portuguese colonial domination."[51] His travels in the early 1960s persuaded him that he could expect local and international support as a leader of a separate anti-colonial rebel group. Nevertheless he encountered difficulties, for once the FNLA's fortunes sank, his search for a new state patron suffered from competition from other still-viable organizations. His failure to find a neighboring state patron may have encouraged him to adopt the Maoist strategy of actually setting up liberated zones inside Angola as bases for further attacks. This action made him attractive to the Chinese, who by the 1960s condemned Soviet "hegemony" in anti-colonial rebel patronage. Zambia's independence in 1964 gave him a rear base, although President Kenneth Kaunda was wary of antagonizing the Portuguese and losing access to the Angolan ports that handled his country's substantial copper exports.[52]

UNITA's leader became a Maoist by circumstance, given his constraints and given that his best competitive strategy argued for launching attacks inside Angola. Accomplishing this in 1966, Savimbi forced the hands of the other anti-colonial rebels. As confrontations between the Portuguese forces and the various rebel groups intensified, the Maoist Savimbi entered into tacit deals with the Portuguese colonialists to focus their offensives against his rivals. He also was accused of arranging commercial deals between UNITA and Portuguese officers.[53] Savimbi switched to a strategy that resembles that of the warlord rebels of the 1990s, insofar as he relied on his political connections to accumulate wealth to build a personal armed political following. In the short term, his strategy played a significant role in preventing both the FNLA and the MPLA from establishing large liberated zones, despite the latter's improved diplomatic fortunes.

[51] UNITA Central Committee, *Angola – Seventh Year* ([place of publication unknown]: UNITA, 1968), 8.
[52] Detailed in Fred Bridgland, *Jonas Savimbi: A Key to Africa* (Edinburgh: Mainstream, 1986).
[53] William Minter, *Operation Timber: Pages from the Savimbi Dossier* (Trenton, NJ: Africana World Press, 1988).

By the time of the 1974 coup in Portugal, Angola still had three first-generation anti-colonial rebel groups. This contention and shifting alliances created opportunities for ambitious rebel leaders and Portuguese forces to exploit diverging interests among combatants, ultimately to the advantage of the Portuguese security forces. For example, in 1965 Alexandre Taty, while serving as GRAE minister of armaments, attempted a coup against Roberto. He briefly sought association with the MPLA before joining the Portuguese in Cabinda; with him he took about 1,200 fighters, who became the core of the Portuguese Tropas Especiais counterinsurgency force. Portuguese forces also exploited local ethnic tensions aggravated by contention among rival rebel groups. By 1974 the number of rebels inside Angola had risen to 22,000. They fought against an estimated 60,000 locally recruited militias fighting on behalf of Portuguese forces. Combatants on both sides compensated themselves through looting local communities and settling personal scores in the course of battle.[54] By now, the anti-colonial rebel ideologues were losing their ability to control externally supplied resources to reinforce their broad anti-colonial political programs and discipline rivals and upstarts, all necessary tasks if they were to subsume these diverse personal and ethnic communal motives for fighting.

The effectiveness of the Portuguese counterinsurgency, particularly in its exploitation of the diverse interests of rebel fighters and factions, meant that the sudden Portuguese withdrawal in 1974 left a political vacuum in the country. Instead of being an opportunity to be seized, the growing vacuum encouraged defections and instability. Just before the Portuguese coup, Daniel Chipenda used his command of MPLA eastern forces to make a bid for leadership. Each rebel group urgently sought outside patronage through playing on Cold War ideological competition. In reality, each shared the single goal of controlling the capital city by the announced 11 November 1975 handover of sovereignty. Alongside them was a terrain littered with freelance militias that were heirs to the collapsing Portuguese counterinsurgency forces. On the international level, the war had become a competition of superpower proxies. Angola also continued to be an arena for politicians in neighboring states to try to use rebels to influence the internal politics of their own countries. Within Angola, factional competition raised fears of ethnic marginalization. Anxious about their fate once the Portuguese

---

[54] John Cann, *Counterinsurgency in Africa* (Westport, CT: Greenwood Press, 1997), 96–99.

left, political elites jockeyed for position in various coalitions. Meanwhile individuals had to decide how best to defend themselves and their communities from growing insecurity, which the more aggrieved or enterprising saw as an opportunity to grab loot and settle personal scores.

Foreign patronage helped each rebel group to assert some discipline over the diverse forces in the areas that each controlled. The FNLA drew the worst lot, finding their American supporters – their MPLA rivals already had Soviet and Cuban support – reluctant to permit even clandestine aid in the wake of US military and political failure in its war in Vietnam. UNITA had already claimed South African backing on the basis of its capacity to occupy highland areas of Angola and, later, on the basis of a promise that it would prohibit the South West Africa People's Liberation Organization (SWAPO) from using Angolan territory as a base from which to liberate South African–held Namibia. As it turned out, Soviet aid proved the most effective, aiding the MPLA's expansion from 1,500 fighters in 1973 to about 7,000 by June 1975.[55] Its opposition to Mobutu also positioned the movement to recruit anti-Mobutu Katanga gendarmes who earlier had fought as a proxy of the Portuguese colonial security services. This odd ideological alliance highlighted how the internationalization and militarization of internal rivalries in African states were overwhelming efforts of rebel ideologues to assert political programs while fighting. Superpower and regional power stakes in these conflicts made for a very harsh terrain for any rebels interested in pursuing a consistent ideological program while still receiving external support. In this regard, the wider context of conflict that once prized ideological rebels now penalized them. At its core, fighting in Angola was beginning to resemble the wars of the future that followed state collapse that are examined in subsequent chapters.

The fierce competition among the liberation movements reflected the political agendas of regimes in neighboring states. Mobutu's decision to help the FNLA reflected his bad relations with the Congo-Brazzaville government, which, in addition to supporting the MPLA, gave aid to the anti-Mobutu Comité National de Libération. In retaliation Mobutu supported the Luis Franque faction of FLEC against the Congo-Brazzaville–aligned N'Zita Henriques faction. Thus, by the mid-1970s, both countries supported rival Angolan nationalists as well

---

[55] John Marcum, *The Angolan Revolution, Volume II: Exile Politics and Guerrilla Warfare, 1962–1976* (Cambridge, MA: MIT Press, 1978), 253.

as rivals to those groups! Roberto's FNLA was virtually destroyed by 1976 as he lost his foreign backers. UNITA regrouped, but by that time the Maoist Savimbi was allied with apartheid South Africa's army. Once American aid resumed in 1985 under the Reagan Doctrine, Congo-Zaire again served as a conduit, but its destination was UNITA. Cuban military officers and soldiers, with Soviet support, assisted the MPLA government. During this time, fighting was particularly intense, culminating in the 1987 battle of Cuito Cuanavale in southern Angola.

The South African Defence Force (SADF) helped UNITA maintain control of a liberated zone in southern Angola as a buffer along the northern border of South African–controlled Namibia to prevent the infiltration of SWAPO fighters. Prior to the 1987 battle, South African forces shot down Soviet aircraft and downed a helicopter carrying ten Soviet advisors. South African trainers assisted UNITA and deployed the 32 Buffalo Battalion, formed in 1975 from former FNLA insurgents when their organization fell apart. Thus when an Angolan government force of 18,000 and their Cuban advisors attacked UNITA in September 1987, they came into direct contact with SADF forces.[56] This battle was among the larger engagements of conventional military forces in sub-Saharan Africa since the end of the Second World War. The US undersecretary for Africa reported that 8,000 UNITA fighters and 4,000 SADF troops mauled the Angolan government force, killing 4,000. He concluded, "The 1987 campaign represented a stunning humiliation for the Soviet Union, its arms and its strategy."[57] Although the American diplomat claimed this event as a success for the Reagan Doctrine, this situation was short-lived. In fact, MPLA and Cuban forces had blocked further South African advances toward the capital and eventually called into question the South African military's long-term capacity to control the border between Angola and Namibia.

From Anti-Colonial Rebels to Warlords

These battles in Angola and the pattern of state support of rebel proxies in cross-border battles belied the promises made back in 1963 at the initiation of the OAU that African governments would respect existing international borders. Although none of these rebel backers wanted to

[56] For details of the battle from a South African perspective, see Col. Jan Breytenbach, *They Live by the Sword* (Alborton: Lemur, 1990).
[57] Chester Crocker, *High Noon in Southern Africa* (New York: Norton, 1992), 360.

change these borders, they were engaging in a type of interstate warfare through proxies that would become especially well developed in sub-Saharan Africa as the twentieth century came to a close. This political use of rebels on behalf of the interests of regimes that were politically divided and that asserted their authority through patronage rather than through strong state institutions would become a major factor in shaping the character of rebel warfare. This is a story that will be picked up in the fifth chapter. Meanwhile, Angola's fate took a different turn.

The 1988 New York Accords ended large-scale outside military aid to Angola's government and UNITA. The agreement established the UN Angola Verification Mission (UNAVEM) to oversee disarmament and an election. The end of the Cold War meant that all major state backers pushed their clients to compromise. At first glance, this agreement should have reduced the number of outside sources of aid for rebels, thus forcing them to centralize their organizations and appeals for limited sources of support. But Savimbi discovered that he could use UNITA's territorial control and organization to mine diamonds and to conduct other commercial operations. From 1992 to 1998 the revenue from these enterprises was between $2 billion and $3.7 billion, giving UNITA resources to continue fighting without bowing to the political or ideological demands of an outside patron.[58] No longer needing to cater to the agendas of the socialist Soviet Union, the OAU Liberation Committee, or the South African government, Savimbi was free to develop an independent strategy. Self-help of this sort empowered members of his organization who were good at making commercial connections with foreign businesses – usually of the shady and illicit variety – and disadvantaged ideologues whose pronouncements no longer attracted outside aid. UNITA's leaders adapted to exploit the illicit commercial connections that they inherited from South African security forces and through UNITA's alliance with Zaire's President Mobutu until he was overthrown in 1997. No longer performing as a state-in-waiting in the southeast, UNITA focused its territorial conquests on Angola's northeast, the site of the alluvial diamond mines and the Congo-Zaire frontier.

UNITA reneged on the New York agreement and by 1993 held five of eighteen provincial capitals. Although it still received supplies from

---

[58] For the low end, see A. Tony Hodges, *Angola from Afro-Stalinism to Petro-Diamond Capitalism* (London: James Currey, 2001), 153; for the high end, see Global Witness, *A Rough Trade, the Role of Companies and Governments in the Angolan Conflict* (London: Global Witness, 1998), 4.

Congo-Zaire, UNITA used its income from diamond mining to purchase the weapons that now flooded international markets as the Soviet Union collapsed and its former allies demobilized large portions of their armies. The war had become a competition of resources: The MPLA government controlled oil and UNITA had diamonds. The MPLA government prevailed, but at a cost of 750,000 Angolans killed after independence in 1975, about 7 percent of the country's population. The government's oil income of about $2 billion a year played a large role in the outcome. Equally important was the MPLA's claim to the sovereignty of the Angolan state, which gave it the legal standing that banks required for their loans against future production of oil. This gave the MPLA government the means to raise quick cash to buy weapons. It could lobby in international venues like the UN by virtue of its membership in that organization. This status paid off in the form of UN resolutions that imposed sanctions on UNITA in 1998. This followed the 1997 UN ban on travel for UNITA officials, the call to shut down their overseas offices, and a ban on flights in their liberated zone. In 1999 the MPLA government launched an offensive from this favorable international position, and Savimbi was killed in battle on 22 February 2002, effectively ending the war.

The case of Angola is especially useful for showing the transition from anti-colonial struggles to something more like a warlord type of rebel war. Moreover, some of the same individuals occupied key positions in these different phases and kinds of warfare. The UNITA leader, for example, was the grandson of Sakaita Savimbi, the heroic leader of the 1902 Ovimbundu rebellion against Portuguese rule. Thus he drew on a deep reservoir of legitimacy in his community. As a successful anti-colonial rebel leader in the 1960s and 1970s, he was proficient at establishing liberated zones while his rivals struggled with one another for foreign patronage. By the 1990s, he almost completely jettisoned his programmatic and ideological stances, preserving only his drive to become the next president of Angola. When the Angolan government forces killed him in 2002, he was a sixty-seven-year old guerrilla fighter with thirty-six years of experience in armed struggle. Once he was dead, UNITA's military organization immediately fell apart, suggesting that the rebel group could not produce a program or a charismatic successor who could revive a strategy that could knit together the community's diverse grievances under a single political idea.

Although war in Angola became much more than an anti-colonial rebellion, the next chapter shows how the anti-colonial pattern of warfare was not yet exhausted. The struggle against the minority rule regimes in southern Africa – Rhodesia, Namibia, and South Africa – followed in the anti-colonial pattern of an international context that was inclined to help ideologically oriented leaders suppress factional splits and maintain political direction in their rebel movements. The next chapter also illustrates the lesson that the character of rebel organizations in Africa tends to reflect the character of the states in which they fight. The reliance of the minority rule states on bureaucratic institutions to assert their authority and to fight was well suited to the rebel guerrilla tactics that had served the anti-colonial rebels when they fought Portuguese forces. Bureaucratically formidable that they were, these states turned out to be less than effective in controlling fields of leverage, the social networks and territories that rebels needed to build liberated zones and to mobilize non-combatants in struggles that focused on the control of the population.

CHAPTER 3

Majority Rule Rebels

The rebels who fought white-dominated regimes for majority rule in Rhodesia (Zimbabwe), South West Africa (Namibia), and South Africa tried to present themselves as deserving international recognition. From the 1960s through the early 1990s international politics greatly influenced how these rebels presented their goals and strategies to their followers and the rest of the world. As in the case of the anti-colonial rebels, external supporters pressed rival rebel groups to show evidence of popular support in a particular country and to unify into a single organization, although often there was disagreement among these backers as to which rebel group was to be preferred. Rebel leaders knew that they had to convey an image of unity, through either agreement or superior performance on the battlefield, if they were to attract the money and diplomatic backing required to fight their wars. The link between socialist ideology and the organization of rebels and their strategies was evident too. Many majority rule rebels also sought rear bases and solidified their personal and operational ties to their anti-colonial brethren as those rebels came to power in the wake of the Portuguese withdrawal in 1974.

The regional politics of majority rule left its imprint on rebel organizations. Internal politics of the Zimbabwe African National Union (ZANU) and the Zimbabwe African People's Union (ZAPU) reflected the necessity for these movements to align their ideas with those of Tanzanian President Julius Nyerere and Zambian President Kenneth Kaunda to secure their backing. Both rebel groups had to weigh the consequences of cooperating with or ignoring FRELIMO in neighboring Mozambique or South Africa's African National Congress (ANC). The politics and strategies of the South West Africa People's Liberation Organisation (SWAPO) were indelibly shaped by its use of Angola as a base after the victory of the Movimento Popular de Libertação de Angola (MPLA). SWAPO's political agenda mirrored those of the victorious Angolan anti-colonial rebels on which it relied for survival and military support. The ANC's internal strategies and organization also were affected by its reliance on the hospitality of the governments in what became known as the frontline states.

In all three countries, majority rule rebellions occurred in the context of growing international condemnation and sanctions against the white-dominated governments. Global rejection of white minority rule – known as apartheid in South Africa – gave the UN a central role in conferring global legitimacy on favored rebel groups, much like the Organization of African Unity (OAU) Liberation Committee had for anti-colonial rebels who fought European occupiers. SWAPO even gained UN recognition as the "sole and authentic representative of the Namibian people," a semi-sovereign status as a state-in-waiting.[1] UN support included financial support for SWAPO's New York office and operating expenses for the Council for Namibia, established in 1974. The UN resources contributed to SWAPO's dominance by providing the basis of patronage and the institutional apparatus for the rebel leadership to discipline fighters, attract supporters, and advertise their claims. The UN-funded Institute for Namibia in Lusaka, Zambia, allowed SWAPO to regulate access to educational opportunities. The UN refugee camps in Angola provided SWAPO with a rear base. Its World Food Program (WFP) and World Health Organization (WHO) channeled operations through SWAPO. Well into the 1980s, in southern Africa at least, international attention and resources helped limit majority rule rebel fragmentation and strengthened the positions of ideologically focused and politically articulate leaderships.

At the same time, the origins and factional battles of these rebels reflected the domestic politics of their home states. In this respect

---

[1] United Nations General Assembly, "Situation in Namibia Resulting from the Illegal Occupation of the Territory by South Africa," Resolution 31/146, 20 Dec 1976, art 2. The 12 Dec 1973 General Assembly Resolution 3111 recognized SWAPO simply as "authentic." South Africa's ANC and Pan-African Congress (PAC) also received UN recognition as interlocutors, as did the Palestinian Liberation Organization.

the rebels who fought white minority regimes differed from the anti-colonial rebels in the Portuguese colonies. The divide-and-rule strategies of the counterinsurgency efforts of Rhodesia and South Africa shaped how insurgents organized, how they fought, how effectively they controlled rivals, and how they enforced their agendas on their own fighters and supporters. The overwhelming military capacity of these regimes, especially in South Africa, forced rebels to rely especially heavily on external support to carry out their struggles. In the case of the ANC, such external dependence forced its members to reconsider their strategies, limiting the ANC's capacity to control other rebel groups inside South Africa. Where they were able to establish themselves, the bureaucratic repressive apparatus of these states and their formidable military capabilities forced these rebels to seek protection from social networks and associations among non-combatants. Because these states exercised authority more through institutions and less through manipulating their social relationships, sensible rebel strategies included finding protection in these relationships and pursuing a population-centric approach to mobilize people beyond the reach of these bureaucracies.

Majority rule rebels faced regimes that could draw on the support of many white citizens who also were involved in the day-to-day tasks of governance. Many of these people considered themselves to be African. After all, Dutch settlers arrived in South Africa in 1652, only thirty-two years after the Plymouth Colony in Massachusetts was established. This white minority exercised much more power in local politics than European settlers ever did in the authoritarian administrations of the Portuguese colonies. Although white settlers at best accounted for 5 percent of the total population in Rhodesia (Zimbabwe), they had enjoyed local self-government since 1923. Their government controlled the military and civil instruments of repression. This formed the basis on which Prime Minister Ian Smith made his Unilateral Declaration of Independence (UDI) from the British Crown in November 1965 to counter claims of majority rule rebels to the right to control the sovereignty of Rhodesia. Similar struggles took place over the control of Namibia, which the South African apartheid government treated as a province of their country. White South Africans had enjoyed self-rule since 1910 as a dominion of the British Empire on the model of Canada, New Zealand, and Australia. Thus, in Rhodesia and South Africa, rebels fought against governments that regarded themselves as rulers of independent countries. In contrast to Portugal's colonies, these regimes were politically stronger, controlled the coercive arms of the state for their own purposes, and could rely on substantial numbers of supporters in all regions of the country and in all agencies of the government.

Tanzanian President Julius Nyerere recognized the significance of this distinction between white minority regimes and colonies. "South Africa's strongest defense against international criticism of her policies," he wrote in 1966, "is the legality of her government, the recognized sovereignty of the state, and the doctrine that internal affairs of any nation are outside the competence of the United Nations."[2] Rhodesia's white minority regime had less standing in international diplomatic circles, because not all states recognized the UDI government. Leaders in neighboring states, however, understood that intervention in the affairs of these militarily powerful states would increase the risk that they would respond in kind. Consequently the battle for majority rule took place even more intensely in the international political realm compared to anti-colonial struggles. The majority rule rebels had to persuade the rest of the world to reject white minority rule as thoroughly as they had rejected colonial rule by the 1960s. Moreover they had to get foreign officials to renounce their recognition of the sovereign rights of such governments to defend themselves. Neither South Africa nor Rhodesia faced this kind of diplomatic rejection in the 1960s, although even then majority rule rebels benefited from the growing discrediting of white minority rule in world opinion.

Majority rule rebels who struggled against white minority regimes had distinctive patterns of recruitment of leaders, cadres, and fighters. These rebel organizations, especially their leadership and their strategic choices, reflected the domestic characters of the white settler regimes in southern Africa. In particular, rebels operated in the context of a much greater urbanization among the African population than in Angola, Mozambique, or Guinea, and this had a decisive impact on recruitment patterns. By 1959 Rhodesia's segregated education system served 80 percent of seven- to fifteen-year-old African children, very high by African standards of that time. Primary and secondary schools were operated mainly by religious missions, although the state provided limited funding (about the same amount as provided for white pupils, who were one-sixteenth as numerous). In that same year, the country had twenty-four African secondary schools organized on

---

[2] Julius Nyerere, "Rhodesia in the Context of Southern Africa," *Foreign Affairs* 44:3 (1966): 382.

the internationally recognized British Cambridge system.[3] This differed
radically from South Africa, where "Bantu education" was designed to
produce unskilled and semi-skilled laborers, and gave Rhodesia's early
rebels a state-provided venue for ideological discussion that strengthened the roles of political commissars and cadres. Again, the bureaucratically effective state unintentionally provided the social spaces for
centrally organized rebels to organize and challenge its authority over
the population.

Educational horizons may have been more limited for black South
African students; nevertheless there were 209,000 secondary school
students there in 1974. Yet 50 percent of school-age South Africans
were not enrolled at all, many of them living in urban areas where more
fortunate youth were becoming increasingly politicized in their classrooms. The system of Bantu universities – Fort Hare, the University of
the North, and the University of Zululand – produced a steady stream
of potential recruits to the cause of liberation.[4] From the perspective
of scholars like Samuel Huntington, who worried about the stability of
rapidly changing societies, South Africa represented the worst possible
situation. It was proficient at producing a politicized class of educated
people. Its apartheid system severely blocked their upward mobility
at the same time that its restrictions on physical movement put them
in close proximity to the urban unemployed, whose expectations of
eventual liberation were reaching new heights.[5]

The economies of both Rhodesia and South Africa failed to absorb
the school graduates produced by their relatively capable educational
systems. In 1971 about 80 percent of junior secondary certificate holders in Rhodesia remained unemployed six months after graduation.[6]
As a result a steady stream of politicized and otherwise unemployed
students joined the guerrilla ranks. In the late 1970s the disruption of
the education system in Rhodesia caused by rebel occupation of parts
of the country forced the government to abandon schools that had
served another quarter million students, some of whom then joined the

---

[3] Franklin Parker, "Education in the Federation of Rhodesia and Nyasaland, 1961,"
Journal of Negro Education 30:3 (1961): 289.
[4] Yeyedwa Zungu, "Education for Africans in South Africa," *Journal of Negro Education*
46:3 (1977): 213.
[5] Samuel Huntington, *Political Order in Changing Societies* (New Haven, CT: Yale University Press, 1968), 55.
[6] Chengetai Zvobgo, "African Education in Zimbabwe: The Colonial Inheritance of the
New State, 1899–1979," *Issue* 11:3 (1981): 14.

liberation struggle. Likewise, in South Africa the 1976 urban insurrection disrupted the education of hundreds of thousands of primary- and secondary-level students, generating more recruits for the exiled majority rule rebels and for the resistance movements inside the country. In contrast, by independence in 1975, Mozambique's Lourenço Marques University had admitted only forty African students. When FRELIMO was launched in 1961, Mondlane reported that there were only 6,928 African pupils in primary schools, about half of one percent of age eligible Mozambicans. By the late 1960s, when FRELIMO started to occupy substantial parts of the Niassa district, there were still no secondary schools for Africans.[7] Thus FRELIMO leaders did not have to deal with the same kinds of political demands and social expectations among recruits that their counterparts in other territories faced in their struggles against the white minority regimes.

Education systems in the white minority–ruled states generated more politically involved cadres and fighters, compared to earlier anti-colonial struggles. International agencies contributed to the education of majority rule rebel fighters to a greater degree than they had to anti-colonial movements. The UN High Commission for Refugees (UNHCR) helped coordinate the education of refugees, sponsoring schools that employed teachers supportive of the majority rule rebellions. In the late 1970s, the UNHCR helped to place 800 student refugees from frontline states in African universities. These services, along with food and health care, not only added to the reservoir of recruits; they also created social spaces where rebel fighters and cadres could develop expectations and political debates that strengthened the rebellion, while also posing challenges of control to the majority rule rebel leaderships. But this fragmenting tendency occurred within a context in which the majority rule rebels' dependence on externally supplied resources and opportunities still favored the ideologically articulate among the rebels.

In all three countries, recruits with primary and secondary education pressed demands for political discussions and debates within the majority rule rebel ranks. Periodically they launched violent challenges to incumbent leaders, which were regularly put down with brutal force. Such challenges, along with the more probing counterinsurgency strategies of these states, pushed rebel leaders to search for traitors in their ranks. Although factional splits within the small coterie of highly educated leaders were a persistent problem, foreign support for "official"

[7] Eduardo Mondlane, *The Struggle for Mozambique* (London: Zed, 1983), 65.

rebels put resources in the hands of leaders to limit such challenges. Rebel leaders faced even more serious challenges from the rank and filers. Often the outcome was a high degree of paranoia among rebel leaders, who used authoritarian and violent methods as well as political indoctrination and promises of improved future status to control their members.

The internal and international realms of rebel politics in southern Africa pushed majority rule rebels to adopt centralized state-like organizations, as their anti-colonial brethren had done. Majority rule rebels tried to carve out liberated zones where they could act as states-in-waiting. Even though they faced formidable security forces, this type of confrontation enhanced the value of tightly knit, disciplined organizations in fighting these regimes. Secrecy and suppression of dissent were important survival strategies that reduced their vulnerabilities to these threats and had the effect of further centralizing the rebel organizations. These defenses naturally clashed with the expectations of debate and influence of many rank-and-file members. Like other rebel groups in this book, the policies of these rebels reflected the domestic and international contexts of their times, especially with regard to their distinctive channels for gaining access to political and material resources. As the evolution of warfare in Africa shows, changing circumstances and opportunities governed which grievances became operative and the extent to which rebel leaders were able (or cared) to articulate a grand political narrative.

Zimbabwe's Struggle

Majority rule rebel politics in Rhodesia – renamed Zimbabwe in 1980 – began much like that of other African rebels in the 1950s. Several urban-based political parties emerged out of a general strike in 1948. In 1957 Zimbabwe's African National Congress, led by Jason Moyo, merged with James Chikerema's City Youth League (CYL) to form the Southern Rhodesian ANC. Like Mozambican and Angolan organizations, this predecessor of Zimbabwean majority rule rebel groups presented an external image of unity that concealed factional divides centered on the personalities of the original founders. Its compromise leader, Joshua Nkomo, headed the new alliance.[8] Its political wing, the National

---

[8] Christopher Nyangoni and Gideon Nyandoro (eds.), *Zimbabwe Independence Movements: Select Documents* (London: Rex Collings, 1979).

Democratic Party, survived only to 1960, when the white minority government banned it. A year later Nkomo emerged as the leader of ZAPU
and went on to play a major role throughout the liberation struggle.

Nkomo launched his political career while at a foreign university,
just as many anti-colonial rebel leaders had done. After graduating
from Fort Hare University College in South Africa in 1948, he helped
to organize a railway workers union. In 1955 he went to the United
States, where he trained as a Methodist minister for three years. Meanwhile, he maintained his Fort Hare network, which later helped him to
coordinate other Fort Hare graduates who joined Zimbabwe's liberation
struggle. Among these contacts were Robert Mugabe, who later became
Zimbabwe's first African president; Herbert Chitepo, who qualified in
1954 as a barrister in London; and Robert Sobukwe, the founder of
South Africa's Pan-African Congress (PAC). Another distinguished
Fort Hare alumnus was Kenneth Kaunda, who took office as the first
president of Zambia in 1964, just as Zimbabwe's majority rule rebels
had to find a rear base in a neighboring state.

Like his anti-colonial rebel counterparts, Nkomo traveled the world
in search of patrons who would help him end white minority rule and
become the leader of Zimbabwe. He considered using peaceful political
means if this would accomplish his goal, but when the white minority
government refused to negotiate majority rule, he sought foreign support for an armed struggle. In 1958 he stayed in Egypt as President
Nasser's guest. That year he attended the All-African People's Organisation meeting in Accra, where he met other nationalist leaders who
enjoyed Ghanaian president Kwame Nkrumah's favor. He was elected
to the executive committee of the Soviet-backed Afro-Asian People's
Solidarity Organisation (AAPSO) at its 1960 meeting in Conakry, after
which he traveled to the Soviet Union in 1961 and China in 1962.

Nkomo took help from wherever he could get it. He considered the
Swedish International Development Agency "the most generous of all
donors of food and clothing for our refugees" and thought that "the
Friedrich Ebert Foundation of West Germany was extremely helpful."
The UN-schooled refugees in Zambia supported ZAPU. The Commonwealth Secretariat's Special Fund gave aid to refugees too, and
in the mid-1970s Libya's President Qaddafi became a minor patron
of Nkomo. Even London-based Roland "Tiny" Rowland, head of the
Lonrho (short for London-Rhodesia) conglomerate, provided "generous contributions" in the form of personal funds and air tickets.[9]

---

[9] Joshua Nkomo, *The Story of My Life* (London: Methuen, 1984), 181–85.

Nkomo's Soviet connection proved to be most valuable in terms of gaining access to weapons and military training. Once Zambia became independent in 1964, Nkomo was able to negotiate the transfer of arms supplies to the ZAPU's armed wing, the Zimbabwe People's Revolutionary Army (ZIPRA), via the Soviet ambassador in Lusaka. But Soviet aid brought with it bad advice. Soviet advisers urged Nkomo to turn ZIPRA into a conventional army using Soviet weapons to invade Rhodesia and create a liberated zone. They thought that this would give ZAPU leverage to force a peace settlement on its own terms while growing global condemnation of the white minority regime left it in an increasingly marginal position.[10] This had worked in Mozambique and Angola, where anti-colonial rebel forces served as the basis for building a strong Marxist political party. Nkomo's ZAPU, however, never posed a serious threat to the Rhodesian armed forces in a head-to-head match on the battlefield. It was a rival majority rule rebel group, the ZANU, that eventually won the battle against the powerful Rhodesian security forces.

Still, Nkomo's ties to foreign backers and command over their resources left ZAPU vulnerable to factional splits. Tensions came to a head in August 1963, when Reverend Ndabaningi Sithole and Robert Mugabe left to establish ZANU. In 1964 the white minority government's ban of nationalist political organizations shifted this open competition into friendly states – primarily Zambia – that bordered Rhodesia, in which the rebels sought to establish rear bases from which to launch armed struggle. Prominent rebel leaders, including Nkomo, Mugabe, and Sithole, were arrested and spent the next decade in prison.

President Kaunda's support for ZAPU helped it to maintain its leading role in the liberation struggle, even as internal battles weakened the organization. It was lucky for Nkomo that the old Southern Rhodesian ANC had lent its political support to Kaunda to break up the old white-dominated Central African Federation out of which Zambia emerged. During his 1960s travels, Nkomo had done Kaunda numerous favors when he was active in the Pan-African Movement of East, Central, and Southern Africa (PAFMECSA). In 1962, Nkomo urged PAFMECSA to support Kaunda's bid to lead Zambia's independence movement, marginalizing the older and more established Harry Nkumbula. In turn PAFMECSA recognized ZAPU as the legitimate nationalist movement for Zimbabwe. Once the OAU Liberation

[10] Christopher Andrew and Vasili Mitrokhin, *The World Was Going Our Way: The KGB and the Battle for the Third World* (New York: Basic Books, 2005), 460–61; and Nkomo, *Story of My Life*, 175–76.

Committee was formed in 1963, PAFMECSA's recognition helped ZAPU to dominate the diplomatic spotlight as the legitimate recipient of foreign aid.[11] Meanwhile, the initial failure of ZAPU to infiltrate Rhodesia to carry out military operations caused some African leaders to doubt its capacity to lead Rhodesia to majority rule. This failure lent substance to ZANU statements condemning "kitchen revolutionaries" preoccupied with factional squabbles and to an extended diplomatic effort to try to get Great Britain to force the white rulers of its old colony to negotiate a turn to majority rule. Moreover ZANU followed up this criticism with its own efforts to bring the fight to Rhodesia.[12]

The first major Zimbabwe African National Liberation Army (ZANLA) operation took place on 28 April 1966, now celebrated as Chimurenga Day, the start of the rebel war. This venture distinguished ZANU's army from its ZAPU rivals. A liberation struggle inside Rhodesia that relied on a strategy of controlling and mobilizing noncombatants made more sense for ZANU, drawing as it did from an ethnic Shona base that made up more than three-fourths of Rhodesia's population. Although this support base widened perceptions of ethnic splits, it helped the rebels to dominate the field of battle and to exploit the local-level social networks and relationships that the bureaucratic Rhodesian state had a hard time controlling.

ZANU also needed an external strategy. Before his imprisonment in 1964, Mugabe used his contacts with Nkrumah when he worked as a teacher in Ghana to secure help with military training for fighters. Mugabe's colleague and ZANU Central Committee member Herbert Chitepo had gained the personal confidence of Nyerere when he had served as Tanzania's director of public prosecution.[13] Nyerere's influence over the OAU Liberation Committee, based in his capital, also meant that ZANU gained recognition alongside ZAPU. Although initially ZANU's infiltration into Rhodesia met with crushing responses from the Rhodesian security forces, it nevertheless convinced foreign backers that it was serious about fighting for control of the population.

ZANLA incursions now pressured ZAPU to operate in Rhodesia. At first ZAPU seemed poised to meet this challenge as the favored majority rule rebels of the Zambian president. In August 1967 ZIPRA staged

---

[11] William Cyrus Reed, "International Politics and National Liberation: ZANU and the Politics of Contested Sovereignty in Zimbabwe," *African Studies Review* 36:2 (1993): 36–37.

[12] "Kitchen Revolutionaries," *Zimbabwe News* [Journal of ZANU] 3:2 (1968): 1–2.

[13] Reed, "International Politics and National Liberation, 38.

its incursion in cooperation with ANC fighters from South Africa. In the following year two more incursions brought the intervention of a combined force of South African police and Rhodesian armed forces, which quickly defeated ZIPRA units. Meanwhile, ZAPU had to manage more internal splits. After Nkomo's imprisonment in 1964, James Chikerema, the head of the old CYL, became the operational leader of ZAPU, while Jason Moyo, the leader of the old Southern Rhodesian ANC, took over planning for military operations. But factional divisions remained. Some observers associated Moyo with ethnic Ndebeles and Chikerema with ethnic Shona.[14]

Early in 1971, rivalry within the majority rule rebel leadership erupted in violence. Young commanders led by Walter Mtimkulu kidnapped top ZAPU political and military leaders. Chikerema left ZAPU to join with Nathan Shamuyarira, leader of a splinter ZANU group, to form the new Front for the Liberation of Zimbabwe (FROLIZI). This marked a turning point in the development of the rebellion that diverged significantly from the experiences of the anti-colonial rebellions. Increasingly, ZAPU and ZANU leaders found that they were attracting capable cadres from within Rhodesia who joined the insurgency as a result of their politicization there. These independently minded recruits complained that the rebellion was not unified enough or moving fast enough.

Such debates raised the anxieties of foreign backers, who pressed for a single majority rule rebel group to assume the mantle of sovereignty once Rhodesian forces were beaten. Once the 1974 coup in Portugal confirmed that the Frente de Libertação de Moçambique (FRELIMO) would inherit state power in Mozambique, its leader, Samora Machel, encouraged unity among the Zimbabwean rebel groups. In December 1974 Kaunda and Machel presided over the Lusaka National Unity Accord, in which ZAPU, ZANU, and FROLIZI, along with several unarmed nationalist groups inside Rhodesia, agreed to join forces. Pressured by South African officials, the Rhodesian government had released Nkomo, Mugabe, and Sithole to participate in the unity talks. Nevertheless factional politics still drove events. A month earlier in Lusaka, junior ZANU commanders had rebelled against what they claimed were the luxurious excesses of their superiors. The leader of the group, a graduate of the University of Rhodesia law school,

---

[14] Simbi Mubako, "The Quest for Unity in the Zimbabwe Liberation Movement," *Issue* 5:1 (1975): 10.

complained that university graduates had to serve under less educated commanders.[15] A consequence of this revolt was the assassination of High Command Chairman Herbert Chitepo on 18 March 1975. Rhodesian officials saw the strategic value in promoting further splits by bringing Mugabe and Sithole back into the day-to-day politics of ZANU.

The violent contestation among the majority rule rebels tried the patience of Presidents Kaunda and Nyerere. Both Zambia and Tanzania imprisoned the remaining ZANU High Command and outlawed groups that did not recognize the Unity Accord. Both presidents supported efforts to unify the two majority rule rebel organizations into a new command, the Zimbabwe People's Army (ZIPA). Under the watchful eyes of the OAU Liberation Committee and leaders of other frontline states, ZANU and ZAPU signed a unity agreement to form the Patriotic Front (PF) on 9 October 1976. Although this did not translate into real cooperation on the ground, it highlighted the extent to which the outside world insisted on the formation of a single group as the bearer of legitimate sovereignty and as a government-in-waiting to take eventual control of Rhodesia. Well into 1979, Machel and Kaunda continued to meet over efforts to maintain at least the façade of PF unity. External efforts, however, did produce sincere moves toward unity. Negotiations took place to recognize Alfred "Nikita" Mangena from ZAPU and Rex Nhongo from ZANU as the commanders of ZIPA, but then Mozambique's President Machel used his army to imprison rebellious ZIPA commanders when they refused to recognize Mugabe's authority. In the end, the diplomatic effort to gain greater rebel unity created a short-lived faction and a platform from which a new set of politically ambitious commanders sought external support.

Despite all efforts, externally driven efforts to unify majority rule rebel groups failed to heal internal rifts. The January 1977 letter bomb assassination of Moyo in Botswana revealed the same kinds of factional rivalries within ZAPU that had beset the Partido Africano da Independência da Guiné e Cabo Verde (PAIGC) in Guinea and FRELIMO in Mozambique, especially after Nkomo resumed control of ZAPU after his release from prison. Nkomo's frustrated Soviet backers resented Nkomo's personal ambitions and propensity for in-fighting, and they saw him as a "man without ideology." Their flirtations with other rebel leaders showed that political programs still mattered to

---

[15] For a ZANU perspective, see A. M. Chidoda, "Kaunda's Chitepo Commission Report," *Zimbabwe News*, June 1976, 28–30.

outside backers.[16] In 1977 factional fighting broke out again at ZAPU's Lusaka headquarters. Shortly thereafter, in June 1978, Alfred "Nikita" Mangena (who had returned from his unity effort) was wounded in a failed assassination attempt, only to die later in Zambia when his car drove over a landmine.

Many smaller conflicts took place over issues of personality, ethnic backing, strategy, and bold opportunist moves within the overall liberation struggle. In this regard Rhodesia's liberation insurgencies showed many of the factionalizing tendencies that characterized warlord rebels, but in a domestic political and international context that muted these tendencies. For now, external patrons on all sides pressed their favored rebel group toward at least making an overt pretence of unified effort. In 1975 Mozambique's independence added a new dimension, introducing viable majority rule rebel backers to the mix and giving more options to rival rebel leaders. Although Machel may have preferred a single unified insurgency, collaboration between Rhodesian security forces and Portuguese colonial authorities against FRELIMO in the recent past, coupled with their support for what became the Resistência Nacional Moçambicana (RENAMO) inside Mozambique, convinced him that he needed to help a friendly regime to come to power in Rhodesia. It made sense for Machel to support Mugabe, whose ethnic kinsmen occupied both sides of the Rhodesia-Mozambique border. Mugabe's movement was both ideologically compatible and militarily prepared for the double purpose of liberating Mozambique's neighbor while simultaneously policing borderlands that Machel's own government found difficult to control. Like the appearance of multiple state patrons in Angola's anti-colonial struggle, the proliferation of external backers had the effect of entangling the war in state-to-state rivalries as well as in the personal agendas of individual rebel leaders.

The new regional base strengthened Mugabe and ZANU. Released from having to appeal for Kaunda's favor against his preference for ZAPU, Mugabe could concentrate on opening a new front in Rhodesia. His capacity to operate inside of Rhodesia was not sufficient to convince the Soviets to switch their support to his movement, but this did not matter so long as ZIPRA stayed bottled up in Zambia with its ZAPU leadership and while Kaunda feared unleashing his guests against the tactically superior Rhodesians. Repeated Rhodesian attacks inside Zambia, and Rhodesia's effort to harm the country economically, led to greater caution on Kaunda's part. Meanwhile, ZANLA units

---

[16] "Rhodesia: Diplomatic Acrobatics," *Africa Confidential* 19:18 (8 Sept 1978): 2–3.

moved inside Rhodesia, where they ultimately established the strongest position by the time that the white minority government finally conceded to the demand to hold elections. This success also attracted ZIPA fighters to ZANLA's banner. This support was more widely felt too, as Mugabe won 63 percent of the votes in the April 1980 presidential election and became the leader of the country that the new government declared would be called Zimbabwe.

The defeat of Rhodesian forces ultimately hinged on the support given by foreign states to the majority rule rebel group that seemed most capable of forming a viable government in an independent, majority-ruled Zimbabwe. Although it is hard to know if Nkomo could have executed a more successful military plan, Soviet aid and Kaunda's offer of refuge in Zambia played an important negative role in how ZAPU devised strategy and how ZIPRA fought. As Nkomo explained after ZAPU failed to inherit power in Zimbabwe, "By the end of the war we had tank crews, and even complete flying staff and maintenance staff for a squadron of combat aircraft, who had passed out of Soviet training schools."[17] FRELIMO backing had served ZANU much better, for this addressed the Rhodesian threat to Mozambique via its use of ZANU as a proxy, even if in the short term this risked further Rhodesian support for RENAMO's fight against ZANU's Mozambique hosts. Moreover, ZANU's backers in Mozambique had themselves only recently been guerrilla fighters and appeared to share Mugabe's clearer understanding of the need to control communities and to cultivate local supporters inside Rhodesia.

Upon gaining access to cross-border bases after Mozambique's independence in 1975, ZANLA fighters focused on exercising effective political control over people inside Rhodesia. Several fighters explained,

> First there is the commander. His job is to lead. Then comes the political commissar. His job is to introduce us to the masses and instruct them in who we are, what we are doing and why. Then there is the man in charge of security. He finds out who is on our side, who is for our case and who are the sell-outs.

Others recounted the effort to connect local grievances and problems to the liberation struggle:

> We would get into an area, study the problems . . . and then teach the people about their problems, how we can solve them by fighting the enemy.[18]

[17] Nkomo, *Story of My Life*, 175.
[18] Quotes in David Lan, *Guns and Rain: Guerrillas and Spirit Mediums in Zimbabwe* (London: James Currey, 1985), 127–28.

This effort included gaining the support of local spirit mediums – religious leaders whose roles included maintaining people's links with ancestors, land, and the production of that land. Thus the ZANU and its ZANLA armed wing successfully linked very local community complaints to a broad political agenda. This political strategy also mobilized some of the same religious practices and beliefs, such as personal invulnerability to bullets, that some outside observers of later warlord and parochial rebels in Chapters 5 and 6 associated with disorder and an absence of political programs.

ZANU's Rhodesian foes understood the political and military threat that rebel support among religious leaders could pose, and in 1973 Internal Affairs officers compiled a country-wide list of spirit mediums, separatist church leaders, and sacred places.[19] But unlike these rebels, Rhodesian officials had a poor record of actually recruiting these notables to their side, particularly once rebels succeeded in convincing these local leaders that the rebels would win and address community complaints, particularly about control over land. Rhodesian government control on the ground instead rested on the effectiveness of military operations and the concentration of non-combatants in protected villages where they could be monitored. Manpower shortages due to the limited numbers of recruits available among the quarter-million-strong white settler population pushed the Rhodesian military and police forces to deploy small mobile tracking units ("sticks") that could move around the countryside at least as rapidly and silently as their rebel foes. These units and special intelligence details were very good at collecting information to identify, track, and kill rebels. Security forces operated among civilians inside Rhodesia, posing as insurgents to gauge local community support for the liberation struggle and to identify specific individuals who aided the fake rebels. Employing divide-and-rule tactics, the fake rebels tried to pit real rebels against local people through accusing enthusiastic ZANLA supporters of being police informants. Likewise, "tame terrorists" (captured guerrillas whose information had resulted in deaths of comrades and who thus would receive nasty receptions when they returned) were deployed to pose as ZANLA fighters to collect information from sympathetic local people. These irregular warfare efforts were backed by the willingness of Rhodesian authorities by 1976–77 to devote 23 percent of the state budget to military expenditures to support 60,000 men under arms. But ultimately Rhodesian armed counterinsurgency innovations were not matched with an

---

[19] Jakkie Cilliers, *Counter-Insurgency in Rhodesia* (London: Croom Helm, 1985), 165.

effective political strategy to gain popular support for their fight against
the rebels.[20]

The Rhodesian security forces also proved to be adept at launching attacks into neighboring countries to strike at rebels' rear bases.
In August 1976, a Rhodesian attack on a ZANLA base in Mozambique, which also served as a UN refugee camp, killed 1,000 pur-
ported guerrillas, including all of the patients in a hospital.[21] This
combination of conventional and irregular warfare and its capacity
to strike deep into the territory of neighboring states and to move
throughout Rhodesia meant that ZANU faced periodic challenges to
its control over liberated zones. Rhodesian military forces were very
adept at launching attacks hundreds of kilometers into the territories
of neighboring states and were successful at disrupting rebel operations and exposing the governments that hosted these rebels to direct
retaliation for their actions. These attacks involved antiquated helicopters and even small civilian Cessna aircraft that Rhodesian forces
converted to military use. But the failure of Rhodesian authorities to
couple their military capacity to physically control territory with an
effective program to recruit and mobilize loyal communities meant
that they were never able to raise a significant force of home guard
militias to fight the rebels as the Portuguese had with the Angolan
fletchas. The Rhodesian authorities were reluctant to foster a class of
African small farmers if that meant taking land away from white commercial farmers. The Rhodesian regime's significant coercive advantage (Map 4) was not sustainable without a political strategy to gain
wide support from non-combatants, particularly given its manpower
constraints.[22]

Non-combatants particularly suffered in areas of contested control,
but this ultimately favored the rebels. Where ZANLA competed with
Rhodesian security forces for control of territory there was always the
possibility that informers, acting on any number of motivations (personal or family security, monetary gain, or personal retribution), could
betray the guerrilla fighters. In places where ZANLA and ZANU could

[20] Ron Reid Daly, *Selous Scouts: Top Secret War* (Alberton: Galago, 1982), 24–26; Bruce
    Hoffman, Jennifer Taw, and David Arnold, *Lessons for Contemporary Counterinsurgen-
    cies: The Rhodesian Experience* (Santa Monica, CA: RAND, 1991), 19–24.
[21] Lawrence Cline, *Pseudo Operations and Counterinsurgency: Lessons from Other Countries*
    (Carlisle, PA: US Army War College, 2005), 12.
[22] Terence Ranger, *Peasant Consciousness and Guerrilla War in Zimbabwe: A Comparative
    Study* (Berkeley: University of California Press, 1985), 265–67.

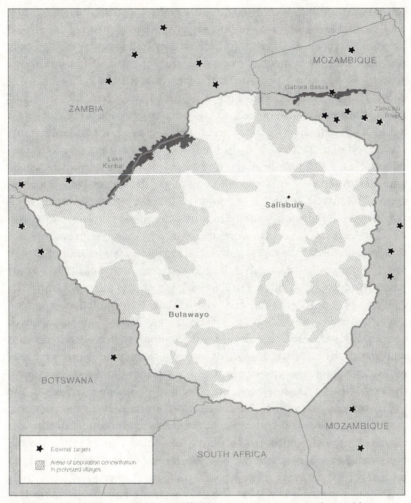

MAP 4. The Rhodesian Counter-Offensive, 1976–1979. Based on Jakkie Cilliers, *Counter-Insurgency in Rhodesia* (London: Croom Helm, 1985), 91 and Bruce Hoffman, Jennifer M. Taw, and David Arnold, *Lessons for Contemporary Counterinsurgencies: The Rhodesian Experience* (Santa Monica, CA: RAND, 1991), 78.

not maintain consistent control, they had to make local people more afraid of the rebel army than of the state security forces to prevent informers and to encourage them to take risks to keep fighters supplied. One commander later recalled, "We were convinced, either we educate them, and they accept us . . . or if they refuse to accept us out of fear [of the enemy] then we instill fear."[23] ZANLA leaders recognized that they needed to maintain as continuous a presence as possible to get local help to "detect enemy agents." To do so they had to resort to physically restricting the movement of people in and out of ZANLA-controlled areas.[24] But as noted previously, the lack of a Rhodesian government political strategy to capitalize on non-combatants' grievances or concerns about mistreatment meant that coercive guerrilla tactics were less apt to cause defections to the government side, as most non-combatants concluded that they had little option but to support the guerrillas. This government failure made all the more convincing the narrative that the guerrillas fought for majority rule and to get the repressive Rhodesian state off the backs of ordinary people so that they could advance.

The Rhodesian state's failure to provide would-be collaborators with a real stake in the success of a counterinsurgency campaign and the fact that international pressures against the Rhodesian state did not evince much popular confidence that the minority regime would hold out for long created opportunities for ZANLA to use violence to advance its cause.[25] This dearth of political choices facing the population enhanced the effectiveness of the rebels' "coercive mobilization" of segments of communities through exploiting local tensions, such as dissatisfaction with gender roles, disgruntlement at gerontocracy, and property disputes, to convince some people to side with them and to help control the rest.[26] But alongside these coercive and parochial elements in the micro-politics of conflict, the consistent commitment to the narrative of majority rule and the promise of access to land, reinforced through external support, continued to play a key role in shaping the overall outcome. Again, international and domestic political contexts played critical roles in shaping rebel organization and behavior.

Close examination of local conditions shows how overlapping layers of motivations and interests operated beneath the majority rule rebels' ideological narrative. Terence Ranger noted that "peasants often excused guerrillas of responsibility for unjust punishments or extortionate demands, blaming these on young boys and girls (the *mujibas*) who

---

[23] David Moore, "Democracy, Violence, and Identity in Zimbabwe: The War of National Liberation from the Realms of Dissent," *Canadian Journal of African Studies* 29:3 (1995): 387.

[24] Justin Nyoka, "Inside Free Zimbabwe," *Zimbabwe News*, Dec 1978, 18–20.

[25] Cilliers, *Counter-Insurgency in Rhodesia*, 49.

[26] Norma Kriger, *Zimbabwe's Guerrilla War: Peasant Voices* (New York: Cambridge University Press, 1992), 7–9.

acted as go-betweens."[27] These go-betweens used rebel affiliations to challenge otherwise untouchable elders, settle personal scores, or to elevate their status in other ways. Similar problems appeared in South Africa, where youth were used as enforcers during the anti-apartheid movement, particularly into the 1980s. This tapped a reservoir of personal grievances and ambitions among rank-and-file rebel fighters and later created serious problems of discipline. It is this local dimension of conflict that plays a much more prominent role in causing what in the aggregate looks like a collection of self-interested and instrumental uses of violence that characterize warlord rebellions that lack strong ideological programs or demanding external supporters. Even success brought these problems: "There were such large numbers of guerrillas that the population has difficulty supplying their needs.... In such stressful circumstances some comrades were more prone to commit spontaneous acts of violence against civilians. They also made what peasants perceived as arbitrary demands."[28]

The defining feature of anti-colonial and majority rule rebels, at least in the ideal, was the drive for unity that submerged and contained factional and personal differences within the organization and political narrative of the wider armed struggle – a feature that distinguished it from later types of armed conflict. Majority rule rebel leaders had to satisfy the leaders of frontline states that they would at least preserve a façade of common purpose. This was a requirement that these leaders were willing to enforce. Once ZANLA held territory in Rhodesia, Mugabe's international travels attracted greater international attention than they had before. In its 1978 summit, the OAU withdrew support from the 1976 unity agreement and gave exclusive recognition to ZANU. Ethiopia and Cuba provided military training; the World Council of Churches organized support of various kinds; and the UNHCR helped set up social services, including in a series of ZANU-run refugee camps housing 35,000 refugees in Mozambique.[29] The international dimension of their struggle extended to ZANU's admission to the Non-Aligned Movement at its 1979 conference in Havana, a status previously

[27] Terence Ranger, "Bandits and Guerrillas: The Case of Zimbabwe," in Donald Crummey (ed.), *Bandits, Rebellion and Social Protest in Africa* (London: James Currey, 1986), 385.

[28] David Maxwell, "Local Politics and the War of Liberation in North-East Zimbabwe," *Journal of Southern African Studies* 19:3 (Sept 1993): 380.

[29] "Statement of the United Nations High Commissioner for Refugees to the Economic and Social Council," 27 July 1977.

reserved for sovereign states.[30] Once ZANU achieved this favorable position, British officials intervened to negotiate the handover of power in 1980, making it even more important that ZANU maintain discipline and internal control to gain a clear victory in an internationally mediated election.

Although other local agendas within the wider rebel war in the Zimbabwean conflict could have emerged to shape the overall conflict more along the lines of a warlord or parochial rebel conflict, in this case the centralized majority rule rebels were able to contain and subsume the differing agendas under a broad political program. The ZANU-dominated government after 1980 was able to benefit from this experience as a sort of state-in-waiting prior to the end of the white minority regime. In this regard, it resembled the state that it fought, even if its political agenda was quite different. This relationship changed in the 1990s, when Zimbabwe's army became involved in fighting in Congo's war (Chapter 5). But during the heyday of majority rule rebel struggles, the bureaucratic nature of the states that they fought would shape the organization and aims of the rebels in the other southern African countries to which we now turn.

Namibia's Liberation

SWAPO emerged as the standard-bearer for Namibian self-determination and majority rule by the early 1960s. Unlike ZANU and ZAPU, SWAPO was able to crush most rival organizations. It also confronted a more formidable array of state security forces, which prevented it from establishing durable liberated zones inside Namibia at the same time that this pressure forced the rebel organization to police its own ranks and root out suspected informers and critics. Fierce attacks from South African security forces and the South African Defence Force (SADF), one of the world's more capable militaries of that time, drove it into deep dependence on alliances with friendly regimes in other African states, especially its MPLA hosts in Angola after 1974. Central to SWAPO strategy was securing and then increasing international diplomatic support for its position as the sole legitimate majority rule rebel organization for Namibia; this strategy

---

[30] Reed, "International Politics and National Liberation," 47–51.

eventually led to a UN-supervised election in November 1989 and independence in March 1990.

Namibia's majority rule activists started out aiming to acquire anti-colonial credentials. Before the First World War, Namibia (referred to as South West Africa before independence) had been a German colony. Then it was legally transformed into a League of Nations mandate, which was taken over by the UN as a trusteeship after the Second World War. The League of Nations and then the UN assigned the administration of the former German colony to South Africa but retained supervisory powers. This international recognition of the territory as one held "in trust" meant that world opinion would play an even bigger role in the strategies of these majority rule rebels. SWAPO had little choice, given the formidable military capacities of their South African foes. The UN General Assembly played a direct role in this conflict, having rebuffed an attempt by South Africa to annex the territory, and ordering that it be included under the trusteeship system. This arrangement required South Africa to provide the UN with information about administration and development, which South Africa refused to do. Moreover, in the 1950s and 1960s South Africa introduced the apartheid system to South West Africa, which angered the UN and its increasing numbers of new African member states. International displeasure with South Africa's domestic politics played a key role in the strategies of majority rule rebels, both within what was to become Namibia and in exile.

Like their ZAPU and ZANU colleagues, many Namibian rebel leaders had acquired their education at Fort Hare College in South Africa, which gave them political experience and contacts with that country's anti-apartheid movement. Jarire Tundu Kozonguizi had participated in ANC student branch discussions during his student days. In 1952 he and two other classmates returned to South West Africa and founded the South West African Student Body (later renamed the South West Africa Progressive Association). Seven years later Kozonguizi used the new organization as a platform to address a petition to the UN to protest that South Africa did not fulfill its obligations as the UN's trustee of the territory. While Kozonguizi was away on this trip to the UN, several other organizations were organized to take up the mission of liberating the country from South African rule

In this instance liberation did not mean just liberation from foreign rule; it also meant liberation from white minority rule. The Ovambo ethnic group in the northern region of the country especially resented constraints on their legal capacities to move and to seek employment once they had signed contracts as migrant laborers. Their settlement in urban areas was tightly controlled, and those who had moved to Windhoek, the capital, found themselves the targets of a resettlement plan in the late 1950s. Their grievances found expression in the formation of the Ovambo People's Congress among Namibian workers in Cape Town in 1957. Renamed the Ovambo People's Organisation (OPO) two years later, this group campaigned for the civil rights of workers and urban migrants.

The leadership of the OPO emerged out of the classrooms and workplaces that provided them with places to discuss politics and to share ideas about organizing to improve their status and abolish minority rule. The irony of this situation was that the militarily powerful South African authorities ran a state that produced an economy and institutions that had numerous pockets in which critics could marshal supporters. For example, one OPO founder, Andimba Herman Toivo Ja Toivo, studied at the Finnish Mission Industrial School in northern Namibia before joining the Native Military Corps of the South African army. His associate, Sam Nujoma, later the head of SWAPO and Namibia's first president, lived precariously in Windhoek, where he worked for the railway. In April 1959 Nujoma became the OPO leader and attracted a following after leading a strike at a fish cannery. The forced removal of the African residents of Windhoek to a new location generated further popular support for the OPO. When in December 1959 the security forces killed eleven African protesters, this event became decisive in launching the struggle for majority rule.[31]

Nujoma fled to the soon-to-be-independent Tanzania, where he obtained Nyerere's support. In April 1960, OPO changed its name to SWAPO to stress the theme of national unity articulated by most anti-colonial rebels and called on the UN to intervene on its behalf. It opened offices in New York, Dar es Salaam, and Stockholm. This international strategy produced results. In 1968 the UN General Assembly terminated South Africa's mandate, calling on South Africa to turn over administration to the UN's new Council for Namibia, appointed to prepare the country for independence. Three years later the International Court of Justice reaffirmed the illegality of South Africa's occupation. SWAPO convinced the UN to recognize it as the sole authentic

---

[31] David Soggot, *Namibia, the Violent Heritage* (New York: St. Martin's Press, 1986), 24–32.

representative of the Namibian people in 1973, effectively criminalizing South Africa's rule in Namibia. UN funding and services to SWAPO would become especially important in the late 1970s and 1980s, when Angolan independence paved the way for the establishment of SWAPO bases just outside of Namibia. Nujoma was very effective at seeking international support, and once receiving it, he dominated the political scene to ensure that SWAPO monopolized its benefits. Thus despite the fact that it controlled no territory inside Namibia, it had become an effective state-in-waiting in an international legal sense by 1973. When one recalls that in the same year the PAIGC already controlled about 80 percent of Guinea-Bissau's territory before it got international support for its declaration of independence, SWAPO's extraordinary political achievement was critical compensation for its military incapacity to hold any real liberated zones.

Nujoma recognized that the diplomatic approach was important for rallying international support, but that it would not end South African rule or white minority privilege in Namibia. The Sharpeville massacre in South Africa in 1960, which had followed the harsh repression inside Namibia after the 1959 protests, convinced Nujoma that SWAPO would have to engage in armed resistance of some kind despite its lack of a sizeable fighting force. Because SWAPO was unable to confront South African forces directly, it formulated a strategy of "armed propaganda" and hit-and-run attacks. In 1962 it dispatched several hundred fighters to Egypt for training as a rebel force, for which he received OAU Liberation Committee support in 1963. This pushed the Caprivi African National Union (CANU), named for the narrow strip of Namibian territory connecting Namibia to the banks of the Zambezi River and the Zambian border, to join SWAPO in 1964. That same year Zambia became independent, thus giving SWAPO a friendly border from which to launch attacks into Namibia, which they did in August 1966. Initially the South African police easily rebuffed these attacks. Not until after the Portuguese coup in 1974, when SWAPO gained access to bases in MPLA-controlled areas of Angola, did its People's Liberation Army of Namibia (PLAN) (founded in 1962 and more seriously organized in 1969) manage to mount notable strikes in Namibia.

Meanwhile, the SWAPO Youth League (SYL) and labor unions operated inside Namibia among workers and students. In 1973 and 1974 a wave of detentions, coupled with brighter prospects for SWAPO inside Angola, drew recruits, disproportionately from urban areas, northward. By the time that SWAPO moved its headquarters to Luanda in 1975, there were more than 6,000 rebels in Angola. The internal political situation in Namibia also favored SWAPO. In 1978 South African officials tried to create an electoral coalition that excluded SWAPO. Although this political tactic was intended to appease international demands and the UN Security Council Resolution 435, which demanded that elections be held to prepare the country for independence, in reality South African officials wanted to create a *cordon sanitaire* of conservative and moderate states around itself. Ultimately, this strategy failed, for it drove politicized and frustrated youth, many facing a tough job market, unable to find employment in line with their expectations and skills, north to SWAPO. A conscription law enacted in 1980 requiring all African males over the age of sixteen to register for military service encouraged still more to flee.

The extension of the formal UN recognition of SWAPO in the 1970s enabled these majority rule rebels to participate in the operation of some UN agencies. The UN Institute for Namibia in Lusaka was founded in 1976 and appointed as its director Hage Geingob, a member of the SWAPO Central Committee and former UN political affairs officer, who later became prime minister of Namibia. Direct UN funding for relief operations in SWAPO camps helped the organization to mount attacks from Angola. SWAPO also benefited from the fact that no other state bordering Namibia would host a rival majority rule rebel group. This monopoly over international diplomatic support and the flow of externally supplied resources gave SWAPO's leaders control over the assets needed to launch and sustain a rebellion. SWAPO's otherwise vulnerable and militarily confounded leadership thus had the tools to manage would-be faction leaders and to impose its own political agenda on those who wanted to participate in the rebellion and who hoped for a position in the majority rule dispensation that was sure to come.

The supportive international environment for SWAPO also protected the rebels from many of the military consequences of its inability to create liberated zones inside Namibia and its paranoid responses to South African military attacks on its bases that led it to repress cadres suspected of collaborating with the enemy. In a 1977 Defence White Paper, South Africa adopted a "total national strategy" in the wake of the independence of Angola and Mozambique that included a broad counterinsurgency program against SWAPO and its South African counterparts. This included convincing prisoners to act as informers and deployment of "pseudo-terrorists" who would mix with genuine rebels to spy on their operations and attack supporters. South African officers had learned some of these methods from working with Rhodesia's Selous Scouts and Portuguese colonial officials and *fletchas* units in Angola before 1975. One such organization, Koevoet, was formed in 1979. During the next ten years Koevoet trackers and commandoes killed, by its own count, 3,225 PLAN fighters, suffering a loss of 161 of its own members. Koevoet benefited from the fact that many SWAPO recruits were from urban areas; the South African security forces, primarily the police in this instance, pursued a viable political strategy in appealing to rural notables and offering to use state resources to help protect their status and authority, a marked contrast to their Rhodesian counterparts. Koevoet also offered bounties to members, about three quarters of whom were Africans, for killed and captured SWAPO fighters.[32] These tactics applied local knowledge and skills to tracking fighters who entered Namibia from Angola.

Ultimately, this military success was subordinated to the international pressure on South Africa to end its rule in Namibia. SWAPO thus won at the ballot box in the 1989 election, when it received 55 percent of the vote, enough to assume control of the government but not the two-thirds percent necessary to amend the constitution. The international community's support was critical to reach this outcome, given that SWAPO never was able to sustain liberated zones from which to organize forces to seize state power. People in Namibia who experienced the restrictions and repression of the South African government had to look as much for international help as to SWAPO to bring them majority rule. The critical role of international support is even more evident when one considers the effectiveness of the South African security forces. These security forces were able to mount direct regular warfare attacks on SWAPO's rear bases and on its MPLA backers in Angola and were able to fight an effective irregular warfare campaign through Koevoet that even included groups of "pseudo-guerrillas" who were dressed and equipped like PLAN fighters. This was a very effective tactic to sow suspicion in the ranks of real guerrillas and leave local people uncertain as to whether any guerrilla was a real PLAN member; it thus undermined the rebels' capacity to conduct the kinds of political work within local communities that had been such an effective part of ZANU's strategy inside Rhodesia by the late 1970s. But this

[32] Peter Stiff, *The Covert War: Koevoet Operations in Namibia 1979–1989* (Alberton: Galago, 2004), 13, 492–93.

South African military capacity on the ground could not prevail over the international support that SWAPO enjoyed.

The tactical effectiveness of South African military pressure became manifest in SWAPO leadership's obsession with the threat of spies and traitors. Without international support, it is uncertain whether SWAPO could have survived. The sudden surge of new recruits in the 1980s, most arriving in SWAPO camps unbidden, introduced new and independent political views and demands. Arguments about strategy and accusations of leadership inflexibility and privilege increased. In western Zambia, several SYL leaders, led by Information Secretary Andreas Shipanga, called for a congress to debate SWAPO strategies. SWAPO's leadership turned on their critics and, with help from Zambian military forces, drove out up to 2,000 dissidents, or about half of their active military force.[33] This was not the first time that SWAPO had summarily disposed of its critics. The Kongwa crisis of the late 1960s saw the killing and expulsion of SWAPO recruits who dared to criticize leaders' decisions and demanded more internal debate. Then the 1980–81 "SWAPO spy drama" resulted in the arrest of 1,000 members who were accused of serving as South African spies. Some were killed, and the rest were kept in detention camps.[34] By then, SWAPO's alliance with Angola's MPLA government protected it from the negative military consequences of detentions and killings of some of its most educated and skilled fighters. As a result, less well educated commanders had freer rein to suppress challenges from the better educated new arrivals under their command.

International politics took a turn away from SWAPO's favor when the Reagan administration in the United States decided to support SADF attacks into Angola. The SADF's aim was to weaken the Angolan MPLA, help União Nacional para a Independência Total de Angola (UNITA) rebels, and attack SWAPO bases inside Angola. This threat to SWAPO followed the general decision of the US government to support the South Africans as part of a broader strategy of helping rebels in Afghanistan and in Nicaragua fight against governments that were aligned with the Soviet Union. Angola was a prime US target, having received considerable Cuban military aid, and by the late 1980s, Cuba

---

[33] Colin Leys and John Saul, "Liberation without Democracy? The Swapo Crisis of 1976," *Journal of Southern African Studies* 20:1 (1994): 124.

[34] Colin Leys and John Saul, "SWAPO inside Namibia," in Colin Leys and John Saul, *Namibia's Liberation Struggle: The Two-Edged Sword* (London: James Currey, 1995), 55.

was estimated to have about 50,000 troops inside Angola. Through 1987–88, MPLA defenders battled against a South African–supported UNITA force. This involved the largest conventional military battle in Africa since the Second World War, which took place in February 1988 as 8,000 South African and UNITA soldiers faced 10,000 defenders. Enough white South African soldiers were killed to cause critics at home to question the utility and expense of the campaign, particularly once it was clear that South African aircraft were vulnerable to Cuban and Soviet missiles.

Once it became apparent that the South Africans could not end the conflict on their terms, but more important, as US-Soviet relations thawed as the Soviet leader Gorbachev undertook reforms, US negotiators began to press the South Africans to withdraw. Under the framework of the December 1988 New York Accords between Angola, Cuba, and South Africa, the latter two committed to withdrawing from Angola. Another provision of this agreement required that South Africa organize UN-supervised elections in Namibia under the terms of UN Resolution 435. Once again, the global environment of international diplomacy ultimately determined the fate of SWAPO insurgents as they took power in independent Namibia on 21 March 1990, a prize that they won in the voting booth rather than on the battlefield.[35]

The South African Struggle against Apartheid

The increasing international rejection of minority rule also played a major role in the fates of majority rule rebels in South Africa itself and shaped the transition to majority rule in April 1994. Neither the ANC nor the PAC, South Africa's two main majority rule rebel groups, could sustain administrative or military organizations inside South Africa to produce anything like a classic liberated zone. From the 1976 Soweto uprising to the sustained popular confrontation with the South African state throughout the 1980s, these rebels could not impose control over most of the major revolts inside South Africa. This intensified their reliance on international recognition of their leadership in the South African struggle and their need to encourage outsiders to criminalize the apartheid regime's behavior if they were to control their recruits and

[35] Chester Crocker, *High Noon in Southern Africa: Making Peace in a Rough Neighborhood* (New York: W.W. Norton, 1993).

limit factional splits. Like their SWAPO colleagues, the ANC and PAC in exile had to incorporate a large number of educated recruits who, in the 1980s, fled urban areas where their political ideas, strategies, and criticisms had developed within a very different set of circumstances than those faced by older cadres.

The ANC was formed in 1912 among members of the African elite to campaign for their civil rights. In 1944 the founding of the ANC Youth League under the leadership of Nelson Mandela, Oliver Tambo, and Walter Sisulu brought to the fore a new generation of leaders to challenge the laws that reinforced white minority privilege. Fort Hare University educated many of these leaders, as it had some of the early SWAPO leaders. Both Mandela and Tambo were expelled from Fort Hare in 1940 for organizing students. Thereafter Mandela became a clerk in a law firm, completed his degree at the University of South Africa, and then pursued his law degree at the University of Witwatersrand in Johannesburg. Here he came into contact with white liberals and white members of the South African Communist Party (SACP), which became a long-time partner of the ANC in its struggle. Among his fellow law students was Joe Slovo, who was later head of SACP; head of the ANC's armed wing, Umkhonto we Sizwe ("Spear of the Nation," or MK); and finally a post-apartheid minister in Mandela's government.[36] He also met Ruth First, daughter of founding members of the SACP and future wife of Slovo.

The victory of the National Party in the 1948 whites-only election signaled the advent of the official policy of apartheid, which further curtailed the rights of non-whites to move about the country and engage in political activities. The ANC continued to pursue a path of non-violent resistance in its Defiance Campaign in December 1951 that was inspired by the successful campaign of Indian independence leader Mahatma Gandhi, who had initially developed the strategy of non-violent civil disobedience in South Africa, where he had practiced law and campaigned for the civil rights of the Indian community. Following Gandhi's lead, the ANC asserted a non-racial character in its 1955 Freedom Charter, which summed up its goals: "South Africa belongs to all who live in it, black and white . . . only a democratic state, based on the will of all of the people, can secure to all their birthright without distinction of color, race, sex or belief."[37]

---

[36] Anthony Sampson, *Mandela: The Authorized Biography* (New York: Alfred A. Knopf, 1999), 36.

[37] ANC, Freedom Charter, http://www.anc.org.za/show.php?id=72, accessed 17 April 2011.

From the start of its campaign for majority rule, the ANC faced official repression. As the South African state intensified its oppression and curtailed African political activity, the ANC leadership faced the dilemma of deciding whether they could afford a non-violent strategy when their meetings were continuously disrupted and their leaders banned from public activities or imprisoned. Despite these difficulties, which included new laws prohibiting political meetings related to the Defiance Campaign, the 100,000-member ANC reaffirmed its broad non-racial commitment to equal rights in the Freedom Charter. While entering into a number of open alliances with other political groups, the ANC secretly allied with the SACP at these meetings to broaden its political reach. Mandela justified his support for this decision: "For many decades the communists were the only political group in South Africa who were prepared to eat with us; talk with us, live and work with us."[38] The decision to join forces with the Soviet-aligned SACP, although borne partly of personal connections and the considerable organizing talents of the now-outlawed party, also shaped the ANC's reliance on eastern bloc supplies and training during its years of struggle.

The apartheid regime's continuing crackdown encouraged other activists to find fault with the ANC's non-violent approach. From 1956 to 1961 the "Treason Trial" kept ANC activists, including Mandela, occupied in court, although all 156 defendants were eventually acquitted. In March 1960 the Sharpeville massacre took place, in which the police killed at least sixty-nine people who were protesting the passing of restrictions on their mobility. After the massacre, the government banned the ANC and PAC and passed legislation that further curtailed and criminalized opposition of all kinds. The 1962 Sabotage Act and 1967 Terrorism Act broadened the authority of security forces to detain people for their political activities and to break up nascent protest groups. Meanwhile the proliferation of newly independent African states offered the prospect of foreign support for more radical nationalist African activists outside the ANC's alliance. In 1959 these "Africanists" – activists who wanted to build mass revolutionary movements inside South Africa on the basis of shared African culture and the experience of repression under apartheid – created the PAC under the leadership of Robert Sobukwe, another Fort Hare graduate. They disparaged the non-violent approach of the ANC, doubting that

---

[38] Nelson Mandela, *Long Walk to Freedom* (Boston: Little, Brown, 1994), 123.

this strategy would gain adequate international attention or prod the conscience of South Africa's white citizens.

The ANC responded to the rival campaign and to government repression with the formation of the MK, under the leadership of Mandela and Slovo. Its aims were to bring the ANC's struggle to the attention of potential recruits, to form the basis for a classic guerrilla war to organize and consolidate bases for resistance and struggle, and to sabotage and attack government targets. After the first MK attacks, the ensuing official repression and passage of draconian new laws showed that the ANC had gravely underestimated the force of the apartheid regime's response, especially in its willingness to recruit informers and use torture to collect information about the armed wing. Moreover the arrest of Mandela and other ANC and MK leaders successfully removed many leaders and forced most of the rest into exile (including Slovo).

Repression pushed the ANC to consider more seriously an exile strategy based on cultivating foreign support for its campaign, much like anti-colonial rebels were doing at the time. Tambo, who had fled into exile in 1960, had established an office in London. The Sharpeville massacre that same year brought the issue of apartheid South Africa to international attention. In 1963 the UN General Assembly condemned repression inside South Africa and voted for economic sanctions against the white minority regimes. The Security Council members (except France) even supported an arms embargo against South Africa. Meanwhile ANC cooperation with the SACP and white liberals raised doubts among some nationalist African governments that favored a more militant approach, especially in Ghana, where the ANC competed with the PAC for support.[39] Although the ANC initially received no direct Soviet assistance, the MK did, which helped the then-exiled leadership sustain the semblance of an armed struggle.[40]

At this juncture, prospects for armed struggle in southern African did not appear very bright. Most majority rule rebels had fled South Africa; neighboring countries still remained in hostile Portuguese or white minority hands; and the SADF could easily intimidate its newly independent neighbors. Consequently the ANC and PAC were forced to look more closely at the viability of their strategies. At the ANC's Morogoro Conference held in Tanzania in 1969, many activists argued that small, fast-moving groups of rebels could attack enemy targets,

[39] "Moulding the Revolution," *African Communist* 38 (3rd quarter 1969), 27.
[40] Andrew and Mitrokhin, *The World Was Going Our Way*, 443.

serve as a focus for popular discontent, and spark a general uprising. This strategy, called *foco* (Spanish for focus), was inspired by the ideas of Ernesto "Che" Guevara and Régis Debray that the armed struggle itself would bring popular support to the rebels who, left to themselves, were too weak to overthrow a regime. ANC activists argued for the mobilization of popular forces in South Africa's urban areas and among dispossessed landless rural people. In what became known as the Strategy and Tactics document, they stated: "The correct course was to launch a campaign based upon the urban working class in which people of the townships would take the place of the jungles and mountains."[41] Confrontation with the state would bring reprisals, which would further politicize the people and weaken their tolerance for everyday state administration in favor of supporting the new revolutionary liberated zones.[42] But after 1964, militants recognized that a careful international diplomatic strategy, coupled with visible signs of successful resistance inside South Africa, was essential for the success of such a geographically isolated rebellion. "Destruction of the military structure created an organizational vacuum," the conferees acknowledged, "which, with commendable initiative, was filled by the External Mission of the African National Congress" and its ties to rebels and governments across the continent.[43]

Slovo maintained that a careful strategy had to be grounded on the control of exiled leaders and the tight discipline of fighters within a strong party organization. It had to build on the good relations that the SACP maintained with Moscow, which promised access to military supplies and training. The ANC non-racial stance and the prospect that a rebel victory would bring a Soviet-style communist party to power in South Africa also isolated the PAC from Soviet support. Thus many ANC leaders at the 1969 conference agreed that they would need a tightly knit vanguard movement to launch the liberation struggle from exile. Meanwhile they needed to establish relations with other insurgent groups. In August 1967 ANC fighters participated in the Wankie incursion of ZAPU into Rhodesia, its first major combat. The Rhodesian forces quickly defeated this effort, and by the end of the

---

[41] Stephen Ellis and Tsepo Sechaba, *Comrades against Apartheid: The ANC and the South African Communist Party in Exile* (London: James Currey, 1992), 58.

[42] Ernesto [Che] Guevara, *Che Guevara on Guerrilla Warfare* (New York: Praeger, 1961); and Régis Debray, *Revolution in the Revolution? Armed Struggle and Political Struggle in Latin America* (New York: Monthly Review Press, 1967).

[43] "The Historic ANC Conference," *Mayibuye* 3:10 (May 1969): 1.

1960s, it seemed that the ANC had become practically irrelevant in South Africa, at least in the eyes of the security forces there.

The repressive capacity of South African state security forces underscored the dangers inherent in ANC's exile strategy. These security forces were proficient at detecting and breaking up organized ANC and MK cells. But the nature of South African society – its industrialized economy, with its need to educate even its manual workforce, and its ruthless segregation of Africans – created social spaces for activists to discuss politics and to organize. Inside South Africa, this new crop of anti-apartheid militants ignored or discounted ANC tactics. For example, Steve Biko, the founder of the South African Students' Organisation (SASO), turned instead to mobilizing rural people whose land had been confiscated as more of them were forced into Bantustan labor reserves. This reminded Biko of Mao's strategy of mobilizing peasants who experienced consequences of state repression but still lived isolated enough from the security services that they could organize for resistance. Biko's ideas also attracted youths who were more interested in the ideas of Pan-African solidarity that had grown around the anti-colonial struggle than in the multiracial Marxist perspectives of the ANC and the SACP.[44] This development increased ANC anxiety, especially because the South African Police (SAP) had captured or killed many of the infiltrators that they sent into the country. Ultimately, however, SASO activists who had to flee the country were left with little choice but to affiliate with the ANC if they wished to remain engaged in the anti-apartheid rebellion. By the mid-1970s, state repression had dealt serious blows to SASO's domestic organization, and this increased the flow of activists into exile.

The 1974 Portuguese coup and the rise to power of FRELIMO in Mozambique meant that the ANC could move their MK operations to Maputo, the Mozambique capital, and organize right on the South African border. The ANC escalated attacks inside South Africa, but it never succeeded in establishing a liberated zone or even seriously challenging state control in border areas. In response to the new constellation of southern African politics – the increase in rebel attacks, the rise to power of FRELIMO and the MPLA in the old Portuguese colonies, and the faltering Rhodesian defense – the South African government declared a "Total National Strategy." South African officials used the

---

[44] Gail Gerhart, *Black Power in South Africa: The Evolution of an Ideology* (Berkeley: University of California Press, 1978).

term "revolutionary struggle" in internal deliberations to describe the threat against them, which they believed was directed from Moscow.[45] The South African strategy focused on reversing the stages of guerrilla war through targeting ANC and PAC fighters to further disrupt their efforts to create liberated zones, while coordinating state efforts to provide basic social services in target communities. Coupled with very modest political reforms, this strategy aimed to control and cultivate support for the government within the communities that could be mobilized to inform on anti-apartheid activists and support the security services.

Until this point in the evolution of warfare in Africa, the anti-colonial rebels and their supporters had excelled in building international networks, which ANC and other majority rule rebels sought to exploit. But by the mid-1970s, the South African security forces organized their own international counter-network. As noted earlier, South African security forces collaborated with Rhodesian counterinsurgency efforts. In Namibia the government directly organized groups like Koevoet and other paramilitaries to track and infiltrate guerrilla units. Inside South Africa, the SAP organized death squads, and commanders received immunity to carry out clandestine operations. Their commanders included people like SAP Colonel Theunis Swanepoel, who was among a dozen police who had trained with the French during their repression of the anti-colonial struggle in Algeria. Security services received visitors such as the Argentine officers who would become involved in the "Dirty War" against guerrillas in that country in the late 1970s.[46]

The SADF role in the Total National Strategy was to destabilize states around South Africa that dared to harbor South African majority rule rebels. This strategy included attacking ANC and PAC bases and sponsoring antigovernment insurgents like RENAMO in Mozambique. These attacks, combined with South African intimidation of neighboring state governments, meant that the ANC found itself fighting for its survival in places that it originally planned would be its rear bases, not the forward areas of conflict. The South African government also tried to create constituencies of supporters among Africans. They executed this political strategy more effectively than their Rhodesian counterparts and found some success in cultivating the leadership of ethnically

[45] Stephen Ellis, "The Historical Significance of South Africa's Third Force," *Journal of Modern African Studies* 24:2 (1998): 264.

[46] Ibid., 271.

defined Bantustans, or territories inside South Africa in which local strongmen were invited to exercise authority and were given resources to build their own patronage networks, on which many in these impoverished territories depended.

With the 1976 Soweto uprising in South Africa, the difficulty of the ANC's position became even more evident. Although this revolt of youth in the urban township swept away many apartheid structures in the immediate area, it created a sort of liberated zone that was neither the product of ANC efforts nor followed ANC plans, and at least initially was beyond the capacity of the government to manage. Because the ANC lacked an MK base inside South Africa and did not have the capacity to confront South African security forces, its leadership had to evolve a new strategy for liberating their country from apartheid rule. ANC strategists now turned to community organizations that would act in place of the "missing guerrillas." In their absence, local South African human rights groups, church organizations, labor unions, and other associations had developed their own ideas about liberation and pursued independent political platforms. Many of these groups had joined together in January 1983 to form the United Democratic Front (UDF) under the leadership of Reverend Allan Boesak. Ironically, some of these groups arose in response to the modest political reforms under the Total National Strategy but nevertheless became fierce critics of the government and its policies.

Meanwhile, armed groups inside South Africa, some of which were affiliated with the UDF, began to attack local government administrators under the slogan, "the country must be ungovernable." In the context of this breakdown of law and order, groups began to kill suspected police informers after hasty appearances in their people's courts; some were summarily killed on the force of suspicion and local rumor. This gave some of these militia members, known as "comrades," opportunities to settle personal scores and, in places like Natal province, attack members of Inkatha, a Zulu-based ethnic association that many of the ANC's supporters believed was collaborating with the apartheid government. The high level of violence convinced many foreign officials, even in the most conservative governments, that the apartheid regime could not survive. Worried about what would replace the apartheid government, key members of South Africa's business elite, some politicians, and journalists even traveled to Lusaka in September 1985 to meet with ANC officials.

In broad terms, the increase in violence against government targets benefited the ANC politically with what seemed to be the start of a people's war that would create liberated zones within South Africa. But the ANC and UDF faced difficulties in controlling the comrades, many of whom seemed to pursue their own agendas, which were often more disruptive and radical than rebel organizers thought appropriate and left non-combatants caught between what looked to many to be violent youth gangs and the security forces of a repressive state. The ANC had to scramble to keep up with these domestic developments if it was to retain political control over the rebellion. Meeting in Zambia in June 1985, the ANC issued the call to "step up our all-round political and military offensive sharply and without delay,"[47] a statement that really reflected the ANC's anxiety to convey a strong image of control within South Africa and avoid any hints of disunity or ineffectiveness to foreign observers at this critical moment.

South African security forces cracked down on these domestic challengers with the July 1985 declaration of a state of emergency. They turned to more forcible repression of domestic opponents with the establishment of the Civil Cooperation Bureau (CCB) in May 1986. The CCB operated as a front for Special Forces operating outside South Africa and as support for police assassinations inside South Africa. This repression helped to drive the UDF and other opposition groups more firmly into the embrace of the ANC as all realized the need for unity and tight organization to maintain underground organizations inside South Africa. Meanwhile, some of the state-sponsored armed groups operated as gangs and vigilantes, while others were linked to ethnically based organizations. Their purpose was to create mayhem in their home communities, thus obstructing the sociopolitical programs of anti-apartheid political organizers. In neighboring states the security forces sponsored pseudo-guerrillas like the Lesotho Liberation Army (LLA) and a "super-ZAPU" to infiltrate real ZAPU units. These groups were attached to the Directorate of Military Intelligence, which recruited African members, many of whom used the backing of their powerful patron to commit atrocities in the course of settling personal scores and to exploit clandestine arms trading and other commercial networks for their personal profit.

[47] "Conference Communiqué: The ANC Is with You," *Sechaba* (Aug 1985): 4.

By the 1980s the South African counterinsurgency strategy was creating surrogate forces that exhibited behavior and organizational structures that began to resemble the warlord model of warfare discussed
in Chapter 5. It started as a sort of Maoist guerrilla warfare strategy
in reverse: a RENAMO-style strategy of what General van der West-
huizen called a policy of destabilization inside South Africa itself. Just
as genuine ANC leaders sought to make areas inside South Africa
ungovernable for the apartheid regime so that they could organize
their own followers, the South African security establishment strove
to make the same communities ungovernable for the ANC and its local
supporters.[48] The South African security services and their surrogates
started to fight more as a sort of rebels-behind-the-rebels, as they used
methods of irregular warfare against majority rule rebels who were
struggling to replace state authority over people with their own. The
government strategy played a key role in generating the violence inside
South Africa that was instrumental in aggravating a serious crime problem that continued to plague South Africa after the end of the apartheid
regime in 1994. Government strategies included arming youth gangs
that fought against the comrades who proclaimed their allegiance to the
ANC. These gangs included ones that were involved in illicit activities
such as drug trafficking; others were affiliated with local strongmen
who collaborated with the apartheid regime. Once armed, some gangs
set up protection rackets and intervened in feuds between businesses
and in other purely local disputes. Police also armed ethnic militias to
use as proxies to fight against ANC-affiliated groups and to create new
centers of political power to compete with the ANC and its allies.[49]

The key element of this strategy was the South African government's
intentional destruction of community organizations and the manipulation of violence within these communities that opposed the apartheid
regime. From the viewpoint of mobilizing people to support a policy or
to follow a particular ideology, this proved to be a very destructive strategy. It used the politics of personal greed, anger, and ambition as tools
to destroy the social space in which community organizing otherwise

---

[48] Nicholas Haysom Mabaringalala, *The Rise of Right-Wing Vigilantes in South Africa*
(Johannesburg: University of Witwatersrand, 1986); and Phyllis Johnson and David
Martin (eds.), *Apartheid Terrorism: The Destruction Report* (London: James Currey,
1989).

[49] Stephen Ellis, "The New Frontiers of Crime in South Africa," in Jean-François Bayart,
Stephen Ellis, and Béatrice Hibou (eds.), *The Criminalization of the State in Africa*
(Bloomington: Indiana University Press, 1999), 59–62.

took place, and it turned target communities into hostile turf for any ideologically motivated rebels. As we will see in subsequent chapters, some features of this strategy resembled that of leaders in some of the most extreme cases of state failure who hosted warlords in places like Congo, Liberia, and Somalia. Ultimately the outcome was different. Communities inside South Africa were not as severely affected by the consequences of this counterinsurgency strategy. Moreover, the ANC international strategy, growing global condemnation of the apartheid regime, and the end of the Cold War played critical roles in shaping the ANC's eventual success. The high levels of state repression of anti-apartheid rebels inside South Africa hindered the development of significant rival rebel groups there and pushed anti-apartheid activists such as those in the UDF to seek closer coordination with the ANC.

Amid a renewed security force crackdown in 1986–87, the exiled ANC leadership lamented "the fact that we are based largely abroad, and lack an underground political base at home,"[50] and they struggled to come up with a strategy to merge with and guide activists who confronted the South African government at home. By that time the only real challenge to SADF in the frontline states came from the Cuban forces in Angola. Elsewhere governments allowed MK and ANC on their soil at the risk of attracting SADF attacks. The SACP journal noted that

> the existence of underground networks of the ANC in countries like Botswana ... is unfairly blamed on the connivance of those countries. In other words, those countries have to spend a large slice of their meager resources to hunt down people who are hardly their own enemies, and do it more vigorously than the South Africans do in their own country.[51]

Mikhail Gorbachev's rise to power in the Soviet Union in 1985 prompted a major shift in ANC fortunes. The following year the Soviet foreign minister suggested that the ANC would be better off negotiating with their adversary, a response to developments in other parts of southern Africa.[52] The 1988 New York agreement that led to Cuban and South African disengagement from Angola and to Namibia's independence in 1990 required that the ANC close its bases in Angola and move to Zambia, Tanzania, and Uganda. The SACP held out against

---

[50] Ronnie Kasrils, "The Revolutionary Army: A Discussion Article," *Sechaba* (Sept 1988): 3.

[51] Tebogo Kgobe, "Is South Africa Suited for Guerilla Warfare?" *African Communist*, 117 (2nd quarter 1989): 26.

[52] Allister Sparks, *The Mind of South Africa* (London: Heinemann, 1990), 364.

the "revisionism" of its Soviet patrons and in June 1989 held its seventh congress in Havana, where it advocated adapting the East German model to South Africa! By this time, however, ANC activists conceded that the global context of their struggle had changed. "Since we are confronted with conditions under which absolute victory is impossible," wrote one ANC commander in its official journal, "we can conclude that the outcome of any negotiation that can be successfully conducted must end up in partial victories for warring parties."[53]

On 2 February 1990 Nelson Mandela was released from prison after confinement for more than a quarter century. The government of F. W. DeKlerk began a process of engagement with majority rule rebels and community activists to write a new constitution. Agreement was reached; both sides claimed partial victory. South Africa's first democratic majority rule elections were held in April 1994, resulting in victory for the ANC and the installation of Nelson Mandela as the first president of post-apartheid South Africa. White South Africans, including many who continued to work in the government service, kept their positions of economic privilege. Many who committed human rights violations and even broke South African law were granted amnesties. Thus political stalemate had engendered racial tolerance and grudging cooperation, hardly the situation that many observers expected to follow the end of apartheid and minority rule.

Much credit for bringing apartheid to an end goes to the international strategy developed by a loose coalition of grassroots activist groups working toward majority rule in South Africa. Commonwealth and UN pressure on South Africa combined with the divestment campaign in the United States to change the government's hard-line policy. In August 1985 Chase Manhattan announced that it would leave South Africa in the wake of the declaration of a state of emergency. The departure of Chase and other Western banks severely undercut South Africa's strategy of borrowing to help pay for its policies of destabilization of neighboring countries and internal repression. Although South African exports of gold and other minerals, about 58 percent of total exports in the late 1980s, were relatively immune from sanctions, the growing isolation of the government and the domestic economy nevertheless made the end of apartheid increasingly acceptable for the country's commercial classes.

---

[53] Alex Mashinini, "People's War and Negotiations," *Sechaba* (Aug 1988): 27.

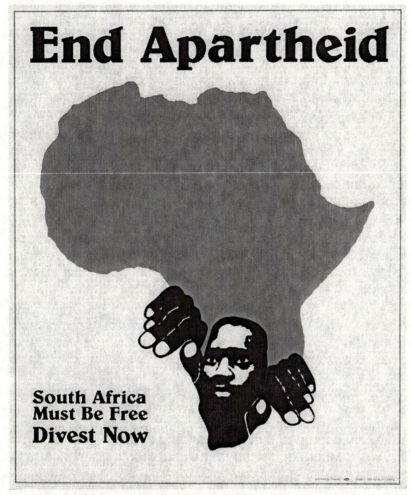

FIGURE 3. End Apartheid poster. Credit: Lincoln Cushing, Inkworks Press, Berkeley, California [printer].

The bulk of the white South African political elite recognized that continued intransigence on the part of the government and the continuation of counterinsurgency efforts risked plunging the country into a wider civil war. According to Ellis, more than 14,000 were killed in political violence between 1990 and 1994, a number exceeding the domestic death toll throughout the entire struggle up to that point.[54] As

[54] Ellis, "Historical Significance of South Africa's Third Force," 263.

the government edged toward negotiations, some members of its security services started to migrate into extremist groups like the Afrikaner Weerstandsbeweging that advocated the creation of a separate white homeland from which to continue their fight. On 10 April 1993, the assassination of Chris Hani, the head of the MK and from 1991 the leader of the SACP, risked unleashing the anger of young militants. Nelson Mandela appealed for calm in a decidedly presidential manner. These dangers, along with the recognition that the ANC leadership no longer could call on international support for a socialist agenda, convinced leading government officials that they could negotiate an end to the apartheid regime and save their own fortunes and freedoms.

This final act of the liberation of an African country from a tenacious and violent regime marked a watershed. Now all of Africa had been liberated from alien rule, and where white minorities had ruled, they now had to accommodate themselves to rule by Africans. The nature of the ANC's exile and the factors that pressed other rebel groups to accept its leading role preserved a level of political discipline and popular legitimacy that eased the post-conflict transition. The victory of these rebels preserved South Africa from further descent into the kinds of turmoil and destruction of autonomous social space – of fields of leverage – that were becoming the centerpiece of the apartheid state's counterinsurgency strategy. The irony of this situation was that this strategy of the apartheid regime, presenting itself as a bulwark against disorder and violence, was creating conditions, which we will consider in greater depth in Chapter 5, that led to the collapse of state order and the emergence of protracted warlord conflicts. But this victory did not end internal warfare in Africa. As colonial rule and apartheid were defeated, Africa was producing its own crop of oppressive and violent leaders. This in turn produced critics, both among the educated elite and at the grass roots, who called for their overthrow. Some of these people took up arms against these rulers of independent African countries and set out to reform the bases for governing their countries. These reform rebels are the subject of the next chapter.

CHAPTER 4

Reform Rebels

By the late 1970s a new type of rebel struggled against despotism and repression – reform rebels.[1] Their targets were indigenous African rulers such as Uganda's Idi Amin (1971–79) and Ethiopia's Mengistu Haile-Mariam (1975–91). Leaders of these new rebels promised to fight against repressive African governments to bring about a "second liberation" to implement new ideas of governance in areas that they controlled.[2] They adapted the anti-colonial rhetoric of national emancipation and a new societal order. Like anti-colonial and majority rule rebels, reform rebels accepted existing borders. Even Eritreans who fought to create a separate country argued that Eritrea's status as a former Italian colony (1896–1941) and its 1950 UN-sponsored federation with Ethiopia entitled it to separate statehood, and that Eritrea's independence was just the last stage of decolonization.

These rebels faced a difficult environment in which their appearances seemed to be at odds with the idea in this book that rebel behavior and organization reflect the broader political context in which they fight. Yoweri Museveni's National Resistance Movement (NRM), the Eritrean People's Liberation Front (EPLF) and Tigray People's Liberation Front (TPLF) in Ethiopia, and the Rwandan Patriotic Front (RPF) lacked the international support that their anti-colonial and majority rule counterparts enjoyed. Those rebels could reasonably count on

---

[1] This term is adapted from "reform insurgencies" in Christopher Clapham, "Introduction: Analysing African Insurgencies," in Christopher Clapham (ed.), *African Guerrillas* (Oxford: James Currey, 1998): 1–18.

[2] Larry Diamond, "The Second Liberation," *Africa Report* 37:6 (1992): 38–41.

support from the OAU Liberation Committee and the UN Decolonization Committee, provided that they could convince outsiders of their capacity to fight alien rule. As Chapters 2 and 3 showed, other sources of international aid favored leaders who were able to unify competing factions, control fighters, and sell a global audience on their plans for liberation. But during this later period, even if rebel leaders could master these organizational challenges, international backing was scarce. Moreover, the political environment seemed to favor the fractious and narrow agendas of ethnic strongmen and heads of political cliques that could interfere with reform rebels' efforts to mobilize people in liberated zones or promote new political visions. That groups such as Uganda's NRM, Eritrea's EPLF, Ethiopia's TPLF, and Rwanda's RPF could emerge and survive at all, much less fight their way to power, is a significant development. Their performance in these conditions highlighted the importance of accommodating to local conditions to devise new strategies for building effective African rebel groups. They also benefited from significant external opportunities. But first we turn to the conditions that tested these reform rebel leaders.

The Difficult International Context

By the mid-1970s, ending minority rule in Rhodesia (Zimbabwe), Namibia, and South Africa was the only task that remained for the OAU Liberation Committee and the UN Decolonization Committee. Liberation in their terms meant expelling alien rulers, not overthrowing indigenous governments that were members in good standing in these organizations. The real threats to most newly independent states came from internal challengers who were of less concern to the UN and the OAU. By the late 1980s the probability that an African president would face a successful coup d'état had reached 60 percent.[3] From then on formal international intervention, usually from other African states, usually occurred to protect these incumbent regimes. In the 1960s and 1970s Guinea's president sent soldiers to Sierra Leone and Liberia to shield fellow presidents from rebellious army officers and protestors. Senegal intervened in Gambia in 1981 to thwart a coup attempt, as

---

[3] Patrick McGowan, "African Military Coups d'État, 1956–2001: Frequency, Trends and Distribution," *Journal of Modern African Studies* 41:2 (2001): 339–70.

did Tanzanian soldiers sent to Zambia and Mozambique in the late 1970s.[4] French military bases and aid to former colonies also helped to prop up unstable regimes, mostly in west and central Africa. Nigerian-led interventions in the 1990s supported governments in Sierra Leone and Liberia against armed opponents. The point here is that, although they did not intervene to suppress truly popular rebel forces, leaders of African states demonstrated through their interventions to protect governments that they were not interested in joining a global project to reform other African states, whether by force or otherwise. This restraint, which would weaken by the 1990s, was in sharp contrast to their very public rhetorical and material aid to the rebels who fought colonial and apartheid rule.

Exceptions to this trend against uninvited intervention did occur, and when it did, it only made conditions more difficult for ideology- and program-driven rebels like the reform rebels. As seen in the second chapter, President Mobutu of Zaire aided UNITA rebels until the early 1990s against the government of Angola. The apartheid states provided cross-border backing for rebels fighting against governments in independent states. In the 1960s Portuguese, Rhodesian, and South African counterinsurgency experts supported militias that asserted ethnic and personal agendas to undermine the broader ideological programs of majority rule rebels. Such support aggravated rivalries and tensions within armed groups, which relieved pressures on these regimes. Other leaders broke this rule, as when Libya's Muammar Qaddafi supported antigovernment rebels to increase his influence south of the Sahara. His support was important in Liberia and Sierra Leone in the late 1980s and early 1990s, and Qaddafi's efforts to target Sudan's president, Jaafar Nimeiri (1969–85), faced wide regional and international condemnation.[5]

The international policies of Ethiopia, Sudan, and other countries in northeast Africa also challenged this mutual accommodation and supported armed ethnic rebels and narrow political cliques, which deepens the mystery of how and why reform rebels could survive in this political environment. Ethiopia's rulers pursued a *realpolitik* to keep their large and ethnically diverse country intact around its

---

[4] Arnold Hughes and Roy May, "Armies on Loan: Toward an Explanation of Transnational Intervention among African States: 1960–85," in Simon Baynham (ed.), *Military Power and Politics in Black Africa* (New York: St. Martin's Press, 1986), 177–202.

[5] Oye Ogunbadejo, "Qaddafi and Africa's International Relations," *Journal of Modern African Studies* 24:1 (1986): 33–68.

ethnic Amharic core; this tactic was born of a deep suspicion that neighboring states promoted fragmentation along its periphery to reduce Ethiopia's regional influence. Some Ethiopian officials used rebel groups as proxies against neighbors to address this problem of political control. Somali government attempts to detach Ethiopia's ethnic Somali Ogaden region from the country in its 1977 military campaign and the 1993 international recognition of Eritrea's separation and independence lend substance to these fears of foreign meddling. Fragmentation also beset neighboring Sudan, Africa's largest country. Fighting broke out in 1955, one year before independence from British colonial rule. Successive regimes exercised limited control over this vast territory and its diverse communities. Successful coups in 1969, 1985, and 1989 dragged local power brokers and their armed militias further into capital-based politics in support of different factions. These Sudanese regimes became prolific backers of rebels in neighboring countries that they believed helped antigovernment rebels inside Sudan. Sudan and Uganda share a frontier with weak levels of government control that serves as a base for rebels that both governments have supported against each other. Likewise Ethiopian relations with Eritrea after 1998 and for decades with Somalia feature the reciprocal sponsorship of rebels to meddle in the domestic affairs of their neighbors.

These regional geopolitics and domestic factional politics have created particular difficulties for rebel ideologues. This kind of external patronage weakens group discipline, as it gives subordinate commanders opportunities to receive direct aid from benefactors who want to destabilize neighbors and use the organization as a bargaining chip in negotiations (Map 5). Rebel leaders' pursuits of personal ambitions against rival clients help to promote the goals of their patrons. But aid from these regimes often is unreliable, as it is contingent on changes in regional alignments, new international agreements, coups in capitals over which rebel leaders have little influence, or simply patrons' efforts to see that no one proxy grows strong enough to threaten its backer's interests. This support from patrons also is free of the old anti-colonial and anti-apartheid conditions of ideological unity, coordinated effort, or evidence of success on the ground. This releases rebel leaders from having to negotiate with local communities for support or to administer them in liberated zones. It opens doors for enterprising, self-interested, and ideologically flexible rebel leaders – whom we will discuss further

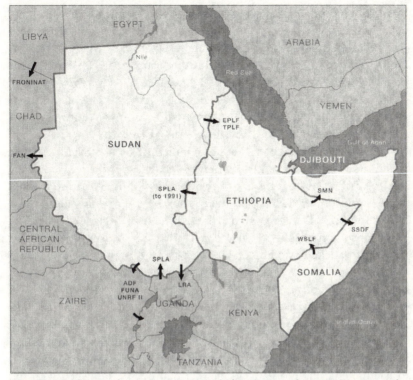

MAP 5. Northeast Africa's Proxy War Rebels, 1970s and 1980s. Drawn on the basis of the text of Chapter 4.

in the next chapter – who are adept at navigating these treacherous political waters.

As one would expect, this politics subordinates rebel organizations and patterns of warfare to the statecraft of neighboring regimes. For example, Idriss Déby took power as president of Chad in 1990 with the support of Mahamat Nour Abdelkerim, a leader of the Tama ethnic community situated on the Chad-Sudan border, and with help from Sudan's government. Nour then moved close to the center of power in Sudan's capital and gained access to many business opportunities, even though he began his ascent as a spokesman for the rural Tama community, which felt marginalized from corridors of power in the distant capital. Nour left Déby's side in 1994 to relocate to Sudan's capital, where he offered to use his influence in the Tama communities for the interests of his new patrons in Khartoum. He became even richer in

Sudan's budding oil industry when he used his position in the Tama community to help the Sudan government to drive the Zaghawa people – Déby's ethnic group – out of Sudan's western province of Darfur. Nour's new patrons promoted him as the head of the Rassemblement pour la démocratie et des libertés (RDL) to try to overthrow Déby's regime, for they reasonably suspected that Chad's president was helping his own ethnic kinsmen in Sudan build their antigovernment rebel group, the Justice and Equality Movement (JEM).[6]

These proxy rebels often tap into popular grievances over marginalization and isolation from the benefits of state power, even when they fight on behalf of corrupt and repressive politicians. Uganda's Allied Democratic Forces (ADF) formed around some of Uganda's Muslim youth who felt that Uganda's government ignored their interests. This opposition began to coalesce in 1991, when Museveni appointed an Iranian-backed candidate as the new mufti of Kampala before a state visit to Iran, a decision that angered a group of students who occupied the central mosque in support of a rival candidate. Several future leaders of the ADF landed in prison, where they forged their ties and recruited followers. By the time that they were released in 1993, these ideologues appeared to be in a good position to begin an Islamic-inspired rebellion against the government. These rebels developed links to Islamic charitable organizations that had been established with the help of Sudan's Hassan al Turabi, who had become the de facto ideologue of the Sudanese government by 1989. When released, the student leaders moved to northwestern Uganda and then to Zaire to establish rear bases with Sudanese aid. This ideological glue and strong personal bonds, forged in the type of isolation that had in an earlier era favored anti-colonial rebels, gave the ADF an initial organizational cohesion and a political narrative that seemed to have decent prospects of success.

By the time the ADF was formally organized in 1996, it had bases in southern Sudan, but ideology was not the basis for Sudan's support. Sudanese aid to this Muslim-based rebel group took place alongside its aid to the Ugandan Lord's Resistance Army (LRA), a rebel group that had emerged from the remnants of Alice Lakwana's Holy Spirit Movement, based on a blend of missionary Christianity and indigenous cosmology. This lack of ideological discrimination underlined the fact that Sudan's government would back any rebels who served its main

[6] Simon Massey and Roy May, "Commentary: The Crisis in Chad," *African Affairs* 105:416 (2006): 443–49.

aim of extending its influence and enhancing its security, and that it was not interested in spreading a particular political idea. For Sudan's government, the real benefit of aiding the LRA and ADF lay in recruiting both groups to fight the Sudan People's Liberation Army (SPLA) rebels in southern Sudan, and to punish the Ugandan government for supporting the SPLA. Zaire's Mobutu also gave aid to the ADF in anticipation that Ugandan and Rwandan armies would attack rebels based in Zaire.

None of these governments wanted to strengthen their proxies to the extent that they could actually seize state power or pursue separatist agendas. Each gave only enough aid to remind the government in the neighboring country's capital that they could respond in kind to proxy attacks. In practice, this meant that the ADF, for example, became a victim of waning Sudanese diplomatic priorities and faded to insignificance by 1999.[7] Sudanese backing was flexible enough that when the SPLA split in the 1980s, one separatist faction even managed to gain support from Khartoum. Sudanese officials were secure in their confidence that this funding would help widen factional splits in the SPLA well before there was any risk that the aid would actually contribute to splitting apart their own country. UN and foreign government relief operations in war-affected areas also contributed to factional splits when they provided resources that local commanders could control personally.[8]

Hostage to the changing political interests of their patrons and to factional struggles, rebels in these circumstances were not able to offer very much real protection to local people who, in any event, were reluctant to support fickle rebels over whom they had little leverage. The absence of a population-centric approach on the part of rebels meant that governments could afford to be relatively sanguine about the excessive use of violence in counterinsurgency campaigns, because they knew that the rebels had narrow bases of popular support. Thus governments did not hesitate to prop up local militias and bandit groups who preyed on their communities. This general insecurity further weakened and

---

[7] Alex de Waal, "The Politics of Destabilisation in the Horn, 1989–2001," in A. de Waal (ed.), *Islamism and Its Enemies in the Horn of Africa* (Addis Ababa: Shama Books, 2004), 198–200.

[8] Douglas Johnson, *The Root Causes of Sudan's Civil Wars* (Oxford: James Currey 2003), 63. Michael Johnson and Trish Johnson, "Eritrea: The National Question and the Logic of Protracted Struggle," *African Affairs* 80:319 (1981): 181–95.

divided rebels, which left local people without rebels who were effective at addressing their real concerns and mobilizing them to fight an
oppressive state.

It is surprising that successful reform rebels emerged and survived
in this regional political context. Their accomplishments point to the
special conditions and strategies that enabled reform rebel leaders
to articulate new visions of politics, to recruit followers, to manage
resources, to discipline fighters, to create liberated zones, and to launch
assaults on capitals. They discovered how to turn weak state control and
regional rivalries into opportunities to organize. Even so, these environments also empowered competitors who often became serious threats
to designs for reform. The rest of this chapter explores this success,
even as other rebels failed to leave the orbit of regional state politics.
The varied performance of reform rebels on the field of battle and
in their struggles for international acceptance raises issues concerning
the sustainability of armed rebellion in Africa around broad ideological narratives beyond the struggles against colonial and minority rule.
The successes of reform rebels show the critical importance of fields
of leverage – the autonomous social spaces in which articulate rebel
leaders are able to organize other people around a political vision and
convince, discipline, or eliminate those who do not share this interest.
This success also raises the question of whether the circumstances of
the rise to power of successful reform rebels were specific to the 1986–
94 period, that is, from the NRM's arrival in the capital of Uganda
to the RPF's victory in Rwanda. Regardless of the behavior of these
reform rebels once in power, their success in mobilizing broad popular
bases of support, in contrast to the failures of others in the same region
and time period, sheds light on why violence in the service of reform
in state politics is relatively rare in contemporary Africa. But first, we
turn to the reform rebels' successes.

Strategies for Success

Throughout his political career, Uganda's Museveni has written about
how to articulate a coherent reform program, build liberated zones,
and fight a national army. His personal link to anti-colonial liberation
insurgencies shows the influence on Museveni's thinking of the ideas
and actions of anti-colonial rebels, an influence also evident after 1991
in the strategies and statements of the EPLF and TPLF in Ethiopia and

in independent Eritrea, and among Rwanda's RPF leaders. These successes occurred roughly about the same time and in the same region as the failures of other rebels who succumbed to the divisive effects of their regional political environment. Some groups deserve special attention in the following pages – particularly the Somali National Movement (SNM) and the SPLA. Their leaders successfully shifted from predatory behavior in local communities and factional in-fighting toward greater consolidation after the late 1980s.

The leaders of the victorious reform rebels developed the capacity to control the flow of funding from external sources. In some cases a dearth of foreign state backers was responsible for this condition. The Marxist EPLF, for example, received no Soviet aid so long as the Soviet Union provided advice and materiel to their Ethiopian adversaries. Moreover, by the 1980s, China's rejection of its Maoist principles, and especially its new diplomatic stance that, as long as no one aided Taiwanese or Tibetan separatists, China would refrain from helping rebels in other lands, spelled the end of its aid to African rebels. Some aid came from Sudan, although EPLF leaders were wary of Sudan's ties to a rival rebel group. Instead they concentrated on taxing Eritreans abroad to support their campaign. Once established, EPLF leaders could monopolize these resources more easily than those they would have received by subordinating their goals to the internal power politics of regimes in foreign countries.

Reform rebels struggled to control resources that came from outside of Africa. Unlike their anti-colonial and majority rule counterparts, they did not have the benefit of UN offices dedicated to the support of the South West Africa People's Liberation Organization (SWAPO) or FRE-LIMO, Scandinavian official development aid, or private NGOs like the Ford Foundation, all of which made aid conditional on internal unity, political coherence, and performance on the ground. By the 1970s and 1980s a growing array of governments and international NGOs sent relief aid to northeast Africa that they viewed as non-political disaster relief. These outsiders were not critical of the capacity of local rebels to actually govern, and they dealt with whoever they needed to gain access to non-combatants in need. Governments and rebels recognized that these sources of aid added a new strategic dimension to their struggles.[9] A common feature of all successful reform insurgents is their

---

[9] Sarah Kenyon Lischer, "Collateral Damage: Humanitarian Assistance as a Cause of Conflict," *International Security* 28:1 (2003): 79–109; and Jennifer Taw Morrison,

sponsorship of front organizations that appeared to foreign donors to be local NGOs – most donors were reluctant to admit that they were funding rebels. These front organizations collected and then channeled resources to their armed wings and ultimately took credit among local people for the services and other benefits that the foreign resources and organizations provided.

Successful reform rebels also shared a capacity to insulate local community politics from interference from rival rebel groups and foreign states. This was easier for the RPF, because its leaders emerged from among commanders in Museveni's National Resistance Army (NRA) and later in the Ugandan People's Defense Force (UPDF), and they exercised unusual levels of influence in this neighboring state. The others faced exigencies of local politics and harsh struggles for survival against state armies that forced them to seek protection from local authorities – chiefs, local landowners, and elders – who exercised political authority on the ground. It is especially critical that, in return, these people forced reform rebels to heed community interests, essentially gaining a say in how liberated zones would be run in return for lending their capacity to recruit fighters and discipline miscreants. This kind of relationship gave reform rebels strong incentives to discipline their members so that they would refrain from abusing people in these communities. Sometimes this was contingent on co-opting local social structures and the personal ties of individual reform rebel leaders, as in the case of the TPLF, or was provoked by sudden turns of events, as in the late 1980s, when the SNM suddenly faced abandonment by its Ethiopian patrons and fierce attacks from the Somali military.

Like earlier rebel leaders, the reformers and their closest associates emerged from an elite group that was far more educated than most of their fellow citizens. They articulated ideas and recruited cadres and commissars in the relative autonomy of university classrooms and discussion groups. The reform rebel leaders tended to come from African universities, rather than from among the few sent off to Europe or the United States who came back to lead anti-colonial rebellions. Museveni, the son of a provincial notable, wrote that his 1967–70 stint at the University of Dar es Salaam shaped his political ideas and strategies. "It is Dar es Salaam's atmosphere of freedom fighters, socialists, nationalists, and anti-imperialism," wrote the young Museveni, "that

"The Perils of Humanitarian Assistance in Armed Conflicts: Somalia in the 1990s," *Small Wars and Insurgencies* 15:2 (2004): 5–19.

FIGURE 4. Nkrumah Hall, the assembly hall at the University of Dar es Salaam at AfricaFocus. Credit: The African Studies Program, University of Wisconsin.

attracted me rather than the so-called 'academicians' of the University College, Dar es Salaam."[10] While attending university, Museveni and some of his classmates, including John Garang, the future leader of the SPLA, visited Frente de Libertação de Moçambique (FRELIMO) fighters in liberated zones in northern Mozambique. There Museveni met Samora Machel, FRELIMO's secretary of defense and then FRELIMO's leader after Mondlane's murder in 1969. Museveni and a small group of friends launched a failed attack in August 1971 and joined other exiles in an attack in September 1972 against the regime of the dictator Idi Amin, who seized power in a coup in January 1971.[11]

Although university life in Dar es Salaam provided Museveni and others with a venue to discuss politics, Museveni's student network,

[10] Yoweri Museveni, "My Three Years in Tanzania," mimeo, no date. I am grateful to a former NRA fighter who gave me a copy of this in Kampala in June 2001.
[11] Yoweri Museveni, *Sowing the Mustard Seed* (London: Macmillan, 1997), 73.

which expanded to include graduates of Makerere University in Kampala after he gave several talks there, was socially and physically removed from the people that he and his associates wanted to liberate. Even though Amin's violent regime angered many Ugandans, these would-be reform rebels would have failed if they had attempted to transfer the ideas in Museveni's undergraduate thesis – the applicability of Franz Fanon's ideas of revolutionary violence – directly to Ugandan farmers and townspeople. They needed to attract farmers and laborers to join what became the National Resistance Army (NRA) after Museveni and twenty-six other educated men attacked Uganda on 6 February 1981 and fought until they took power in Kampala in January 1986. This core group included a law graduate from the University of Dar es Salaam, a fine arts graduate from Makerere University, a student of veterinary medicine, school teachers, and a number of students who joined the Front for National Salvation (FRONASA) before being absorbed into the NRA.[12] Some of these fighters had experience in the field with FRE-LIMO in Mozambique, but in 1981 they lacked the secure rear base and strong international support for their struggle that their Mozambican anti-colonial colleagues enjoyed earlier in Tanzania, a sign of the critical shift in the international context.

Museveni's fighters faced considerable competition from other rebel groups in the time period around and after their 1981 attack. These included ex-president Tito Okello's backers, who organized a group called the Federal and Democratic Movement of Uganda. Some of ex-president Yusuf Lule's supporters in the Uganda Freedom Fighters joined Museveni's NRA, but this raised the possibility of future factional division. Others formed the Uganda Nationalists Organization to restore a traditional leader. The Uganda Freedom Movement (UFM) also competed for popular support. Meanwhile an ex-minister of Amin's government formed the Uganda National Rescue Front to take up the cause of the West Nile region and other northerners in Uganda.[13]

The NRA's organizational cohesion was important for the fortunes of the future RPF leaders and their Rwandan Patriotic Army (RPA). Fred Rwigyema, the RPA commander until his death in Rwanda in 1990, was among the twenty-six who joined Museveni in the 1981

---

[12] Ondoga ori Amaza, *Museveni's Long March: From Guerrilla to Statesman* (Kampala: Fountain, 1998), 234–41.

[13] Gerard Prunier, "Le phénomène NRM en Ouganda: une expérience révolutionnaire Originale," *Politique Africaine* 23 (1986): 112–14.

attack. He and Museveni's half-brother were classmates in secondary school, which they left together in 1976 to join FRONASA in Mozambique. These two and many other RPF commanders followed Museveni through his campaign against Amin's government to Kampala in 1986. Before his 1990 attack on Rwanda, Rwigyema had served as deputy army commander and deputy minister of defense of Uganda (until November 1989). Paul Kagame, also associated with Museveni at the start of the NRA fight against the 30,000-strong government army, became the acting head of military intelligence in Uganda in late 1989, a position that he used to recruit ethnic Rwandans to join the RPF struggle. From their positions in the NRA and then in the Ugandan military, Rwigyema and Kagame organized the 3,000 or so Rwandan refugees who had joined the NRA, incorporating them into the Rwandan Alliance for National Unity (RANU), which became the RPF in 1987.[14]

The NRA and, after 1986, their country's new army, the UPDF, provided an institutional focus for this group of Rwandans, although it did not eliminate the diverse motivations of the RPF. Some RPF supporters included unlikely leaders, such as a former director of the Rwandan state petroleum firm, a former director of the Kigali Chamber of Commerce, and several others who had fallen out of the Rwandan dictator's patronage networks.[15] Nor was the RPF very appealing to people inside Rwanda, because it was dominated by ethnic Tutsis, who comprised only about 10 percent of the pre-1994 population of Rwanda. Moreover, the fact that many RPF members had spent most of their lives outside of Rwanda was not a recipe for building extensive links with communities inside the country. The presence of a French garrison and close personal ties to the French presidential office gave the Rwandan regime a link to its own powerful backers. Thus the initial failure of the RPF to gain a foothold in Rwanda after their October 1990 invasion, coupled with the deaths of Rwigyema and several other top commanders, did not portend success. After the failure of the invasion, the surviving RPF leaders realized they would have to devise a strategy to gain local and international support beyond the considerable initial advantages of early Ugandan government support, their

---

[14] Gerard Prunier, *The Rwanda Crisis* (New York: Columbia University Press, 1995), 70.

[15] Gerard Prunier, "Éléments pour une histoire du Front patriote rwandais," *Politique Africaine* 51 (1993): 123–27.

battlefield experience, and their networks in that country's military forces.

Successful Eritrean reform rebel leaders also demonstrated the importance of elite networks in insulating early organizers from crippling regime interference and the allures that came with serving as a neighboring regime's proxy. Issayas Afreworki, later president of independent Eritrea, led a group of intellectuals in the late 1960s and early 1970s from the Eritrean Liberation Front (ELF) to form what became the EPLF. He and other Eritrean leaders helped to organize a study circle in the mid-1960s. Afreworki and Haile Woldetensai, another prominent EPLF leader, shared longer ties, having both been active in student politics at the elite Prince Makonnen Secondary School in Asmara before they both entered Haile Selassie University in Addis Ababa and then joined the ELF in 1966. A new group of university students joined the EPLF in the early 1970s in time to play important roles in the insurgency as it faced fierce repression from the Ethiopian military that took power in a coup in 1974.[16] These students were hardly free of divisive tendencies in their own ranks, as they complained of the ELF's "feudalist, comprador and capitalist tendencies," and some split from the organization.[17] As they forged out on their own after 1971, they turned their backs on political and material support from Arab states to take their chances in a splinter group without significant external aid, a situation that pushed them to privilege pragmatic accommodation over their ideological commitments.

The TPLF also developed out of an African scholarly milieu far removed from the experiences of most citizens. One leader recalled that "the university in Addis Ababa became the venue where politically minded teachers and students from all districts of Tigray converged and discussed issues concerning the whole of Tigray."[18] Like EPLF's Afreworki, the TPLF leader Meles Zenawi became a president, in his case after the two rebel groups jointly drove Ethiopia's military regime from power in 1991. Zenawi also was a product of an elite secondary institution, General Wingate Secondary School in Addis Ababa. Old

---

[16] On personal backgrounds, see David Pool, *From Guerrillas to Government: The Eritrean People's Liberation Front* (Athens: Ohio University Press, 2001), 83–84.

[17] Randi Rønning Balsvik, *Haile Sellassie's Students: The Intellectual and Social Background to Revolution, 1952–1974* (Addis Ababa: Addis Ababa University Press, 2005), 281–86.

[18] Aregawi Berhe, "The Origins of the Tigray People's Liberation Front," *African Affairs* 103:413 (2004): 576.

school networks abounded in the TPLF leadership. Sebhat Nega, a key early TPLF recruiter, was a school director in Adwa, the administrative capital of Tigray province, and attended university in Addis Ababa, where he received a degree in agricultural economics in 1964. Like Afreworki's uncle, his father served as a high administrator in the old imperial bureaucracy, which would be important later for bringing provincial patronage networks inherited from the imperial regime over to the TPLF.

Had these educated Tigrayan and Eritrean activists graduated before the mid-1960s, they would have enjoyed decent employment prospects, most likely as civil servants. But the rapid production of degree holders outpaced the economy's capacity to absorb them, and many graduates failed to obtain the state employment to which they felt entitled.[19] For students like Zenawi and Afreworki, the fact that they had not come from the Amharic ethnic core of Ethiopia's multicultural state left them especially disadvantaged in a patronage-based system that suddenly had many more people with skills and connections than positions for them. Those from families that were just entering this competition for status and jobs amid the exponential expansion of secondary school enrolment, which was one hundred times higher in 1969 than in 1951, had huge expectations that education would transform their prospects. But many of the new schools offered substandard instruction, and students struggled to learn in cramped quarters; school certificate examination failure rates climbed from about 40 percent in the mid-1950s to more than 80 percent in the mid-1960s.[20] This created a rapidly growing cadre of students who fell by the wayside, reluctant to return to their families as failures. Instead they hunted in vain for jobs in urban centers, and some joined the reform rebels.

Compared to the founders of reform rebel groups, the leaders of anti-colonial rebel groups earlier faced what seemed like easy paths of upward mobility. Recall that Mondlane left an attractive position as a university professor in the United States and that Cabral could have stayed at the UN. The payoff of success was no less than leading one's country to independence and the chance of presidential office. Most of these rebel leaders and their competitors benefited from international connections acquired through schooling or professional careers, whether they became rebels or followed more conventional careers. At

---

[19] John Markakis and Nega Ayele, *Class and Revolution in Ethiopia* (Nottingham: Spokeman, 1978), 50.

[20] Balsvik, *Haile Sellassie's Students*, 8.

best their reform counterparts had developed regional networks, and although they were no strangers to high status, they faced a much more precarious future. In a context of galloping expectations and the expansion of education, reform rebel leaders had fewer personal options. In each country the development of authoritarian regimes, especially ones that discriminated against particular ethnic groups or that focused privilege on a select group of families, only increased the gap between the aspirations of a new educated class and opportunities for upward mobility.

Still it remained for reform rebel leaders to translate their ideas into actions. Every successful group faced many competitors. They had to gain the allegiance of the people on whose behalf they claimed to fight, while contending with ethnic separatists, rival reformers, and local bandits, some of whom received support from neighboring governments, along with the armies of the regimes that they aimed to overthrow. All successful reform rebels adopted pragmatic strategies and modified rigid ideological blueprints to adjust to the realities of local conditions. They also had to organize their external affairs, an especially difficult task for the EPLF, given the international reluctance to recognize their separatist claims, and do so in ways that did not allow the agendas of foreign governments or other outsiders to override their own objectives.

Successful Domestic Strategies

All rebels have to figure out how to arm their followers, attract more fighters, and, if they wish to rule, translate their ideas into a concrete strategy to administer non-combatants. How they go about getting the necessary resources to accomplish these tasks shapes their organization and behavior. Readily accessible foreign aid can release fighters from the difficult task of convincing local people to hand over resources and willingly lend support. If maintaining fighters rests on material support from an outsider who does not require evidence of their administrative skills or popular support – for example, as proxies for a neighboring state's government to destabilize their common enemy – rebels can loot local people's property. If this behavior creates refugee flows that burden governments, this can be in the interests of those who use these rebels as proxies. Thus to pursue a clear political agenda, reform rebel leaders had to figure out how to control resources and take concrete steps to eliminate their own fighters' incentives to prey on local communities.

This control would also enable rebel leaders to rein in individuals' self-interested motivations and to instead use resources to administer non-combatants and convince recruits to fight for a fairly abstract political idea.

Museveni recognized the importance of identifying and managing individual fighters' motivations. After visiting liberated zones in Mozambique, he wrote: "The person who uses the opportunities that present themselves to seduce peasants' wives or daughters will never win the confidence of the masses."[21] His analysis of FRELIMO's experience stressed the importance of enforcing a code of conduct to prevent fighters from using their weapons to take what they wanted from local people.[22] He gained practical experience with controlling armed fighters when briefly serving as minister for defense after Amin's removal in 1979. At that time he struggled to streamline army recruitment procedures, weed out units that supported local strongmen, and prevent soldiers from using their guns to extort money from citizens, but then he left the government when he lost out in internal power struggles and a rigged election.[23]

Very likely Museveni and his associates benefited in the long run from the fact that they had few sources of external support when they launched their armed attack on 6 February 1981. Tanzanian President Nyerere's reluctance to pick a fight with Milton Obote, the winner of a rigged election in 1980, so soon after the expensive Tanzanian invasion to remove Amin, meant that the NRA was not allowed to establish a rear base on Tanzanian territory. Taking a page from anti-colonial and majority rule rebels, Museveni toured the globe in search of support. Visits to Kenya, Britain, and Libya produced few results. Libya's Muammar Qaddafi already supported the UFM, and Museveni received only token military supplies from him.[24] NRM efforts to recruit foreign activists and diplomats to their cause also met with frustration. "Due to the weakness of our external workers, it has not been possible to get material assistance from outside," Museveni

---

21 Yoweri Museveni, "Fanon's Theory of Violence: Its Verification in Liberated Mozam-
    bique," in N. M. Shamuyarira (ed.), *Essays on the Liberation of Southern Africa* (Dar
    es Salaam: Tanzanian Publishing House, 1972), 8.
22 Pascal Ngoga, "Uganda: The National Resistance Army," in Christopher Clapham
    (ed.), *African Guerrillas* (Oxford: James Currey, 1998), 101–02.
23 A. B. K. Kasozi, *The Social Origins of Violence in Uganda* (Kampala: Fountain, 1994),
    134.
24 Museveni, *Sowing the Mustard Seed*, 141–42.

complained.[25] By this time it had become much harder to organize
support among foreign governments and citizens' groups to overthrow
a recognized government of a majority-ruled African state, compared
to the enthusiasm that had greeted the representatives of earlier anti-
colonial rebels and that majority rule rebels still enjoyed.

Museveni and many NRA fighters lacked ethnic ties with those who
lived in the territory across which the NRA would have to fight to
make their way to the capital. Museveni was from the southwest part
of the country, and some of his associates were actually refugees from
Rwanda. This gave President Obote a basis to claim that the NRA was
only for foreigners and ethnic minorities. Obote tried to exploit local
fears of hosting outsiders in the Luwero Triangle, an ethnically mixed
area close to the capital where the NRA established its base and started
to build a liberated zone. There the presence of Rwandan migrants
and the belief among some people that newcomers were crowding out
"sons of the soil" gave urgency to arguments that the NRA would
try to rally newcomers against community notables. The NRA also
faced competition from two other rebel groups that had supporters in
this area, including the Libyan-backed UFM, which claimed to protect
local ethnic Baganda interests.

Thus as soon as the NRA controlled territory inside Uganda, it
had little option but to come to terms with local community leaders
if it was going to survive, which also meant compromising the political ideas developed in classrooms and late-night discussions. Commanders had to figure out how to incorporate into the NRA agenda
parochial grievances such as ethnic claims and property disputes –
which were seriously at odds with student rhetoric about socialist visions
of modernity overthrowing capitalist imperialism – to make the rebels
as acceptable as possible to local people and to provide these people with a rebel political narrative that they could relate to their own
situations.

The predatory behavior of the Ugandan military against its own citizens helped the NRM cause. Official human rights abuses provided
evidence to local people that the NRM was correct in its analysis of
government corruption and oppression. Government repression and
violence also forced non-combatants to consider more seriously the
prospect that the NRM was better suited to offer them security. People in this region faced an even worse situation after an army brigade

---

[25] National Resistance Movement, *Mission to Freedom* (Kampala: NRM, 1990), 271.

made up mostly of ethnic Acholi soldiers from northern Uganda staged a coup on 27 July 1985 that brought General Tito Okello to power. Okello pursued a ruthless counterinsurgency strategy against the NRA that also targeted non-combatants. Even prior to the 1985 coup, the violence on the part of the unpopular government encouraged NRA commanders to refrain from upsetting local landholders in the Luwero Triangle, while creating a system of elected resistance committees. This innovation enabled the NRM to associate itself with the legitimacy of locally respected individuals who were elected to the NRM adminis-tration of the liberated zone. This incorporated the authority of local leaders – not necessarily previous officeholders; they could simply be people whom others respected – into the NRM administration, and the local leaders incorporated their ideas about local governance and their accommodative mechanisms into the administration of the liberated zone.

The NRA used local institutions to manage community strife – such as youth anger at bossy elders, the ambitions of would-be local warlords, family vendettas, or grudges, which motivated much of the personal violence in other conflicts – before these factors could disrupt local order and spoil NRM relations with these communities. These new positions gave local people whose status and authority had recently been connected to the NRA and its program incentives to use their authority to supervise the behavior of NRA fighters, which saved NRA commanders from taking sides in purely local or personal conflicts. The local linkages also gave NRA commanders more authority to call on communities to provide resources and manpower for their fight.[26] Thus the NRM did not alienate the local elite, even if it singled out government-appointed chiefs for harsh treatment; this strategy also denied the targets of NRM hostility the opportunity either to organize a conservative reaction against NRM influence or to launch the kind of rural bandit gangs that had followed chiefs in Angola and Mozambique who opposed liberation rebels (discussed in Chapter 2).

The tiny size of the NRA in February 1981 pushed it to recruit new leaders locally. A former commander said that that this broadening of the leadership of the NRA limited the opportunities of student groups to "conduct their revolutionary social experiments" that he thought would alienate most people and undermine the NRA's military effectiveness.

[26] Nelson Kasfir, "Guerrillas and Civilian Participation: The National Resistance Army in Uganda," *Journal of Modern African Studies* 43:2 (2005): 284–85.

This also equipped the NRA to serve as a path of upward mobility for members who exhibited leadership skills that came from personal knowledge of local people and their socioeconomic conditions.[27] These features reinforced the tendency – already promoted by revolutionary committees – to treat bad decisions and fighter indiscipline as local community problems and not the result of an intrusive alien insurgent force. The NRA used this support – obtained by providing security to people who, as a consequence, thought of themselves as liberated from an oppressive regime – to press its offensive against Obote's and, after June 1985, Okello's governments and to compete against other rebel groups to be the legitimate representative of the people.

Despite these strategies, NRA forces were forced to retreat before a government offensive in March 1983. The NRA still benefited from its proven interest in administration and prior success in protecting people from the violent government forces. The continued predations of the Ugandan army and the arrival of NRA reinforcements from a western front, under the command of future RPA leader Fred Rwigyema, turned the tide of the war and culminated in the NRA capture of the capital on 26 January 1986. Luck, leadership, and government miscalculation facilitated the NRA success, but the underlying pragmatism of the NRM strategy of administering liberated zones developed primarily thanks to the reform rebels' international marginality and their need to heed the interests of the local people on whom they relied for survival. Government repression was not enough to bring these communities together, as we will see in other instances in the next chapter on warlord rebels. This practice of governance as a strategy of survival was critical in shaping the behavior of these rebels and their relations with communities, as it pushed rebel leaders to undermine support for the ethnic militants and self-aggrandizing looters in their midst who tried to exploit turmoil to their own ends.

TPLF leaders showed a similar pragmatism in crafting a strategy of popular mobilization. In the 1970s, a group of student activists who were originally members of the Tigray National Organization (TNO) continued a reading circle's discussion of the accounts of the other liberation struggles. Their interest in the "dialectical contradictions of society" and "socialist modes of production" that were staples of academic debates found their way into TPLF official documents. The

---

[27] Interviews with a former NRA commander, Entebbe, 10 July 2000, and with another former NRA commander, Kampala, 24 July 2000.

more practical noted, however, that these same ideas, when implemented by the Ethiopian government, generated deep popular anger,
and that this reaction foretold the likely response if the rebels tried to
do the same. Instead, the TNO students focused on observing local
conditions and scouting out potential recruits when they returned to
Tigray during school vacations. This local information proved much
more useful in their discussions about how to organize a rebel group.
The TPLF was formally organized in February 1975 after the 1974
military coup installed the Derg (Amharic for "committee") in power
in Addis Ababa. The Derg, which drew on ideas of radical reform that
animated the TNO student activists, quickly adopted a program drawn
from Soviet-style Marxist-Leninism but that targeted radical educated
youth. This pushed more of the educated youth from Tigray to join the
TPLF.

Once fighting began in 1975, the TPLF faced armed competition from the Tigray Liberation Front (TLF), which, like the TPLF,
promised to redistribute land to peasants. The TLF received support
from the ELF, which opposed the EPLF. Although the ELF received aid
from Sudan and several Arab countries, EPLF influence continued to
grow, and its support for the TPLF helped the latter eliminate the small
group of intellectuals who made up the TLF from the field of competition. According to a former TPLF commander, his group betrayed
unsuspecting TLF leaders who had come to negotiate a merger and
murdered them.[28] The competition also included the Tigray People's
Organization, made up of student radicals who favored outright independence for Tigray, although the TPLF absorbed this organization
more peacefully in 1975.

A more serious challenge came from conservative nationalist mobilization of Teranafit and the Ethiopian Democratic Union (EDU), a
coalition of Tigrayan nobility and local *shifta* (bandits). This organization encompassed multiple agendas, including the restoration of
the nobility's privilege and the personal aims of local notables who
exploited their connections to "noble bandits," and ultimately to their
followers, who were "renowned for their lack of discipline, drunken-
ness, raping, and pillaging, to the point where many peasants . . . insist
that they were not political organizations at all but simply gangs of
marauders." Their presence, however, posed a serious threat to the

---

[28] Kahsay Berhe, *Ethiopia: Democratization and Unity, the Role of the Tigray People's
Liberation Front* (Münster: Verlagshaus Monsenstein und Vannerdat, 2005), 50–51.

students-turned-insurgents. First, in 1975 the TPLF had about 100 poorly equipped and untested fighters, while Teranafit and the EDU mobilized 10,000 followers.[29] Although their leaders told peasants that they would give land to everyone to counter the Derg's promises of land redistribution, the real threat of EDU and Teranafit lay in their capacity to create mayhem and community insecurity as energetic followers from Tigray joined them for personal protection or opportunities to loot. This undermined TPLF efforts to organize a liberated zone. Moreover, aid from conservative anticommunist regimes in Sudan and Saudi Arabia gave various groups of fighters a degree of independence that shielded them from the need to compromise with a broad segment of the local population.

For its part, the TPLF enforced strict rules of conduct to limit its fighters' offenses against communities and built local administrations in liberated zones, thus winning the support of the peasants who benefited from rebel-supplied security and services. In fact this was one of the few options open for building a successful and lasting fighting force in such a difficult environment.[30] This institutional structure would not have been possible if this still-small group had not been able to solve the serious problem of competition among rebel groups that gave free rein to the diverse grievances and ambitions that motivated some people to fight. Outside of on-and-off relations with the EPLF, the TPLF had few external backers. It was briefly linked to the Afar Liberation Front (ALF), which was run by the son of a sultan who had fled the Derg's revolution, but the location of ALF headquarters in Saudi Arabia gave authorities there leverage to redirect ALF connections in favor of their EDU clients. Moreover, the TPLF did not share the ALF agenda of restoring pre-coup notables, and once ALF resources dried up, there was no compelling reason to maintain the relationship.

Ultimately TPLF strategy rested on attracting key people who controlled local patronage networks to bring the would-be *shifta* into groups under TPLF control. A former TPLF leader pointed to the critical role of Gessesew Ayele (also known as Sihule), a former parliamentarian in his late fifties, who had played a major role in starting the TPLF's rebellion. Sihule's support for the TPLF gave the rebels the advantages of the nationalist credentials of Sihule's powerful local family and

---

[29] John Young, *Peasant Revolution in Ethiopia, the Tigray People's Liberation Front, 1975–1991* (New York: Cambridge University Press, 1997), 101–03, quote from 103.

[30] Max Peberdy, *Tigray: Ethiopia's Untold Story* (London: Relief Society of Tigray UK Support Committee, 1985).

the personal prestige of his combat against the Italian invasion before 1941. As an administrator for the Ethiopian empire who enjoyed real prestige at home, Sihule included local *shifta* leaders in his influential personal network. Sihule had made good use of these people when he worked in the pre-1974 government, using them to remind his bosses of the necessity of making deals with local strongmen like him, if they wanted him to continue using his local clout on behalf of the distant state administration. This patronage network gave the TPLF access to and ultimately influence over a set of social relationships that local people considered vital to their long-term security and well-being, but that certainly did not feature positively in the students' early political debates. The site of the start of the TPLF armed campaign on 18 February 1975 was selected "because Sihule had prior knowledge of this area and, more importantly, he had the respect of the people living in the villages adjacent to this terrain."[31] His status meant that he could convince some *shifta* leaders to switch to the TPLF side, linking the provincial tradition of legitimate armed resistance to authority to the TPLF's campaign.[32]

Sensitivity to local sociopolitical structures and conditions enabled the TPLF's local allies to control armed young men who otherwise might have joined the EDU or Teranafit and have preyed on civilians. Instead these youth helped the TPLF in expanding their liberated zones. After 1982 the fierceness of the Ethiopian government's attacks, combined with the reduction of TPLF-controlled territory, made fighter discipline and sensitivity to local people's interests even more important for survival, even if this meant that they had to tolerate local practices and concerns that did not fit insurgent visions about the ideal future reformed society. Once the TPLF and EPLF rejoined forces in 1988, they confronted 500,000 Ethiopian soldiers; against this massive army they went on to capture Addis Ababa in 1991. The end of the Cold War and the Soviet Union's decision to stop backing their African partners were critical in weakening the Derg, but the survival of TPLF links with local people and their support was also critical to the TPLF's survival of the onslaught of Africa's largest army. The government's strategy of trying to use overwhelming conventional force against the rebels, partly a consequence of bad Soviet advice and its abundance of material aid, also left large segments of complex rural social networks. Because the

[31] Quoted in Berhe, "Origins of the Tigray People's Liberation Front," 590.
[32] Berhe, "Origins of the Tigray People's Liberation Front," 576; and Young, *Peasant Revolution in Ethiopia*, 96.

government could not control these networks through brute force, the reform rebels were able to use them to organize.

Ultimately EPLF leaders did not suffer from their status as political outsiders in the regional politics of insurgency once they realized the importance of identifying and responding to local interests as a pragmatic strategy for survival. Perhaps they were more amenable to this local strategy at the outset, once student intellectuals in the 1960s and early 1970s split from the ELF over what they regarded as its subservience to the agendas of Arab countries in return for diplomatic and material support. Their complaints focused on the dominance of Muslims from Eritrea's lowlands who had fled to Egypt to organize the ELF in 1960. These Muslims tried to link the ELF struggle to the Pan-Arab nationalism and anti-Israeli politics of Middle Eastern governments, with the hopes that they would give diplomatic and military support for Eritrean independence. These international connections reflected the dominance of clans that lived on the Eritrea-Sudan border, which had provided officers for Sudan's army in the 1950s and then staff for the ELF in the 1960s. Foreign help reinforced factional differences, as "nationalist sentiment notwithstanding, the use of clan and tribal linkages became part of the process of recruitment into the armed struggle."[33] Such family ties helped to prevent fighters from mistreating people in their home areas but failed to restrain them from abusing other people, including recruits, from more distant communities. Thus Hamid Idris Awate, a bandit leader–turned-insurgent from one of these clans, attacked Ethiopian forces in 1961 but then raided settlements and cattle herders outside the protection of his clan under the guise of "revolutionary taxation."[34] Cross-border support of this sort was tailor-made to reinforce parochial agendas, because it could aggravate the local societal divisions against which groups like the ELF struggled.

From the mid-1960s the more ideologically driven rebels included growing numbers of students and small-town peasants in the largely Christian highlands where some of the students later taught. Some pro-independence students, intellectuals, and urban workers were refugees from attempts to organize the Eritrean Liberation Movement (ELM) in 1958, including office workers and students who believed that the 1957 declaration of Amharic as the official language of Eritrea left

[33] Pool, *From Guerrillas to Government*, 50.
[34] Michael Johnson and Trish Johnson, "Eritrea: The National Question and the Logic of Protracted Struggle," 187.

them at a disadvantage in finding good jobs. By 1962, Ethiopian security forces quickly crushed this radical, urban-based movement.[35] The 1967 execution of twenty-seven Christian fighters for "failure to perform" during an offensive reinforced the association of the ELF with a Muslim identity and energized a dissident faction within the ELF. At the same time, a massive government offensive against the ELF uprooted large numbers of civilians, who fled to Sudan, and this helped change the minds of the few who had previously thought that federation with Ethiopia was a viable option.[36]

Disagreements with other Eritrean nationalists helped to consolidate the bonds between the highland nationalist intellectuals; however, these conflicts also left them isolated. They could not turn to ELF's Arab backers, nor could they interest Soviet-aligned countries in their socialist program for reform, particularly after the 1974 coup, which resulted in the Soviet Union becoming Ethiopia's main military backer. Thus they launched the EPLF, active from 1970 but not formally organized until 1977, in the direction of self-reliance. They simply added denunciations of the "erroneous stands and baseless slanders of the socialist countries" to their condemnations of "Ethiopian imperialism," "US imperialism," and the "reactionary puppet regimes of the region" that aided the ELF.[37]

The EPLF undertook studies and community surveys to identify local grievances and concerns, which provided useful information for establishing village assemblies and introducing land reform in ways that would not alienate villagers. EPLF cadres worked through existing village institutions such as the *baito* committees, which adjudicated land tenure disputes and resolved other conflicts. These institutions served as frameworks for organizing community defense during times of crisis.[38] Once local people agreed that the EPLF was there to protect them, the institutions that protected people from attack and settled local conflicts were more easily grafted onto the rebels' own organization. Much like the NRA in Uganda, personal disputes over land and between families

[35] Edmond Keller, *Revolutionary Ethiopia: From Empire to People's Republic* (Bloomington: Indiana University Press, 1988), 154–55.

[36] John Markakis, "The National Revolution in Eritrea," *Journal of Modern African Studies* 26:1 (1988): 58.

[37] Memorandum, Eritrean People's Liberation Front, 1978, 14–16 (author's personal collection).

[38] Kidane Mengisteab, "African Traditional Institutions of Governance: The Case of Eritrea's Village *Baito*," in Olufemi Vaughan (ed.), *Indigenous Political Structures and Governance in Africa* (Ibadan: Sefer Books, 2003), 210–11.

were subsumed into the locally run administrative structures of the rebel group, and this practice protected the rebels from manipulation by those who wanted to settle personal scores or who were looking for personal aggrandizement. Thus the highland peasantry acquired a stake in ensuring that the EPLF could protect them and the liberated zone from the Ethiopian army, but their support did not require acceptance of all EPLF ideological justifications or nationalist arguments. Also, the presence of the EPLF served the practical purpose of insulating the liberated zone administration from people serving as proxies for outsider or local political entrepreneurs who might otherwise exploit community disputes to challenge the EPLF presence or to enhance their own influence.

The establishment of local stability enabled the EPLF to build hospitals, schools, and workshops in its liberated zone. After the rebels consolidated their own institutions, particularly in sparsely populated areas, they experimented with innovations such as using women as fighters without directly challenging too many community conventions. One scholar estimates that by the mid-1970s, about a third of its membership and an eighth of its frontline fighters were women.[39] This shared interest between local people and rebels provided a basis to connect local people's practical need for protection from a coercive state with the political agenda of the rebels' quest for Eritrean independence.

The RPF in Rwanda provides another model of reform rebel strategy. Unlike the EPLF and TPLF, the RPF lacked strong ties with the people whom it wanted to liberate. Instead the RPF organized among other refugee Rwandans, among whom it defined its goals and built its capacity to overthrow a repressive regime. As discussed earlier, initially RPF leaders were deeply involved in Museveni's effort to rid Uganda first of the regime of Idi Amin and then of Milton Obote. Once the NRM assumed control of the Ugandan government in 1986, the future RPF leaders held positions in the new regime – one scholar lists thirty top RPF figures, all of whom held positions or had responsibilities in the NRA – prior to the RPA attack on Rwanda in October 1990.[40] Paul Kagame, head of the RPF from 1990 and later the president of Rwanda, said, "At the beginning of the war we started with an army that

[39] David Pool, "The Eritrean People's Liberation Front," in Christopher Clapham (ed.), *African Guerrillas* (Oxford: James Currey, 1998), 32.
[40] Elijah Dickens Mushemeza, *The Politics and Empowerment of Banyarwanda Refugees in Uganda, 1959–2001* (Kampala: Fountain, 2007), 133–36.

we stole from Uganda."[41] He used his position as head of NRA military intelligence from November 1989 to June 1990 to organize about 3,000 Rwandan refugees within the NRA and to identify dissenters among RPF refugees in Uganda. This "borrowed" institutional structure, including positions that emphasized strategies of control such as political commissars and intelligence officers in Museveni's army, along with the social autonomy of the tightly knit refugee and rebel fighter community, helped the RPF's articulate group of leaders to organize and plan to attack Rwanda. They hoped that oppressed Rwandans would join the RPA, just as Ugandans had joined the NRA. This goal also appeared to enjoy the support of Museveni himself, as Ugandan aid to this "stolen army" continued after the 1990 invasion at a level that the US State Department undersecretary for Africa noted was "hard to miss."[42]

In fact, in October 1990 the RPF invasion from their Ugandan base frightened many Rwandans who saw that the attack forced them to choose between supporting these foreign invaders and their own authoritarian government. Moreover, even though the international community began to pressure the Rwandan government to hold multiparty elections, the RPF could not reasonably hope to win power in a national election if it were seen as fighting for the cause of an ethnic minority: The narrowness of its demographic base would virtually ensure its defeat. Instead international pressure on the Habyarimana regime to negotiate with the insurgents brought RPF representatives into government office by 1993. Face-to-face talks with Rwandan officials began in 1991 under OAU auspices. The power-sharing government that followed the August 1993 Arusha agreement gave the RPF as many ministerial posts as the old ruling party and promised it half of all army command positions. This remarkable gain reflected the RPF's negotiating skill and discipline at a time when they held only a small strip of territory in the northern part of the country. More critically, this and other internationally sponsored peace negotiations in the 1990s and later marked an important shift away from old diplomatic practices of explicit backing for one side or the other in rebel wars. The practice of inviting all combatant groups to negotiations with the intent of creating a power-sharing government and foreign hostility toward the authoritarian Habyarimana regime enabled the RPF to gain a far larger share

[41] François Misser, "Kagame Speaks," *New African* (July 1993): 17; and idem, *Vers un nouveau Rwanda Etretiens avec Paul Kagamé* (Paris: Editions Karthala, 1995).
[42] Herman Cohen, *Intervention in Africa: Super Power Peacemaking in a Troubled Continent* (New York: St. Martin's Press, 2000), 225.

of power than their military capabilities and domestic popularity would otherwise warrant. At least the RPF's internal cohesion limited factional splits; otherwise, international mediators might have welcomed these factions too.

This agreement left Rwanda government hard-liners with a quarter of the ministry posts, and international pressure forced them to start to share control over the army. It introduced a small UN peacekeeping force to monitor the agreement, but international mediation left the RPF vulnerable to the shifting interests of distant capitals. In a meeting in Uganda, for example, RPF representatives learned from the US ambassador that "the UN is overextended these days in peacekeeping operations. . . . The UN and its member states have other preoccupations these days."[43] Uncertain external protection, coupled with the recognition that winning truly free elections was highly unlikely, gave the RPF contradictory interests vis-à-vis the diplomatic process. On the one hand, diplomacy gave them a measure of power that they could not obtain through armed action. On the other hand, it would deny them ultimate control over the state if the international agreement was fully implemented and Rwanda became a democratic country.

To solve this dilemma the RPF seized power by force while it simultaneously engaged in international mediation. It installed a RPF garrison in the capital under the terms of the Arusha agreement, which put its fighters at the center of political power and gave them a base to destabilize the Habyarimana regime. Dissident RPF officials claim that this strategy included targeted political assassinations, laying landmines, and (in a controversial claim that is not accepted by many experts) even shooting down the president's airplane on 6 April 1994.[44] That tragic event signaled the start of the Rwandan genocide, which resulted in the murder of more than 800,000 people over the next three months.[45] The government's pursuit of genocide left it unable to repel the RPA's

---

[43] Cable, US embassy, Kampala to Department of State, Washington, DC, document 07873, 6 Oct 1993, 2.

[44] Charles Onana and Déo Mushayidi, *Les secrets du génocide rwandais: enquête sur les mystères d'un président* (Paris: Duboiris, 2002), 223–44; and Abdul Ruzibiza, *Rwanda: l'histoire secrète* (Paris: Éditions du Panama, 2005). These allegations also appear in the memoirs of James Gasana, Rwanda's defense minister in 1993: see *Rwanda: Du parti-état à l'état-garnison* (Paris: L'Harmattan, 2002).

[45] The Rwandan genocide was a consequence of the government policy of extermination and is not treated here as an internal war. For a survey of recruitment and organization for genocide, see Scott Strauss, *The Order of Genocide: Race, Power and War in Rwanda* (Ithaca, NY: Cornell University Press, 2006).

second invasion, which installed the RPF government in Kigali in early July 1994.

The RPF's strategy to seize power extended to organizing Rwandan refugees in Uganda, who numbered about 200,000 by 1990, and in other countries. Such large numbers reflected the fact that various Ugandan constitutions contained provisions defining the offspring of refugees as refugees. The decision of the UN High Commission for Refugees (UNHCR) to provide these refugees with separate schools – often better than those that Ugandan citizens attended – and scholarships gave some refugees the education that they needed to emigrate to wealthier countries, from which they later provided support to the RPF.[46] Some became targets of attacks in the 1980s by youth militias attached to Obote's political party, which further reinforced their marginalization. Although Obote tried to incite local people to attack refugees over land disputes to recruit support for his government against Museveni's NRA, many of these people identified with Museveni's struggle rather than with an ethnic Tutsi or Rwandan exile cause.[47] After Museveni's NRA came to power, naturalization as Ugandan citizens seemed to be a viable option, but many refugees faced few options within the local rural economies where the refugee camps were located, even though refugee status brought UNHCR scholarships not available to others in Uganda. Therefore many second-generation refugees, including those who joined the NRA and then the RPA, excelled academically. Education gave them access to skills that enabled many to move to other African countries, to Europe, and to North America, from where they could contribute financially to the RPF. Others concluded that even though joining the RPF was very risky, it gave them the opportunity to use their skills and offered them the possibility of managerial positions in a government some day.

Reform Rebels and Foreign Relations

The RPF's relations with international mediators and the Ugandan government showed that external support did not necessarily interfere with reform rebel efforts to suppress factional splits and discipline followers or pursue wider political goals, nor did it necessarily interfere with

[46] Mushemeza, *The Politics and Empowerment*, 84 and 107.
[47] Catherine Watson, *Exile from Rwanda: Background to an Invasion* (Washington, DC: US Committee for Refugees, 1991), 6–10.

rebels' considerations of the interests of local populations. Where rebels had the capacity to manage their political relationships and the balance of power between different groups, they could shape how resources were used, seeking out, blocking, and channeling resources in ways that promoted their group interests. All of these rebels exploited the autonomous fields of leverage for political organizing that they found, either in school classrooms, distant provincial political establishments, another state's security services, or refugee camps. This autonomy from the politics of the capital and the capacity to buffer and manage aid from foreign regimes benefited reform rebels. This next section examines several particularly successful cases in which rebels further leveraged this autonomy in their clever organization of overseas supporters so that they could dominate this source of income, reaping many of the advantages provided by the OAU Liberation Committee and UN policies of channeling money and political support to favored rebel movements. Reform rebel leaders, especially in the EPLF and TPLF, created their own means to collect funds from overseas members of their communities and set up their own NGOs to coordinate foreign aid.

These successful rebel foreign relations enabled reform rebels to convince a critical mass of non-combatants that they were bringing services and protection to particular communities, as they learned to manipulate international humanitarian and relief organizations. The capacity to shape the opinions of a distant public and attract resources made it a lot harder for rival groups to challenge these rebels once they became established. Unlike rebels who had to incorporate the political agendas of their patrons directly into their own operations and strategies in return for aid, the management of diasporas and NGOs as advocates for their causes allowed reform rebels to appeal directly to people in foreign countries, including refugees from their own communities, and gain access to their resources. Thus reform rebels overcame some of the diplomatic constraints imposed by the international recognition of incumbent governments – in contrast to international condemnation of colonial and apartheid regimes.

The EPLF leaders were innovators in managing their own foreign relations. They faced a number of serious disadvantages: unlike SWAPO's UN-funded Institute for Namibia or FRELIMO's Ford Foundation–funded Eduardo Mondlane Institute, they did not have the support of international organizations committed to the liberation of their specific homeland. Nor did they have the patronage of a superpower backing them in the early days of their struggles. To remedy this, they supported their own international agency, the Eritrean Relief Association (ERA), in 1975 to operate as an auxiliary to local government institutions established in EPLF-liberated zones to provide health, education, and agricultural services. The ERA grew from the personal connections that Lutheran catechists Woldeab Weldemariam and Redagezghi Ghebremedhin had built with Scandinavian Lutheran NGOs, which convinced the International Committee of the Red Cross (ICRC) in 1976 to channel its food aid to Eritrean refugees in EPLF-controlled areas through the ERA. Such connections yielded overseas contributions of about one million dollars in 1980, which grew to tens of millions of dollars by 1985. By 1988, when the EPLF and TPLF joined forces to oust the Ethiopian government, the ERA attracted about $100 million ($175 million in 2011 dollars).[48]

The ERA's role as a provider of social services and its image as a local NGO appealed to the Scandinavian NGOs and the ICRC. None of these foreign organizations wished formal association with a separatist rebel group that fought a recognized sovereign regime. Instead they appreciated that their new partners could use their aid to actually provide services to local people. Some Scandinavian NGOs went on to mobilize more foreign support for the ERA and by extension the EPLF, and to provide humanitarian aid to the TPLF. In 1981 these and other sympathetic foreigners set up the Emergency Relief Desk (ERD) in Khartoum (which Sudan's government permitted to support rebels in neighboring countries), to ease cross-border relief operations and foreigners' visits to liberated zones without directly implicating them in EPLF and TPLF causes.[49] By 1984 the official US Agency for International Development (USAID) channeled its food aid through the ERD and on to the ERA for distribution to refugee camps and in liberated zones. The ERA also set up committees in Western countries to provide information about the EPLF, recruit sympathetic visitors, and provide a point of contact for new sources of aid.

In the early 1980s the TPLF and its supporters duplicated this institutional framework through their Relief Society of Tigray (REST),

---

[48] William DeMars, "Helping People in a People's War: Humanitarian Organizations and the Ethiopian Conflict, 1980–1988," PhD dissertation, University of Notre Dame, 1993, 69–70.

[49] Mark Duffield and John Prendergast, *Without Troops and Tanks: Humanitarian Intervention in Ethiopia and Eritrea* (Trenton, NJ: Red Sea Press, 1994).

which by the mid-1980s had caught up to the ERA in donations from foreigners. REST was particularly effective in coordinating overseas activists not only to collect contributions but also to publicize the insurgent cause. This coordination began with the visit to Tigray of members of the British organization War on Want, a NGO that became sympathetic to the TPLF cause as their activist members in Britain decided that the TPLF's practice of socialism was more progressive than that of the Ethiopian regime.[50] In Britain these arguments boosted the legitimacy of the TPLF struggle, and through organizations like REST, more activists were able to visit liberated zones to see this preferred form of socialism in practice. The legitimacy of such organizational ties was enhanced in 1984 when Oxfam UK began to coordinate its programs through REST so as to avoid working directly with the TPLF. Some NGOs like Oxfam included workers who were sympathetic to rebel causes. For example, a former Oxfam manager relates how during the 1980s his predecessors in the NGO's office in Zambia provided small amounts of assistance through intermediaries to the ANC, even though these rebels did not have a humanitarian aid wing.[51]

International endorsements from non-state international actors became critical for attracting other NGO aid and advancing the political argument that officials in non-African countries should take more interest in TPLF fortunes. In 1984–85 REST publicity became especially important as Ethiopian offensives pushed more than 200,000 refugees into Sudan and displaced about 800,000 people inside Ethiopia. These refugees became magnets for aid rather than burdens for TPLF efforts to provide security and services. After members of the REST-UK Support Committee visited liberated zones in Tigray, their report noted that "because the rules of diplomacy dictate that the governments of the world deal only with fellow governments, virtually all official aid from the EEC, Britain, etc., is going to camps in Dergue-controlled areas."[52] The committee appealed to people in Britain to donate directly to this network of aid to overcome this perceived injustice.[53] By 1985 support

---

[50] James Firebrace and Gayle Smith, *The Hidden Revolution: An Analysis of Social Change in Tigray (Northern Ethiopia) Based upon Eyewitness Accounts* (London: War on Want, 1982).

[51] Robin Palmer, "Oxfam's Support for the ANC in Zambia in the 1980s," Robin Palmer (ed.), *A House in Zambia: Recollections of the ANC and Oxfam at 250 Zambezi Road, Lusaka, 1967–97* (Lusaka: Bookworld, 2008), 45–50.

[52] Peberdy, *Tigray*, 58. See also Kirsty Wright, *Famine in Tigray: An Eyewitness Account* (London: REST/UK, 1983), 72–73.

[53] Peberdy, *Tigray*.

FIGURE 5. Map of Torit (Southern Sudan). Photograph by L. J. M. Seymour.

for NGOs that addressed the needs of refugees and displaced people reached the $100 million level, matching the resources that flowed to the ERA.

The SPLA and the Oromo Liberation Front (OLF) adopted this model with the Sudan Relief and Rehabilitation Association (SRRA) and the Oromo Relief Association (ORA). The ORA received less than 10 percent of the volume of ERD aid during the mid-1980s, primarily because its parent rebel group neither controlled significant areas in ethnic Oromo areas of Ethiopia nor maintained social service agencies. In 1985 the SRRA was organized to take advantage of this new source of support; however, the SPLA did not concentrate on setting up an institutional infrastructure to provide services, at least initially, which made "rebel NGOs" much less attractive to foreign humanitarian relief workers. After the SPLA started to set up more permanent administrative structures in the 1990s in its liberated zones, this changed. The SRRA then catered to United Nations Children's Fund (UNICEF) interests in setting up centralized service centers, grafting its own community development committees, which had become a form of SPLA administration, onto the externally designed model of local development.[54]

---

[54] Author's observations during a visit to SPLA-held areas of Bahr al Ghazal province, June 2003.

Rebel organizations catering to foreign NGOs provided access to refugees and others under their control in exchange for resources and collaborated in creating the appearance that their humanitarian operations were politically and militarily impartial. The reengineered institutions equipped NGOs, UN agencies, and the ICRC with seemingly "neutral" partners whom they could use to reach rebel-held areas. The reform rebels took credit for food aid and social services that foreigners paid for, but that were distributed under the watch of their own front organizations. Now rebels could control resources without having to accept the political directives attached to aid from neighboring states. Rebel NGOs also insulated foreign NGOs and international organizations from direct involvement in the factional politics of the reform rebels and limited the appearance of direct contact with rebels, which might hinder their relations with governments or their own donors. These arrangements served dual military and humanitarian goals: Once the EPLF and TPLF, and eventually the SPLA, could feed and protect populations in liberated zones, the flow of refugees across the Sudan border decreased. Meanwhile, with regard to the EPLF and TPLF, Sudanese authorities could harness foreign-financed relief and development efforts to their project of weakening the Ethiopian regime. Foreign NGOs still could tell their donors that their aid had a real impact on local people's lives and that they were helping local people to take responsibility for improving their own situations.

Just as anti-colonial and majority rule rebels had to impress foreign governments, these reform rebels had to demonstrate to foreign visitors that they ran genuine liberated zones. Very likely this relationship strengthened the position of reform-minded and more educated leaders – for example, those with a foreign education and who could speak European languages – as it contributed to an overall strategy of building liberated zones. This affected interests and the conduct of warfare in the lower levels of rebel hierarchies. For example, as the TPLF and EPLF distributed foreign food aid through the village committees that they had set up, they could promote the fortunes of the local people who supported their agendas and suppress any disruption to rebel-provided security and services – a powerful disciplinary tool.[55] Reliable overseas interlocutors and sympathetic foreigners also gave the rebels a channel for presenting their cause in overseas capitals.

---

[55] Gayle Smith, Counting Quintals: Report on a Field Monitoring Visit to Tigray (Utrecht: Dutch Interchurch Aid, 1983), 67–76; Gayle Smith, "The Famine This Time," *Middle East Report* 166 (1990): 13.

Western NGOs were especially prized. Unlike direct aid from states, this sort of aid was not vulnerable to shifts in the foreign policies of distant governments. Western NGOs operated independently, sometimes even in defiance of their home governments' policies. In comparison to anti-colonial and majority rule rebels, they provided the reform rebels with greater leverage to mobilize sympathetic citizens in democratic countries to pressure their government officials on behalf of their rebel friends. Organizations like ERA and REST, for example, provided sympathizers with a steady stream of information about the plight of civilians in areas under their control.

Using NGOs to develop international relations brought reform rebels into more direct contact with overseas members of their own national communities. Many among the estimated 180,000 Eritreans in North America, Europe, and the Middle East contributed to the EPLF's struggle. By the early 1980s these collections had become a regular 2 percent tax on their gross earnings. High levels of EPLF control on the ground and the threat that the EPLF could prohibit abstainers' entry into Eritrean liberated zones or into an independent Eritrea once the EPLF came to power gave overseas Eritreans an incentive to contribute to EPLF coffers. Support committees attached to the humanitarian aid effort took the initiative, organizing annual cultural festivals as venues for visiting EPLF dignitaries to mobilize supporters.[56] The TPFL, RPF, and SPLA tapped ethnic kinsmen through cultural organizations in conjunction with annual folklore events and political strategy meetings, but these new avenues to overseas resources were only open to rebel groups that had established liberated zones and could maintain reliable relations with outsiders by virtue of their own stable institutions and disciplined fighters.

From Failure to Success

The success of reform rebels notwithstanding, the regional politics of rebellion in northeast Africa caused most rebel leaders to succumb to the lure of resources and personal advance as they accepted the agendas of regimes that used them as proxies to destabilize neighbors. As a consequence, these rebels as a whole lost the flexibility that they needed to

---

[56] Tekle Woldemikael, "Political Mobilization and Nationalist Movements, the Case of the Eritrean People's Liberation Front," *Africa Today* 38:2 (1991): 31–42.

establish effective, unified organizations and political programs. Reform rebels avoided this by operating at a relative remove from regional politics and ultimately benefited from their marginalization, or in the case of the RPF, from their ability to exploit the organizational interests and needs of their Ugandan backers. Desperation and the capacity to craft their own strategies to attract and control resources and people reinforced those who promoted political agendas within these rebel organizations. The RPF aside, this gave them the capacity to build administrations that incorporated local authorities and convinced communities that the insurgents could protect them. Did reform rebels require fortuitous circumstances for success, or could individual leaders have crafted new strategies to change their relations with local people? The experiences of the Somali National Movement (SNM) and the SPLA show that not all proxy rebels were fated to remain hostage to the agendas of distant patrons and the interests of opportunist leaders. But these cases show that, although leadership and clever strategies play important roles, breaking free from this path also required the wherewithal to exploit major shifts in regional politics that forced these groups to find new strategies to get the resources that they needed to survive.

The SNM formed in 1981 amid a series of antigovernment demonstrations in northern Somalia and in the wider regional context in which governments tried to influence a crowded field of proxy rebels in neighboring states. Prior to Somalia's loss of the irredentist war in 1977–78 to bring ethnic Somalis in eastern Ethiopia into an expanded Somalia, President Siad Barre backed the Western Somali Liberation Front (WSLF) in Ethiopia, the Northern Frontier District Liberation Front (NFDLF) in northeastern Kenya, and the Front de Libération de la Côte des Somalis (FLCS) in Djibouti. After turning back Barre's attack, Ethiopia's President Mengistu responded in kind with support for the Somali Salvation Democratic Front (SSDF), the Somali Patriotic Movement (SPM), and most consequentially for our considerations, the SNM.

Mengistu kept a watchful eye on his SNM clients, many of whom included defectors from Somalia's army, high-level politicians, and civil servants, and insisted that their headquarters be based in Ethiopia's capital. An early SNM chairman complained that Mengistu was mostly interested in using these rebels as a bargaining chip and to threaten Barre. Ethiopian security forces monitored SNM leaders to make sure that none became powerful enough to challenge the interests of their patron and took advantage of their client organization's dependence on them to arrest people selectively and pass information to leaders who would best serve Mengistu's interests.[57] Mengistu meddled in factional competition within the SNM, selectively pitting one against the other, while keeping the organization just strong enough that it could be used to threaten his enemy to the east or as a bargaining chip.[58]

The SNM's initial fate was to be a bargaining chip. Mengistu's patronage ended suddenly in April 1988, after setbacks in the Ethiopian regime's battle against the Somali government–backed EPLF. He forced the SNM off Ethiopian territory in exchange for the Somali president's pledge to end his support for the EPLF and several other rebel groups. Barre took advantage of this change of events to launch a violent offensive against opposition supporters in Somalia's north. Despite this harsh Somali government attack, SNM leaders knew that they had to move; otherwise the same Ethiopian security forces that had monitored them over the past seven years would kill them. Their return to Somali territory and into refugee centers in this time of crisis forced SNM leaders to negotiate with local clan elders who, despite the turmoil of this period, retained enough authority within their communities-on-the-move to manage the distribution of food in the camps. Moreover some elders played key roles in organizing remittances from abroad. They had taken on these roles several years earlier when harsh government regulations had undermined the formal banking sector. Families had to find alternative means to receive cash from their loved ones who were working overseas. Trusted clan elders and their connections to kinsmen outside of Somalia were the best way for family members to guarantee that money would find its way to intended recipients, even after they also had been forced to flee to refugee camps.[59]

This joint control over resources forced SNM leaders to recognize that they could not get access to the money that they needed to buy guns unless they incorporated local systems of remittance transfers into their own organization. But to control this enough to prevent rivals from gaining access to the resources, they had to continue to consult with non-combatants, who could fairly easily withhold their cooperation. One SNM official reported that this arrangement disadvantaged SNM leaders such as those drawn from the old Somali army, Islamists,

[57] Interview, former high-level SNM official, Hargeisa, 24 June 2006.

[58] Daniel Compagnon, "Dynamiques de mobilization, dissidence armée et rebellion populaire: le cas du Mouvement National Somalien (1981–1990)," *Africa* 47 (1992): 503–30.

[59] Interview, former SNM commander, Hargeisa, 22 June 2006.

socialist ideologues, hard-line nationalists, and clan chauvinists, because those with exotic ideologies or authoritarian habits were less adept at talking to local authorities.[60] This set the pattern for political relations to the extent that when SNM backers made their unilateral declaration of independence for the Republic of Somaliland on 18 May 1991, after a series of inter-clan conferences, it incorporated the "Guurti," the customary organization of clan elders, into the new legislature.

This situation reduced the scope of action for opportunist commanders, as local communities could cut them off from resources. This happened in 1992 and 1994, when two commanders tried to loot local communities to pay followers and buy guns. Apparently they thought that if they could create their own militias, they could fight their way into wider Somali politics, be included in internationally sponsored conflict resolution efforts, and eventually claim a stake in an interim government in the Somali capital. Instead the new Somaliland government forbade participation in peace negotiations connected to the wider Somali conflict, claiming that this gave incentives to opportunists to defect and use violence against their own communities in pursuit of political power in a distant city.[61] Sharing control with local authorities also helped discipline SNM fighters. As a visitor to the area in 1988 observed, SNM fighters had to be careful about whom they attacked, "because their clan and family backgrounds have to be taken into account, and the same holds for any person they might kill."[62] In other words, social sanctions were strong enough to prevent misbehavior. This is not to say that these rebels became an exemplar of human rights observance or democratic governance. It is remarkable, however, the extent to which their organization shifted from a status as a proxy dependent on Ethiopian support, harboring a collection of factions, some of which were predatory in their behavior toward non-combatants, to a rebel group that had to rely on local support for its survival and that built an effective administration.

The SPLA exhibited similar shifts at about the same time. It also suffered the sudden disappearance of its Ethiopian patron. From 1983 it had used Ethiopia as a rear base, while Mengistu used the rebel group to try to destabilize Sudan's government, which in turn supported anti-Mengistu Ethiopians and various separatist rebels. Like the early SNM,

---

[60] Interview, former member of SNM Central Committee, Borama (Somaliland), 25 June 2006.

[61] Interview, Somaliland government official, Hargeisa, 24 June 2006.

[62] Gerard Prunier, "A Candid View of the Somali National Movement," *Horn of Africa* 14 (1991): 107–20.

FIGURE 6. Frontline SPLA at Torit. Photograph by L. J. M. Seymour.

the SPLA relied on Ethiopian security services to police the organization for dissenters but also suffered the whims of the Ethiopian dictator's favor. When Mengistu's regime crumbled in 1991, the SPLA was left without its main patron, and once forced into Sudanese territory, the rival Nasir faction split from the SPLA to create its own Southern Sudan Independence Movement (SSIM).[63] A prominent scholar of Sudan points out that the availability of foreign relief aid facilitated this split, as the new separatist faction could receive benefits directly and, ironically, also gained support from the Sudanese government to fight the SPLA.[64]

By 1994 the SPLA received more support from the Ugandan government but also had to address the problem of its unpopularity in many southern Sudanese communities. That year it held a conference that adopted a seemingly liberal constitution, which helped to reassure the international community that the SPLA was committed to democratic rule and the establishment of local government institutions in liberated zones.[65] This apparent shift also equipped the SPLA to address the demands of US officials. By 1997 US aid flowed through the Sudan

[63] Peter Nyaba, *The Politics of Liberation in South Sudan: An Insider's View* (Kampala: Fountain, 1997).

[64] Johnson, *Root Causes of Sudan's Civil Wars*, 63.

[65] Claire Metelits, "Reformed Rebels? Democratization, Global Norms and the Sudan People's Liberation Army," *Africa Today* 51 (2004): 65–82.

FIGURE 7. Billboard: The Final Walk to Freedom. Photograph by Miklos Gosztonyi.

Transitional Assistance Rehabilitation (STAR) program to SPLA local institutions, and by the end of the 1990s the United States gave about $100 million annually to SPLA-controlled areas. The SPLA's direct relationship with STAR allowed the SPLA to channel aid to supporters and, in turn, caused local people to appeal to SPLA-backed institutions and not to breakaway factions for the services that this aid provided.

The SPLA reforms and a series of "consultations" held through the late 1990s also helped the SPLA integrate their local associates into new administrative structures, demonstrating the link between successful rebel foreign policy and rebel organizations on the ground. Their previous reliance on local chiefs to recruit and discipline fighters meant that many of these authorities found prominent positions in the new administration. Although this did not lead to real democratic reform in southern Sudan, it helped the SPLA to solidify its control of communities and suppress rival rebel groups. This high degree of control ensured that the SPLA was accepted as the sole rebel group representing southern Sudan in the internationally mediated peace agreement, signed in 2005. Under the terms of this agreement, a referendum was

FIGURE 8. John Garang statue at the SPLA Headquarters. Photograph by Miklos Gosztonyi.

held in southern Sudan in January 2011 that determined that the region should become an independent country.

Ingredients of Success

Each successful reform rebel group started as a small group of activists, usually far more educated than their fellow citizens, who then launched small attacks that were supposed to spark widespread rebellions of oppressed people. Each pragmatically evolved into an organization committed to holding and organizing liberated zones. The experiences of these organizations bear out Mao's famous observation: "Because guerrilla warfare basically derives from the masses and is supported by them, it can neither exist nor flourish if it separates itself from their sympathies and cooperation."[66] This task was made easier for the EPLF and TPLF in Ethiopia by a government that insisted on imposing ideas for the reorganization of society on unwilling citizens.

---

[66] Mao Tse-tung (trans. Samuel Griffith), *On Guerrilla Warfare* (New York: Praeger, 1961), 45.

There and elsewhere widespread official human rights abuses and government inability or unwillingness to protect communities contributed
to this evolution; however, abusive and oppressive government is not
a sufficient cause of reform rebel behavior. More important was the
capacity of these rebels to get popular support, usually born out of
desperation and narrowed choices, coupled with leaders willing to jet-
tison rigid attachment to ideologies and political programs. Above all,
leaders of these rebels had to find and develop the political fields of
leverage – political spaces that they could manage and control – to
channel resources, so that their organizations did not become the focus
of intragroup competition or ignore the interests of local populations.
These factors and the new political relationships that they helped to create defeated a momentum toward disorganization and insecurity at a
local level and narrowed the organizational space, limiting the exploitation of opportunists and others with short-term views that focused
mainly on advancing their personal interests at the expense of broader
organizational goals.

The evolution of former proxy rebels into rebels who built liberated
zones and, in the case of the SNM, created their own state and bid
for diplomatic recognition shows that resources alone do not determine
the behavior of rebels. As examples in the next chapter show, other
Somali rebels looted local communities while they relied on incomes
from trade and extortion. The SNM could have followed that path, but
the critical moment of survival forced them to include local community
authorities – clan elders – in their survival strategies. This, like the
SLPA's expulsion from Ethiopia, forced rebels into alliances with people
who already exercised local authority and enjoyed sufficient respect to
convince communities that their lives would be more secure if reform
rebels won. Success also depended on their capacity to master their
international and regional contexts, whether accidentally – through the
circumstance of marginalization at critical points, as was the case for
the early NRM, the TPLF, and the EPLF, or through organizational
insulation and privileged ties to an exclusive patron, as illustrated by
the RPF relations to Uganda – or actively – as demonstrated by the
NRM's ability to push aside a negotiated settlement at the last minute
(1985–86) or by the TPLF's and EPLF's institutional innovations in
coordinating foreign relief aid.

Why are reform rebels so scarce on the African scene? It is not likely
that people in Africa are afflicted by an absence of ideological thought.
Instead the capacity to find political and social space to build effective

organizations and experiment with political ideas appears to be critical
to reform rebel success. This space has grown narrower in many countries since 1994, as the next chapter shows. Moreover the changing
nature of international conflict resolution makes it harder to maintain
rebel cohesion. Most outside mediators want to end conflicts through
the creation of coalition governments. As is argued in the preceding
pages, this prospect of shared power, accessible through force of arms
and not through success in running administrations in liberated zones,
encourages opportunist individuals and factions within what might otherwise have been more program-based rebels. This is particularly true
when rebel leaders face other challenges that limit their capacity to
control fighters and address the factional tendencies that arise at some
point in nearly all of the rebel groups that appear in this book.

The narrowing of the sociopolitical space to construct rebel organizations appears to choke off prospects for contemporary reform insurgencies. This evolution accords with a major message of this book:
that the nature of politics in the states in which they fight plays a key
role in shaping the organization and behavior of rebels. The international context matters too, but ultimately, as strategies of reform rebels
show, this seems to be manageable. In fact, the irony of the reform
rebel experience lies in the relative ease with which leaders can manage
the networks and connections to international society, provided they are
able to carve out some autonomy of action in their regional and national
political environments. Thus the realm of politics within the country –
especially how the rulers that the rebels battle exercise their own authority – emerges as the most important determinant. At first glance, the
relatively weak institutional capabilities of many African states might
be expected to provide ample social space and incentives for reformist
rebels to organize. There are widespread complaints about corrupt and
incompetent state administrations, the predations of individual officials, blocked paths of upward mobility for the educated who lack good
political connections, and the broken promises of government reform.
In fact, this space is filled with informal networks of state power, with
clandestine commercial rackets tied to politicians and to armed groups
that operate sometimes as bandits and at other times as enforcers for
politicians.

Leaders of reform rebels found refuge from some of these forces,
but it appears that the arenas for organizing, like the University of Dar
es Salaam in the 1960s, the NRA's Luwero sanctuary, the networks of
alienated local bosses in Tigray, and so forth, are harder to find now. As

African societies have become more urbanized, and as patronage politics has penetrated into more aspects of people's lives in some countries,
the propensity for strife to produce reform rebels has declined. Would-
be reform rebels are crowded out by leaders of politicians' militias, the
business associates of deposed presidents, and the junior bosses in old
political patronage networks who emerge as the main organizers of rebel
organizations. They apply their skills to extracting resources and their
old political networks to the tasks of organizing their own bids for state
power. The next chapter considers these important developments in
the evolution of warfare.

CHAPTER 5

Warlord Rebels

Widespread fighting started in 1996 in Zaire, which in 1997 was renamed the Democratic Republic of Congo. According to one estimate, by 2004 this conflict had killed 3.9 million people from direct violence and the effects of the breakdown of public order.[1] By 1994, four years of fighting in Liberia had driven more than 794,000 people, about 30 percent of the country's population, to seek refuge in neighboring countries.[2] About 30 percent of Sierra Leone's population, or 1.15 million people, were internally displaced or became refugees in 1999, the eighth year of that war.[3] These measures of disorder reflected the failure of warlord rebels to build liberated zones, protect non-combatants, or rally people around convincing political programs as alternatives to corrupt or oppressive regimes. Warlord rebels tended to devote at least as much time to fighting among themselves as to fighting government forces. Much the same can be said of government forces that also suffered factional splits and preyed on their own citizens.

Warlords dominated conflicts in the 1990s and early 2000s in Liberia, Sierra Leone, Côte d'Ivoire, and Guinea-Bissau. They also played major roles in Congo, Somalia, and elsewhere. People in these

[1] Benjamin Coghlan, Richard Brennan, Pascal Ngoy, David Dofana, Brad Otto, Mark Clements, and Tony Stewart, "Mortality in the Democratic Republic of Congo," *Lancet* 367 (7 Jan 2006): 44–51.

[2] Office of the United Nations High Commissioner for Refugees, *Populations of Concern to UNHCR: A Statistical Overview, 1994* (Geneva: UNHCR, 1995), table 7.

[3] United Nations High Commissioner for Refugees, *Refugees and Others of Concern to UNHCR: 1999 Statistical Overview* (Geneva: Registration and Statistical Unit, UNHCR, 2000), 8, 29.

places often saw warlord rebels as at least as corrupt and oppressive
as their often-violent and disorganized governments. Although some
warlords had significant support from communities that stood to benefit if the warlord was able to seize state power, warlords did not court
mass domestic or foreign support. Outsiders, especially African governments, that did support them were not driven by reformist or revolutionary impulses and instead saw these rebels as cheap tools for influ-
encing politics in other countries. By the 1990s, rebel politics shifted
from the university classroom and activist networks that supplied the
leadership of the rebel groups discussed in previous chapters and that
connected them to popular authority figures and grassroots critics to
warlords who emerged out of the internecine struggles of politicians.
A key feature of warlord rebel leaders is that they were products of
the systems of political authority that they fought. Even as they fought
to overthrow regimes to become their country's new political leaders,
there was little that was even vaguely reformist in their public agendas.
As they fought, they just appropriated the existing instruments of political power and used them in even more intensive ways at the expense of
building bureaucratic institutions. Because warlords and governments
ran organizations in much the same way, this meant that both relied on
small units to fight in irregular warfare and that both suffered similar
levels of internecine conflict, faced similarly constant factional splits,
and exhibited a similar disinterest in running liberated zones (or simply
governing).

Global politics in the 1990s did little to block this evolution of
warfare. By the 1990s, there were few foreign backers who cared
whether rebels set up effective liberated zones or fielded commissars to assert political and administrative control over fighters. Many
NGOs professed commitments to political neutrality and negotiated
with whomever controlled access to distressed civilians. Because distress
attracted foreign support, the supply of resources may have encouraged
more predatory behavior on the part of warlords and certainly gave
them few incentives to protect the people under their control. The willingness of many international institutions and foreign governments to
negotiate with all combatants rewarded the violent and predatory behavior of faction leaders, making it easier for subordinates to set up their
own factions. Thus prudent warlords were wary of relying on the would-
be cadres and commissars needed to build staff and control effective
administrations in liberated zones or of recruiting popular and effective commanders to launch offensives. Although this prevented more

able leaders from taking over these rebel groups, it also contributed to military deadlocks. As no single group could deliver the decisive blow to the rest, conflicts tended to drag on. Splits still occurred, but this just produced new groups that were unable to swallow up or defeat the original group. Thus a journalist working in Somalia wrote, "by late 1991 there were nearly 40 distinct bandit groups in the capital alone."[4] Representatives of seven different armed groups signed the 1995 Abuja Accord in an effort to end fighting in Liberia, and Congo's war featured multiple personal networks that produced scores of factions.

This fragmentation empowered armed groups that had agendas other than seizing state power. These groups, called parochial rebels (subject of the next chapter), appeared in many other conflicts, but they played a more significant role in warlord conflicts. Many grew out of the networks and identities of local communities as people organized to defend themselves from the disorder of state collapse and the predations of warlord rebels. Some parochial rebels, often known as militias, who protected communities organized their own relations with commercial networks. Others joined warlord rebels as partners. Some warlords sponsored parochial rebels, just as states sponsored militias to exert influence in places and among people whom they could not control directly.

These interlocking relationships produced very complex conflicts. Many warlord rebel groups broke into multiple factions. These wars were very hard to end because there were so many different combatant groups and there was not a central command, either on the rebel or on the government side, that could issue a command to quit fighting and disarm and disperse. This extensive use of proxies also tangled up broader agendas for fighting with the politics of those who fought for intensely local reasons. The nature of prewar politics, especially its engagement with illicit and criminal businesses, shaped this intersection of interests. Legacies of prewar politics turned access to and control over resources at the expense of political organizing into targets for ambitious individuals. Although membership in warlord rebel groups and militias empowered individuals in a variety of ways, personal advantages that maximized access to resources in this violent and competitive environment and thus elevated the possessor into key positions grew in value out of proportion to other motives for fighting. As

---

[4] Scott Peterson, *Me against My Brother: At War in Somalia, Sudan, and Rwanda* (New York: Routledge, 2000), 21.

before, the evolution of warfare in this direction reflected changes in prewar state politics, a topic to which we turn next.

Warlords and States

Africa's warlords are products of prewar violent systems of personal rule in which presidential power depended on personal control over economic resources, including in illicit trades, to be doled out to loyal associates. Dominating what were ostensibly private or even illegal transactions was a critical tool for managing politics. Regime critics and opponents faced serious organizational obstacles when access to almost any source of income, even an illicit one, was dependent on some sort of accommodation with members of the president's political clique. This high level of control, ironic in that it was a key cause of the bureaucratic incapacity that made these states so weak in institutional terms, gave rulers powerful instruments that they could use to co-opt critics, divide opposition communities, and discipline individual political actors.

Their status as officials of sovereign states gave these rulers the capacity to manipulate regulations and selectively enforce laws to protect their supporters. Some presidents allowed subordinates to carry out transactions that were officially outlawed, and they shielded from outside scrutiny the occasional international outlaw who counted among their business partners. Some presidents allowed their more reliable associates to organize their own militias. Militias were useful coercive political tools to target regime opponents and co-opt young men who were ambitious, angry, bored, or just struggling to survive – the same sort that rebels in previous chapters recruited – and rulers used them as muscle to dominate commercial ventures. Thus even as the bureaucratic capacity of states shrank, holding state office remained as integral as ever to exercising political authority through controlling and regulating other people's access to resources. Even black marketers and others who operated in the old fields of leverage beyond the grasp of tax collectors and state regulations had to come to an accommodation with politicians – who had become the real middlemen who controlled access to all sorts of opportunities.

This exercise of political authority exploited the interdependence of formal and informal dimensions of power. In these systems of authority it became very difficult for individuals to become old-fashioned bandits or outlaws as true outsiders to the political establishment, because the political system had co-opted banditry and outlaw behavior as part of its mechanisms of control. These societies thus lost important fields of leverage, the social space and resources that previously would have harbored and sustained outsiders and critics and would have provided valuable recruits and networks for the ideological rebels discussed in previous chapters. Instead, these networks linked prewar political players to global and regional economic networks and created a milieu that supplied many of the continent's warlords. The appearance of warlords in greater numbers in the 1990s and their behavior as insurgents were directly tied to this evolution of regime politics in some countries in Africa. The power struggles of these middlemen presaged warlord rebellions, and most warlords began as political faction leaders within their own states. But before the 1990s, their competition for power was registered in palace coups and the jockeying of self-aggrandizing insiders within the still-centralized personalist systems of authority.

Prewar presidents in Sierra Leone, Liberia, Somalia, and Zaire (Congo) controlled resources and, in the more extreme cases, exercised coercion in much the same manner as warlords did later. It became difficult to distinguish between regime and criminal syndicates when politicians partnered with foreign businessmen to tap into resources and services from international illicit markets. Government officials and ethnic Lebanese businessmen dominated Sierra Leone's clandestine diamond trade from the mid-1970s. By the early 1980s, they sponsored paramilitaries that outnumbered the country's army by four to one to protect their operations and to assert their authority. "These activities are encouraged from a high level," wrote an observer,[5] and they fused clandestine economies with the exercise of violence for private gain and political authority.

Well-placed individuals launched their own bids for power when presidential control over these networks faltered. The first starter advantage of being or of having been close to the resources and relationships of power shaped the patterns of recruitment and the kinds of agendas that would drive rebellions. A warlord's fighters still could avenge past personal injustices, provide for families, loot, or seek excitement or protection; these reasons for joining were not so different from those in other conflicts. The primary difference lay in the absence of ideological leadership. The dominance of aggressive and enterprising insiders

[5] "Sierra Leone: The Unending Chaos," *Africa Confidential* 23: 21 (20 Oct 1982): 6.

in formal and clandestine economies deprived the old-fashioned rebels of the traditional margins of state power and other protected social enclaves, such as universities, that rebels needed to organize their fight against corrupt regimes and violent and greedy politicians. Even clandestine trades that had historically helped to fund rebel challenges to states were not exempt. As a scholar found in Congo in the 1980s, black market operators usually had to collude with local or regional government officials.[6] Networks that under other circumstances facilitated broad-based ideological rebellions became integral to sustaining warlords.

Ibrahim Abdullah astutely saw the failure of Sierra Leone's university students to lead the rebellion against their corrupt government in the 1990s as a distinctive feature of that conflict. Gangs, some allied with politicians, security forces, and government-backed student agitators, he argued, overwhelmed the students' efforts to organize opposition around an ideological program, despite widespread popular agreement that the country's problems lay in the corrupt administration of the self-interested president and his cronies.[7] These students were not alone in finding the university to be a diminishing platform for rebellion. By the 1980s, economic problems hit universities especially hard. During the 1990s, about 20,000 academic staff emigrated from the continent each year; 10,000 academics from Nigeria were employed in the United States alone at mid-decade.[8] World Bank researchers estimated that at the start of the twenty-first century, one third of Africa's professionals had departed. In an extreme case, every doctor in one graduating class at the University of Zimbabwe left the country.[9]

One does not have to have professors or doctors to launch rebellions. But as is shown in previous chapters, the bulk of Africa's ideologically motivated rebel leadership came from this milieu. Universities provide social spaces for activists to develop ideas and programs, to connect with political players with deep roots in communities in distant provinces, and to figure out how to organize and mobilize people with diverse personal motives for fighting. This pattern of rebel recruitment and

---

[6] Vwakyanakazi Mukohya, "Import and Export in the Second Economy in North Kivu," in Janet MacGaffey (ed.), *The Real Economy of Zaire: The Contribution of Smuggling and Other Unofficial Activities to National Wealth* (Philadelphia: University of Pennsylvania Press, 1991), 43–71.

[7] Ibrahim Abdullah, "Bush Path to Destruction: The Origin and Character of the Revolutionary United Front (RUF/SL)," *Africa Development* 22:3 (1997): 45–76.

[8] Ibrahim Jumare, "The Displacement of the Nigerian Academic Community," *Journal of Asian and African Studies* 32:1 (1997): 113.

[9] Kyle Brown, "Africa's Loss in the Brain Drain," *West Africa*, 27 May 2002, 20.

discipline established ties to communities before fighting began, and this led to more resources. This process was reversed when political bosses with privileged connections to networks that were built around controlling access to resources sought to acquire weapons and attract recruits. These warlords pushed civic oppositions to the margins of politics. Liberia's Movement for Justice in Africa (MOJA) and other prodemocracy movements in the 1980s such as that led by Étienne Tshisekedi in Congo were considerably more effective than warlords at mobilizing large numbers of people to take personal risks to oppose government repression. But once these patronage-based political networks began to break apart, armed conflict followed along the social and economic networks of competition between warlord factions.

Anton Blok described a similar dynamic in his study of Sicilian bandits who operated in the island's criminal networks and colluding state bureaucracies. "Rather than actual champions of the poor and the weak, bandits quite often terrorized those from whose very ranks they managed to rise, and thus helped to suppress them."[10] Blok explained that people who joined these organizations were drawn to collaborations with local strongmen who had good connections to illicit economic opportunities through partnerships with corrupt politicians. These connections, which in many cases became the only realistic path of upward mobility, impeded large-scale organizing among peasants. For individual fighters, their patron's connections gave them closer contact to regional economies and protected them from retaliation from the communities that they jointly exploited. But the local notables were the real beneficiaries of bandit plunder in having co-opted would-be radicals to protect their system of exploitation.[11]

Likewise, in warlord rebellions it was not material resources that shaped the behavior of leaders and fighters so much as relationships in the political systems out of which they emerged. Recruits who would have been rejected or who would have faced harsh discipline in other circumstances found themselves free (or forced) to pursue personal interests that were more avaricious and violent than other leaderships would have tolerated. The irony of this is that the places where individuals might seem to be most receptive to a revolutionary or reform rebel's appeal were those that were least likely to see such a rebellion

---

[10] Anton Blok, "The Peasant and the Brigand: Social Banditry Reconsidered," *Comparative Studies in Society and History* 14:4 (Sept 1972): 496.

[11] Anton Blok, *The Mafia of a Sicilian Village, 1860–1960: A Study of Violent Peasant Entrepreneurs* (Oxford: Blackwell, 1974), 99–102.

develop. In fact, those who pushed political programs were often singled out as special targets of repression and co-optation in conflicts. Jeremy Weinstein observed that "where resources permit, opportunistic rebel leaders crowd out activists."[12] A refugee from Liberia explained how this kind of selection process cowed others, as aggressive fighters created conditions "in which the fear of death and humiliation puts the genuine adults and achievers into their shells. The vacuum is then filled in by the young ones who become dare devils, not caring about death or any related end."[13] Although it is easy to conclude that these fighters come from delinquents focused on fulfilling personal desires, the analysis in previous chapters suggests that some 1990s warlord rebel recruits could have become distinguished liberation fighters in different circumstances. Over time, the material resources available to rebels do not vary hugely. The changes in the social and political contexts in which leaders arise and resources are used are much more significant in producing warlord conflicts. Differences in the governance of prewar states explain why those with broad political programs did not appear in the place of warlords to mobilize widespread popular frustration about corruption and violence, or why people who were otherwise forced to live with the negative personal consequences of collapsing state administrations did not lead rebellions.

Why Warlords in the 1990s?

Some scholars applied the term "warlord" to those fighting in Chad in the late 1970s up to the installation of Hissène Habré as president in 1982. That situation seemed to fit Chinese leader Chiang Kai-shek's denunciation of Chinese rebel warlords in the 1910s and 1920s as consisting of competing armed groups who operated autonomously of the collapsed state, who relied on foreign support to survive, and who lacked political principle and enriched the leaders of rebel groups.[14] But many of Chad's rebel groups had strong ties to clan elders and other authorities whose authority predated the state and who maintained

---

[12] Jeremy Weinstein, *Inside Rebellion* (New York: Cambridge University Press, 2007), 52.

[13] K. Moses Nagbe, *Bulk Challenge: The Story of 4000 Liberians in Search of Refuge* (Cape Coast: Champion, 1996), 53.

[14] Roger Carlton and Roy May, "Warlords and Militarism in Chad," *Review of African Political Economy* 16:45 and 46 (1989), 20.

considerable autonomy in their own local affairs. Many of these groups were ethnic militias that defended local interests, although others fit in the warlord category in that some of their leaders used prior positions in the state to mobilize resources and recruits beyond the reach of the formal institutions of the state to try to overthrow the incumbent regime.

Congo's eastern rebellion in the mid-1960s was a warlord precursor. Amid the breakdown of state authority, the Conseil national de libération (CNL) produced unruly fighters, widespread violence against civilians, and an absence of effectively administered liberated zones. "Once they took over provincial or district headquarters," wrote one scholar, "the first item of business was to occupy the official mansion and to enjoy the privileges of office which included money, tradable commodities such as gold, and a life of pleasure."[15] This behavior frustrated Che Guevara, the Cuban revolutionary leader sent by Fidel Castro to advise these rebels. Guevara complained that Laurent Kabila, then under his tutelage and later a key wartime figure in the 1990s, let "days pass without concerning himself with anything other than political squabbles, and all the signs are that he is too addicted to drink and women." Guevara did not think much of the fighters either; after a successful ambush, "the brilliant victors realized that the greatest prize was on top of the lorry: namely, bottles of beer and whiskey."[16] Here was an emissary who came with political ideas and connections to a foreign patron who could have brought more resources and organizational control, and still Kabila was not swayed. Were it not for his reappearance in the 1990s, Kabila would have remained a footnote to the history of warfare in Africa, a demonstration of how to fail in rebellion in the 1960s.

Kabila's CNL failure in the 1960s in part had to do with the fact that there was a less intensive network of official patronage from which to draw resources, compared to the 1990s. Most of the region's mining economy was still in the hands of foreign firms, protected by Belgian military advisors who led foreign mercenaries to beat back the rebels. President Mobutu's nationalization of major mining operations (1967) and his seizure of smaller firms (1973) to turn over to his political supporters lay in the future, when it laid the foundations for the political

---

[15] Georges Nzongola-Ntalaja, *The Congo from Leopold to Kabila* (New York: Zed Books, 2002), 133.

[16] Ernesto [Che] Guevara, *The African Dream: The Diaries of the Revolutionary War in the Congo* (New York: Grove Press, 1999), 69, 67.

networks that became prizes in fighting in the 1990s. In the 1960s, these resources and their multinational firm exploiters attracted foreign help on Mobutu's behalf. Then French and Moroccan military support broke a separatist rebellion in southeastern Congo in 1977, and Belgian support was critical in ending one in 1978. But unlike the 1960s rebellions, those in the 1970s involved politicians who had been insiders in a regime that was in the process of building its authority on channeling the economy into patronage networks. Had these revolts been allowed to unfold, perhaps warfare would have looked much as it did in the 1990s.

External support for African regimes began to become less reliable in the early 1980s. Soviet officials acknowledged that their aid to Africa's "revolutionaries" actually supported faction-ridden regimes with minimal commitments to real socialist policies. When Ghana's Flight Lieutenant Jerry Rawlings visited Moscow in December 1981 after his coup, Soviet officials "pointed to their own problems which they said made it difficult for them to offer much help, and advised Ghana to go to the IMF," noted a prominent journalist.[17] US officials shored up client regimes throughout the 1980s, pressuring international institutions to make loans to Mobutu's Zaire (Congo) against the advice of IMF experts, and supporting Liberia's dictator Samuel K. Doe after his theft of an election in October 1985. But by 1990, US interest and material support for these regimes was in rapid decline, and the US Congress took more interest in condemning dictators for human rights abuses.

The collapse of the centralized patronage network in the 1990s in Sierra Leone, a country that was less dependent on foreign financial or diplomatic support than Congo or Liberia or Somalia, showed that the sudden withdrawal of foreign backing was not a necessary condition to provoke regime collapse and the outbreak of warlord conflicts. Sierra Leone's politicians financed their own networks through control over legal and illicit diamond trades. But as Sierra Leone's regime faced an armed threat from across the Liberian border in March 1991, global attention was focused elsewhere. The United States and its allies were preoccupied with their attack on Saddam's Iraq, which began on 17 January 1991; just nine days before Somali president Siad Barre had fled Mogadishu in an armored vehicle.

---

[17] Quote in Baffour Agyeman-Duah, "Ghana, 1982–6: The Politics of the P.N.D.C.," *Journal of Modern African Studies* 25:4 (Dec 1987): 631.

Light arms played an important role in warlord conflicts that lacked the kinds of centralized organizations needed to launch frontal assaults or to build more conventional armed forces. Mobile small units of fighters relied heavily on the AK-47 light automatic rifles that were ubiquitous in warlord conflicts. These assault rifles were easy to maintain and use and were relatively inexpensive. The average world price in the mid-1990s stood at about $400 for a new, fully equipped AK-47.[18] The spread of cheap mobile telephones and Internet technology undermined the role of institutions like the Eduardo Mondlane Institute or the United Nations Institute for Namibia that previously used control over global contacts and information to exercise organizational or ideological dominance over recruits to channel them into internationally "approved" rebel groups.

The influx of NGOs to conflict zones helped warlords and promoted rebel fragmentation. Rebels could use the humanitarian crises that they created to attract foreign NGO relief aid. Fighters infiltrated refugee camps and commandeered supplies while commanders used crises to insert themselves into diplomatic efforts to resolve conflicts. Humanitarian justifications for NGO intervention also transformed political issues into moral tasks, obscuring the reasons why people fought and the interests at stake and avoiding arguments about the real impact of their presence. Part of this real impact included NGO help to support populations under warlord control, releasing these rebels from old tasks of administering liberated zones.[19] The delivery of aid thus linked foreign NGO interests to those of the rebels with whom they had to negotiate. This undermined the old system, which drew ambitious commanders to join an "official" rebel group as a condition of outside assistance, because most NGOs did not require that rebels demonstrate their capacity to operate a liberated zone or display a particular ideology or program as a condition for receiving aid.

These developments presented African governments with dilemmas. Officials in Nigeria, for example, were concerned that warlords would undermine regional stability, create humanitarian crises, and provoke interventions by regional rivals. Other rulers sought out relations with warlords to circumvent constraints of their domestic politics. Some officials in Zimbabwe and Uganda, for example, personally benefited

---

[18] Phillip Killicoat, "Weaponomics: The Global Market for Assault Rifles," World Bank Working Paper (Washington, DC: World Bank, April 2007), 21–23.

[19] Sarah Kenyon Lischer, "Collateral Damage: Humanitarian Assistance as a Cause of Conflict," *International Security* 28:1 (Summer 2003): 79–109.

from their governments' intervention in the war in Congo in the late 1990s. This was a double-edged sword, as it helped to maintain existing patronage networks at the same time that it potentially empowered field officers and lower-level politicians to make their own deals with local warlords and perhaps challenge their political patrons back home. Some officials made compelling cases that their countries faced serious security threats from warlords in Congo, even as those directly involved in interventions sometimes benefited from personal ties to warlord rebels. This made interventions especially dangerous, as they tended to deprofessionalize armies as officers and soldiers became tangled up in the politics and commerce associated with their contacts with other armed groups.

Although warlord rebels in the 1990s appeared in environments that had become more accommodating to small, non-ideologically driven armed groups, no single factor appears to have predestined countries to warlord conflicts. As the reader will see in the following discussion, substantial elements of Sierra Leone's conflict were imported from neighboring Liberia. Around the same time, Nigeria's politics suffered an intensified personalization of power and patronage politics under the rule of General Sani Abacha (1994–98) without collapsing into wholesale warlord conflict. Central authority in three states on Guinea's borders collapsed amid factional fighting in the 1990s, but that country did not follow suit. Somalia's conflict has had substantial warlord elements, but not everywhere or at all times.

Although the preceding factors are not sufficient conditions for warlord conflicts, they appear to be necessary ones. The strongest risk factor was political systems with extensive emphasis on patronage and personal loyalties as bases of political authority. Thus O Mais Velho (The Eldest One), the personality cult of Jonas Savimbi of União Nacional para a Independência Total de Angola (UNITA), evolved from a Maoist-inspired anti-colonial rebellion in the 1970s and 1980s, with liberated zones and political indoctrination (even if it occasionally coordinated with Portuguese colonial forces for tactical purposes), to a warlord rebellion that used famine as a weapon of war and shifted its operational focus to the diamond mines to produce revenues for its arms purchases in illicit markets. When government forces killed Savimbi on 22 February 2002, the war ended, as UNITA lacked an institutional framework to succeed him. The stark contrast between the early days of UNITA's Maoist organization and the later days of Savimbi's cult of personality shows the importance of particular political contexts in shaping the organization of rebels and other armed groups. For example, at the same time that UNITA imploded, Eritrean and Ethiopian armies fought a war with front lines and heavy artillery over a contested border that killed between 70,000 and 100,000 soldiers.[20] The highly centralized reform rebels in the previous chapter had become the governments of their states, and they fought one another in ways that contrasted starkly with the warfare of the deeply personalized political networks such as Savimbi's UNITA and in the states in West Africa to which we now turn.

Warlords in West Africa

Before leading the attack of the National Patriotic Front of Liberia (NPFL) against Liberian president Samuel K. Doe's regime in 1989, Charles Taylor emerged in politics as an activist in Liberian student organizations. While at Bentley College in Boston, he earned his BA in economics in 1977 and then served as chairman of the Union of Liberian Associations in the Americas (ULAA). Styling himself a radical Pan-African student activist, Taylor led an occupation of Liberia's UN mission in New York in 1979 during the visit of Liberian President Tolbert. Instead of pressing charges, Tolbert paid for Taylor and the ULAA's secretary-general to visit Liberia to consider working for the government.[21] Tolbert's invitations really were offers of power and personal advantage tied to presidential favor. When prominent critics accepted these invitations, observers would grow cynical about prospects for reform as the onetime activists were seen enjoying the benefits of presidential favor. Nonetheless, Tolbert still faced considerable opposition. In 1973, a group of university students organized MOJA, a West Africa–wide organization in solidarity with the struggles against apartheid and Portuguese colonial rule.[22] Taylor's student activism in the United States also associated him with the Progressive Alliance of Liberia (PAL), an overseas Liberian student group supportive of MOJA's liberation agenda. By 1979, these groups sponsored

[20] Tekeste Negash and Kjetil Tronvoll, *Brothers at War: Making Sense of the Eritrean-Ethiopian War* (Athens: Ohio University Press, 2000), 99–103.

[21] Matthew Brelis, "Rebel's Saga: Mass Jail to Showdown for Power," *Boston Globe*, 31 July 1990, A1.

[22] Togba Nah Tipoteh, *General Report to Second Congress, Movement for Justice in Africa* (Monrovia: MOJA, March 1980).

protests and supported the first serious opposition party candidates seen in Liberian elections in several decades. Taylor's arrival in Monrovia in March 1980 to discuss an official appointment occurred in a context in which students and civic activists might have become the nucleus of a reform rebellion like Uganda's National Resistance Army (NRA) or Ethiopia's Tigray People's Liberation Front (TPLF). But the course of Liberian politics marginalized these activists while it elevated Taylor and others who operated in political insider networks.

Taylor arrived in Liberia in time for the 12 April 1980 coup in which his would-be patron was murdered and the twenty-eight-year-old Sergeant Doe took power. Fortunately for Taylor, his friend Thomas Quiwonkpa was among the coup plotters and became the head of the army. Taylor then became the director of the General Services Agency, the government's overseas procurement office, which gave him personal authority over government contracts. Amid claims that he had stolen money from his office, in 1983 Taylor fled to the United States. The ULAA denounced Taylor in October 1983, branding him part of a "bunch of opportunists who decided to go and get their share of the apple pie in the PRC [Doe] Government."[23] Because the United States had an extradition treaty with Liberia, Doe's foreign minister, Ernest Eastman, and attorney-general, Lavalie Supuwood, asked US authorities to arrest Taylor to face corruption charges back in Liberia. From May 1984, Taylor was held in an American prison, but he escaped in September 1985 and returned to West Africa. By 1990, Eastman had joined Taylor as his spokesman for international affairs, and Supuwood was Taylor's legal advisor.

Taylor fled Liberia as Quiwonkpa's popularity within the army threatened Doe's capacity to use the army and security forces against his enemies. Doe faced another threat from his former rural development minister, Samuel Dokie, who organized a raid from neighboring Guinea on 21 November 1983. When the raid failed, Quiwonkpa, who came from the same region as Dokie, realized that Doe would blame him, so he and his aide-de-camp and future NPFL commander, Prince Johnson, fled to the United States. Quiwonkpa was killed after his own failed coup attempt on 12 November 1985. Government reprisals in his home region killed as many as 3,000 people,[24] including two of

---

[23] Edward Wonkeryor, *Liberia Military Dictatorship: A Fiasco "Revolution"* (Chicago: Strugglers' Community Press, 1985), 167.

[24] Bill Berkeley, *Liberia: A Promise Betrayed, a Report on Human Rights* (New York: Lawyer's Committee on Human Rights, 1986).

Dokie's brothers. This turned these communities into a sympathetic entry point for the NPFL invasion in 1989. By that time there was widespread popular anger against Doe's regime, an organized civilian opposition was growing, and the government was losing control of the situation. But events showed that it was the character of the disintegration of Doe's political network rather than the abundant grievances among most Liberians or the political narratives of Liberian ideologues that weighed most heavily in shaping the rebel groups that emerged.

Doe had enemies across West Africa, many of whom were former members of his political network. Their old positions provided them with important contacts and access to resources when they fled. One government official who fled Liberia in 1982 played a typical role in connecting different political networks. He was married to the daughter of the murdered President Tolbert and was related by marriage to Félix Houphouët-Boigny, the president of Côte d'Ivoire. His daughter was the widow of the slain Liberian president's son, who also was murdered. The widow then joined the entourage of Blaise Compaoré, the head of the Burkina Faso army, who, unlike Quiwonkpa, successfully seized power in 1987. This family history connected the Ivorian president to Doe's enemies and may have made Houphouët-Boigny more willing to provide Taylor's NPFL with a rear base at a time when major international backing for rebels was declining.[25] But first, when Taylor arrived back in West Africa, his contact with Compaoré introduced Taylor to the Libyan leader Muammar Qaddafi, who provided him with an estimated 700 Burkinabes, who fought alongside the NPFL in Liberia.[26]

Taylor's connection to Compaoré helped convince Libyan officials that Taylor was a credible rebel leader, giving him an advantage over other anti-Doe politicians like Joe Wylie, later to join the armed group Liberians United for Reconciliation and Democracy (LURD), and Prince Johnson, an NPFL commander who would later split with Taylor to form the Independent National Patriotic Front of Liberia (INPFL). Support from Libya and Burkina Faso elevated Taylor's prospects over those of more popular Liberian dissidents. Many of them went to Ghana after Doe stole the presidential election that homegrown critics and international pressure had forced on him in 1985. Popular leaders with

---

[25] Stephen Ellis, *The Mask of Anarchy: The Destruction of Liberia and the Religious Dimensions of an African Civil War* (New York: New York University Press, 1999), 66–67.

[26] S. Byron Tarr, "The ECOMOG Initiative in Liberia: A Liberian Perspective," *Issue* 21:1 (1993): 80.

experience in organizing civic activists – like Amos Sawyer, a MOJA leader and a University of Liberia professor with a PhD in political science from Northwestern University, and Jackson Doe (not related to the president), the real winner of the 1985 poll – fled Doe's repression. Ghana's government gave them refuge, and the influence of these activists among Ghana's officials led to Taylor's arrest on at least two occasions when he visited Ghana. The activists portrayed Taylor as corrupt, and one person who met Taylor in Ghana speculated that Taylor was the sort who might finance his rise to power through "the easy option of granting banking facilities to drug barons who have billions of dollars for laundering."[27]

Back in Liberia, the intellectuals and civic activists – the would-be ideological rebels – faced Doe's wrath. Following arrests of student leaders at the University of Liberia in 1981 and 1982, repression in 1984 turned lethal. The university was closed, which meant that the 7,000 or so enrolled at the country's two main universities lost their venue for political discussion and organizing to oppose Doe's one-party dictatorship.[28] Student leaders were jailed, flogged, and threatened with death, while President Doe's Decree 2A banned "student politics in any form or for whatever purpose whatsoever."[29] Professors left for overseas jobs as salaries declined by 85 percent from 1980 to the mid-1990s.[30] In defining the country's political future, the great majority of activists and their supporters in these institutions faced significant obstacles in the form of competition with defectors from Doe's entourage who had moved abroad and who benefited from the personal connections and resources that previous political insider status provided.

Although repression hindered civic opposition, challenges from Doe's former associates were serious, just as an 80 percent reduction of US aid after the stolen presidential election limited his resources. Doe's response was to widen the reach of his patronage network further into smuggling rackets and partnerships with shady foreign operators. This shift in the organization of Doe's patronage network brought to Liberia

---

[27] Kwesi Yankah, "Charles Taylor: Dark Days in Ghana," *Uhuru* [Accra] 5 (1990): 38.

[28] Patrick Seyon, "Liberia," in Damtew Teferra and Philip Altbach (eds.), *African Higher Education* (Bloomington: Indiana University Press, 2003), 381–90.

[29] Berkeley, *Liberia: A Promise Betrayed*, 157.

[30] Anthony Barclay, "The Political Economy of Brain Drain at Institutions of Higher Learning in Conflict Countries: Case of the University of Liberia," *African Issues* 30:1 (2002): 44.

individuals who could do business with Taylor and other warlords after 1989 and helped to strengthen the hand of former insiders who built their warlord rebel groups on the framework of Doe's old associates and their connections. One such associate, a Dutch businessman, later helped Taylor manage the timber industry to finance arms purchases.[31] Doe's old finance minister reemerged during the war as "economic advisor" to Taylor and director of an air transport company accused of transporting arms.[32] Such individuals played multiple roles in Doe's, and then in Taylor's, political networks. Some of them combined roles as government officials (if they were Liberian) with roles as local fixers and as private businessmen with influential overseas contacts.

Rebel leaders and would-be leaders previously encountered in this book did not face such a wide array of well-funded and connected political insiders as competitors while being so limited in their own institutional and material resources. The South African and Rhodesian security forces attempts to use pseudo-guerrillas and other armed groups to make up for resource scarcity and to disrupt and confuse real rebels forced these rebels to focus on short-term survival at the expense of long-term political projects, to the disadvantage of the ideologues who conceived them. But the weeding out process against ideologically inclined would-be rebels with real popular support was much more effective in Liberia and in other venues with warlord rebels. NPFL members like Elmer Johnson, a former Boston University student and US Marine, were able strategists and sought recruits through articulating popular narratives. But this popularity threatened Taylor's leadership. Elmer Johnson died in an ambush behind NPFL lines in June 1990. Civilian politicians held a lot of appeal among the rank and filers drawn to the NPFL soon after the 1989 invasion. When Jackson Doe, the real winner of the 1985 election, appeared behind NPFL lines in mid-1990, "there was a very very big festival in the middle of the war to celebrate that a leader of our people had been saved."[33] But he was not seen again and was presumed to have been murdered.

---

[31] United Nations Security Council, *Report of the Panel of Experts Appointed Pursuant to United Nations Security Council Resolution 1306 (2000), Paragraph 19 in Relation to Sierra Leone* (New York: United Nations, Dec 2000), para. 215.

[32] United Nations Security Council, "List of Individuals Subject to the Measures Imposed by Paragraph 4 of Security Council Resolution 1521 (2003) Concerning Liberia," 2 May 2005. Some of Doe's business relations are detailed in a letter to him, 7 Jan 1989 (copy in author's possession).

[33] Letter of Tom Woewiyu [former associate of Charles Taylor], Monrovia, 19 July 1994.

While the civic opposition was under attack, other ambitious former members of the old political network competed with one another. Prince Johnson split with Taylor early in the war to race to the capital. The arrival of the Nigerian-led Economic Community of West African States Monitoring Force (ECOMOG) in August 1990 denied Johnson and his several hundred fighters the prize of Liberia's presidency, even though Johnson's INPFL later managed to capture and kill Doe. Doe's old information minister, Alhaji G. V. Kromah, emerged in September 1991 as the head of the United Liberation Movement for Democracy (ULIMO), an alliance of former Armed Forces of Liberia (AFL) commanders and about 12,000 recruits from among AFL soldiers and refugees in Guinea and Sierra Leone. ULIMO's first leader was Raleigh Seekie, a deputy finance minister in Doe's regime. In September 1994, AFL commander Roosevelt Johnson took 8,000 fighters to form ULIMO-J, while Kromah's core became ULIMO-K. George Boley organized the Liberia Peace Council (LPC) in 1993 with about 2,500 fighters in southeastern Liberia. After receiving his BA and MA in New York and a PhD in education management in Ohio in the 1970s, Boley was assistant minister for education under Tolbert and then became Doe's advisor. "Boley was de facto head of government in 1980," wrote an observer, "[a]s gatekeeper to Doe, he consciously exploited Doe's distrust of educated people."[34] Old connections from Doe's political network were valuable assets for these men to form their own armed groups in Liberia's war, but of course these also were assets that many of their rivals enjoyed.

Unable to seize the capital, in January 1991 Taylor organized the National Patriotic Reconstruction Assembly Government (NPRAG) at his base in Gbarnga. Controlling at times more than 90 percent of Liberia's territory, Taylor hoped to convince outsiders to recognize the NPFL as the government of Liberia with Taylor as its leader.[35] The NPFL hired Washington lobbyists to represent this claim and had its own agent in suburban Washington. But even the Washington lobbyists did not present a convincing picture of effective administration when they visited NPFL-held territory. "The Taylor forces are

---

[34] S. Byron Tarr, "Founding the Liberia Action Party," *Liberian Studies Journal* 15:1 (1990): 25.

[35] For example, Charles Taylor, "Address to the Nation" (typescript in author's possession, 13 April 1992); and NPRAG, "The Legal Status of the National Patriotic Reconstruction Government as the De Facto Government of the Republic of Liberia" (Gbarnga, photocopy, no date).

not paid – they are all volunteers. Basically they live off the land,"
they reported.[36] NPRAG's own agents recorded popular complaints
of "commanders and their subordinates in the habit of harassing and
brutalizing peaceful citizens."[37] Government courts did not function,
schools were unfunded, and insecurity and poverty provoked the flight
abroad of more than half a million people from NPFL-held territory,
about a third of the population, and the displacement of another third
to areas of Liberia beyond the NPFL's control.[38] Yet when effective
or popular commanders attempted to solve military or administrative
problems, they threatened Taylor's primacy. One, "Strike Force" head
Nixon Gaye, was executed in 1994, just as he was using his popularity to gain control over resources that Taylor needed to sustain his
position.[39]

Internal fragmentation elevated the importance to Taylor of controlling other people's access to commercial channels, much as Doe
had done as president. Taylor invited timber firms back to NPFL-
controlled territory, provided that they accepted NPFL demands for
"contributions" and logistical support.[40] Rubber production and diamond mining added to NPFL finances, and this was managed in much
the same way that Doe had used economic opportunities to reward
his supporters before the war. A visitor to NPFL territory in 1990–91
noted that many local commanders engaged in looting and illicit timber
and mining operations and profited from roadblock tolls. "For them to
talk of opening the roads or uniting with the Monrovia based government only remained an illusion because their business was at stake if
that happened."[41] Other factions faced similar problems in constructing the bureaucratic structures or tolerating the popular leaders that
would be necessary to build functioning liberated zones.

Although the NPFL did a poor job of organizing a liberated zone, it
was an effective backer of Revolutionary United Front (RUF) rebels in

[36] Lester Hyman and H. P. Goldfield, "*Notes on Liberian Fact-Finding Visit*" (Washington, DC: photocopied report, 1991), 4.

[37] NPRAG, *Report from the National Security Committee Submitted to the Conference
Bureau, All-Liberian National Conference* (Gbarnga, photocopy, 25 April 1992), 7.

[38] Human Rights Watch – Africa, "Testimony of Janet Fleischman," Sub-Committee on
Africa, House Foreign Relations Committee, Washington, DC, 18 May 1994.

[39] "Taylor's NPFL in Disarray," *West Africa*, 5 Sept 1994, 1546–47; author's visit to
Liberia at that time.

[40] NPFL memos sent to members of Liberia Timber Association, 1990–92, San Pedro,
Côte d'Ivoire (author's possession).

[41] Bayo Ogunleye, *Behind Rebel Line: Anatomy of Charles Taylor's Hostage Camps* (Enugu:
Delta, 1995), 138.

Sierra Leone. Attacking from Liberia on 23 March 1991, NPFL fighters, including ones from Burkina Faso and Côte d'Ivoire, reportedly
outnumbered their RUF counterparts.[42] Captured fighters "stated that
among the reasons given by Charles Taylor for attacking the country
was that Sierra Leone was being used by ECOMOG, the Nigerian-led
multinational intervention force, as a base to prevent him from becoming President of Liberia."[43] Taylor complained that West African mediation excluded the NPFL and talked to the civic opposition as possible
successors to the dead dictator. Nigerian leaders also were concerned
about Libyan connections to Taylor's NPFL and the example that Taylor might provide to other ambitious former officials who might launch
armed challenges to corrupt regimes. The NPFL was known to have
ties to dissidents from other countries, raising fears that it would meddle
in other countries' domestic politics. Thus when 3,000 ECOMOG soldiers landed in Monrovia in late August 1990, and 7,000 more arrived
by February 1991, they blocked Taylor's capture of Monrovia and
Liberia's presidency.

Grievances against Sierra Leone's corrupt and predatory government were not the primary motivation of many Sierra Leonean recruits
to the RUF who joined while the group was based in Liberia. In August
1990, Taylor told NPFL fighters to arrest ECOMOG country nation-
als, including Sierra Leoneans. Corporal Foday Sankoh, the head of
RUF, had a plan for his detained countrymen. Jailed for several years
in Sierra Leone for a minor role in a 1971 coup attempt, he emerged
in Libya with Taylor in the late 1980s. Sankoh then recruited among
the NPFL's Sierra Leonean detainees in Liberia. Their abuse, followed
by Sankoh's offer of protection, showed them how dangerous it was to
be without protection in a war zone.[44] Some joined voluntarily, such
as Sam Bockarie, an RUF commander and a former illicit diamond
miner who left Sierra Leone to become a hairdresser and professional
nightclub dancer in Liberia. NPFL fighters appeared to act on similar
motivations. A postwar survey of fighters found that about 35 percent
cited the need to protect their families as their primary reason for joining the NPFL. About 20 percent reported that they joined because
they were scared to do otherwise, and about 18 percent reported that

---

[42] Peter da Costa, "The Military Option," *West Africa*, 22 April 1991, 590.
[43] "Campaign against Charles Taylor Launched," *We Yone* [Freetown], 8 Feb 1992, 5.
[44] Scott Stearns, "In Rebel-Held Country," *West Africa*, 15 April 1991, 560–61; Truth
Commission, *Report*, vol. 3, ch. 3 (Freetown: Truth Commission, 2004), 98–102.

they were abducted. Some reported that they received pecuniary incentives such as money, food, and jobs to join the NPFL.[45] Sankoh listed gaining power and revenge as among his motivations for teaming up with the NPFL and then leading the RUF in Sierra Leone.[46] Rather than fashioning themselves as states-in-waiting in the reformist or revolutionary modernist mold of those encountered in previous chapters, these warlord rebels were organized very much like the regimes that they fought. Their main difference was that they intensified the violent and predatory character of the political authorities that they wanted to replace, as they and the fragmenting government forces began to fight among themselves.

Those with ideological and programmatic motivations encountered obstacles, as with Sankoh's (like Taylor's) intolerance of effective and popular commanders. Ibrahim Abdullah notes that student ideologues who fled Sierra Leone for Libya after facing government repression and others who might have become the core of a reform rebellion were killed or fled early in the conflict.[47] Two commanders had complained that NPFL fighters and newer RUF recruits abused local communities and undermined the RUF's appeals to fight the corrupt Sierra Leone government, but they were executed. Their programs threatened Sankoh, whose power ultimately rested on his role as a proxy for Taylor's NPFL and his control over resources. The NPFL's January 1992 "Top 20" operation killed or chased off much of the indigenous political leadership of the RUF.

Like MOJA activists in Liberia, Sierra Leone's ideologues lost out to those with connections to parts of old political networks, or to those who fought their way to these resources. This behavior and its harsh winnowing effect appeared wherever patronage dominated politics. Kukoi Samba Sanyang, the leader of a failed 1981 Gambian coup and later NPFL member,[48] was seen among Gambia's left-wing activists as not "intellectually credible" and concerned with revenge against authorities who blocked his earlier political aspirations. Failing to interest activists, he recruited illiterate disaffected former security force members in a bid

[45] James Pugel, *What the Fighters Say: A Survey of Ex-Combatants in Liberia* (New York: United Nations Development Programme, April 2007), 36.

[46] Ebow Godwin, "Interview with Foday Sankoh," *New African*, Nov 1999, 42–46.

[47] Ibrahim Abdullah, "Bush Path to Destruction: The Origin and Character of the Revolutionary United Front / Sierra Leone," *Journal of Modern African Studies* 36:2 (1998): 203–35.

[48] Ellis, *Mask of Anarchy*, 82.

to punish those who blocked his political aspirations and to appropriate politicians' resources and positions for himself.[49]

Lacking a significant popular base or political program, RUF did not devote a lot of attention to holding or administering territory. An exception to this occurred in October 1992, when RUF began capturing illicit diamond mining operations. This drew army soldiers and commanders into collaboration with RUF, creating "the sobel phenomenon, i.e. soldiers by day becoming rebels by night."[50] New soldiers recruited from among unemployed youth in the capital and provincial towns resembled RUF fighters in their circumstances and showed Sierra Leone's citizens the extent to which their own government's army was now fighting in very much the same manner and for the same purposes as the warlord rebels. Like the army's recruits, some RUF recruits who did not join for protection came from among outcast youth in towns or among those who ran afoul of local chiefs, the main administrative authorities in rural Sierra Leone.[51] These recruits were on the margins of the violent capital-based system of patronage politics whose members looted the country's resources, including diamonds, for the benefit of a narrow political elite. Fighting to occupy diamond mines was a way for youth on any side of this conflict to get access to the resources that financed prewar and wartime patronage, as they tried to force their way into this political system and appropriate their share of the loot.

This scramble within the army and the RUF produced new factions, including the Armed Forces Revolutionary Council (AFRC), which seized power in the capital on 25 May 1997. The AFRC soldiers invited RUF to join them in the capital but failed to receive international recognition. ECOMOG soldiers, in Sierra Leone since 1990 to fight against Taylor's NPFL, forced them out of power in February 1998. More factions appeared among soldiers and their friends, including the West Side Boys, a name reflecting their shared preference with RUF fighters for the music of American hip hop artist Tupac Shakur, based in Los Angeles in the western United States.[52] Once RUF reached

---

[49] Arnold Hughes, "The Attempted Gambian Coup d'État of 30 July 1981," in Arnold Hughes (ed.), *The Gambia: Studies in Society and Politics* (Birmingham: University of Birmingham Centre of West African Studies, 1991), 96–99.

[50] Arthur Abraham, "War and Transition to Peace: A Study of State Conspiracy in Perpetuating Armed Conflict," *Africa Development* 22:3 (1997): 103; David Keen, *Conflict and Collusion in Sierra Leone* (Oxford: James Currey, 2005).

[51] Krijn Peters, *Re-Examining Volunteerism: Youth Combatants in Sierra Leone* (Pretoria: Institute of Strategic Studies, 2004), 26–27.

[52] For rebels' musical preferences, see "Lawless Country," *For Di People* [Freetown], 5 July 2000, 2; see also Mats Utas and Magnus Jörgel, "The West Side Boys: Military

the capital, it also began to split, as commanders staked out their own claims to diamonds and other resources. Like the officials that they chased out, they grafted themselves onto illicit, economy-fueled political networks to underwrite their own power, up to the decisive UN and British intervention in 2000 that effectively ended that war.

Through all of this competitive violence, RUF was responsible for the bulk of recorded human rights abuses during Sierra Leone's decade-long war.[53] Targeting civilians became RUF policy after its removal from the capital in 1998, when commander Sam Bockarie declared RUF's Operation No Living Thing.[54] As it became clear that the bulk of the country's population considered RUF to be a menace, RUF strategy turned to intimidating citizens through amputations and destruction of the remaining administrative capacity of the government. This showed people that the government could not protect them and that they had to tolerate the RUF and renegade army presence. But the RUF gained no real popularity, drawing only 1.7 percent of the popular vote for its presidential candidate in 2002 in the first postwar election.

Patronage politics also shaped conflict in Côte d'Ivoire. This eastern neighbor of Liberia developed a centralized political network under President Houphouët-Boigny when he began helping Taylor and other former Doe associates in the late 1980s. This system provided steady growth and political stability so long as his regime received subventions from France, its former colonial ruler, to help manage the agricultural sector for the benefit of regime insiders. Open-ended French support ended soon after the president's death in December 1993. New constraints on patronage, combined with international pressure to hold multiparty elections, encouraged strongmen in this network to make their own bids for power. Because election campaigns gave them their own platforms to appeal directly to followers, ethnic and populist political strategies became attractive alternative means to preserve or enhance their status in this newly competitive political network.[55]

Navigation in the Sierra Leone Civil War," *Journal of Modern African Studies* 46:3 (2008): 492–93. Utas and Jörgel note that "West Side Boys" was a reference to the Tupac Shakur tune "Hit 'em Up."

[53] Sierra Leone Truth Commission, *Findings*, vol. 2 (Freetown: Truth Commission, 2004), 38–39.

[54] Lansana Gberie, *A Dirty War in West Africa: The RUF and the Destruction of Sierra Leone* (London: Hurst, 2005), 118–55.

[55] Jean-Pierra Dozon, "L'étranger et l'allochtone en Côte d'Ivoire," in Bernard Contamin and Harris Memel-Foté (eds.), *Le modèle ivoirien en questions: crise, réajustements, récompositions* (Paris: Éditions Karthala, 1997), 779–98.

Competition produced political instability. Houphouët-Boigny's successor, Henri Konan-Bedie, was overthrown in December 1999 in the country's first coup, and Robert Gueï was invited to take power. Tension grew when Gueï lost an election to Laurent Gbagbo in October 2000 and Gueï sought Taylor's protection in Liberia. Meanwhile, Burkina Faso's President Compraoré also became enmeshed in the conflict in Côte d'Ivoire, because many populist politicians, including Gbagbo, targeted Burkinabe immigrants to Côte d'Ivoire. Compraoré supported the Forces Nouvelles, which gathered together many who felt cut out of Côte d'Ivoire's politics, and by 2002, occupied the northern 60 percent of the country.[56] Taylor helped two new armed groups along the country's border with Liberia, the Mouvement populaire ivoirien du Grand Ouest (MPIGO) and the Mouvement pour la justice et la paix (MJP). MPIGO and MJP pursued local grievances over the arrival of outsiders who enjoyed support from the old capital-based patronage network. Like the Forces Nouvelles, they mobilized local frustrations about political and economic marginalization. These armed groups succeeded in setting up local administrations and keeping a modicum of order. But to the extent that they relied on regional patrons or moved outside of their areas of core support, they also became instruments of the violent competition to control patronage resources.

Gbagbo was a major figure in this violent reconfiguration of political networks. Like counterparts elsewhere in West Africa, he was an old regime insider. At first, Gbagbo was a regime critic. As leader of the semi-clandestine Front populaire ivoirien (FPI) since 1982, after returning from exile abroad, he emerged as an opposition candidate in the 1990 multiparty election that followed international pressure. But after winning just 18 percent of the vote, Gbagbo accepted Houphouët-Boigny's offer of a cabinet position. This effectively co-opted a visible opposition figure. More significant for Houphouët-Boigny and for the war later was Gbagbo's role as boss of student militias. He had used his position as a professor of history and dean at the Université de Cocody-Abidjan to mobilize student protests. His FPI thus worked closely with the student group Fédération estudiantine et scolaire de Côte d'Ivoire (FESCI)

FESCI connections gave Gbagbo ties to armed group leaders who emerged in 2002 and before, including future Forces Nouvelles

---

[56] Richard Otayek and René Banégas, "Le Burkina Faso dans la crise ivoirienne: effets d'aubaines et incertitudes politique," *Politique Africaine* 89 (March 2003): 78–80.

organizers. The Forces Nouvelles head, Guillaume Soro, was a FESCI leader in the 1990s. Gbagbo's wartime ally, Charles Blé Goudé, target of 2006 UN sanctions for leadership of the violent Congrès Panafricain des jeunes patriots, succeeded Soro as FESCI head. FESCI also provided an early base for Eugène Djué, the head of the pro-Gbagbo Union pour la Libération Totale de la Côte d'Ivoire. The student organization provided these and other "student activists" with connections to clandestine economic activities, as they organized protection rackets and other operations when they were not fighting prewar election campaigns.[57]

Gbagbo aided violent militias against the Taylor-supported MPIGO and MJP in the west through his assistance to the anti-Taylor Movement for Democracy in Liberia (MODEL). Within Côte d'Ivoire, and with help from anti-Taylor forces, he incorporated ex-FESCI leaders into the Forces de Libération du Grand Ouest (FLGO). MODEL and FLGO used their connections to the Ivorian head of state to protect illicit timber operations. Likewise, until Taylor's exile from Liberia in 2003, MPIGO and MJP members joined clandestine operations on the Liberian side of the border.

These and other armed groups in Côte d'Ivoire and the hard-to-follow proliferation of acronyms illustrated the importance of complex prewar and wartime patronage networks in shaping the formation and the alignments of armed groups in this era. Each incorporated fighters with diverse agendas but operated in a political environment that was hostile to the kinds of political demands and programs that previously defined many of Africa's insurgencies. These elements of pre-conflict politics appeared in Somalia too, although as the next section shows, the local social context played a large role in modifying the extent and intensity of warlord rebel group activity.

Somalia's Warlords

Somalia's President Siad Barre (1969–91) also used formal and illicit economy networks to sustain patronage politics. This strategy became more pronounced after the Soviet-backed Ethiopian army thwarted his invasion of Ethiopia's ethnic Somali Ogaden region in 1977–78.

---

[57] Yacouba Konate, "Les enfants de la balle: de la FESCI aux mouvements des patriotes," *Politique Africaine* 89 (March 2003): 49–70.

Barre's growing unpopularity and several coup attempts highlighted the dangers of tolerating much autonomy or efficiency among state officials, and nepotism became the rule. Barre's son commanded the army, his brother became foreign minister, his son-in-law was minister of defense, one daughter served as director general of the central bank, and another daughter was director general of the ministry of finance.[58] Barre also used clans as vehicles to distribute favors. Clans have long played important roles in Somali politics, but they are not immutable. As Barre played favorites and pitted kinship networks against one another for political advantage, everyone began to have a heightened stake in the political fortunes of their own clan or sub-clan. Ideally, one's relatives or a local patron would be in a position to subvert a law or regulation – with approval or at least tolerance from the capital – to channel resources and opportunities in one's direction. This left people watchful that others were not favored at their expense. The overall consequence was that most people operated under the assumption that the politicized logic of kinship was critical in shaping one's personal fortunes. Thus even ardent Somali nationalists needed to pay careful attention to clan affairs. This shows how, once widespread violence broke out, the broader social context could drive individuals to participate in very divisive "clan warfare," even if they retained Pan-Somali irredentist convictions at a personal level.

Manipulating the clandestine economy was central to sustaining Barre's authority. This included diverting foreign aid and contracts, about $1.5 billion (in 2011 dollars) from the United States during the 1980s and $1.8 billion from Italy, southern Somalia's former colonial ruler, to regime favorites.[59] Massive over-counting of refugees from the 1977–78 war and government counterinsurgency campaigns enabled officials to sell or give supplies to supporters, activities that diverted about 75 percent of all aid in the early 1980s.[60] Moreover, a law enacted in 1975 decreed that all land was state owned and required that occupants register their claims. Not surprisingly, "senior army officers, politicians, businessmen, civil servants and relatives of Siad

---

[58] Hussein Ali Dualeh, *From Barre to Aideed: Somalia, Agony of a Nation* (Nairobi: Stellagraphics, 1994), 36. The Letter to the Editor of Ahmed Deria in *Horn of Africa* 3:4 (1980/81): 61–67 lists fifty-three family members and close associates of Barre who occupied official positions.

[59] Refugee Policy Group, "Hope Restored? Humanitarian Aid in Somalia" (Nov 1994), 7.

[60] Jonathan Tucker, "The Politics of Refugees in Somalia," *Horn of Africa* 5:3 (1984): 22.

Barre acquired large estates . . . in the most fertile areas."[61] Some new "owners" brought kinsmen from cities or distant provinces to work on their farms, sometimes with help from foreign donors who wanted to promote commercial agriculture. A foreign scholar working in the south in 1988 found in her research site that all registered landowners had been government officials and that 75 percent were not from that area. Three quarters of the households that she surveyed feared losing their land to savvy urbanites and people with political connections.[62]

Assertive new landowners further entangled clan identities with Barre's political system as they undermined the authority of the local councils and elders who had previously resolved land disputes and allocated land to young men. Some beneficiaries mobilized militias to protect their new assets, and by the late 1980s militias proliferated in the southern regions of Somalia. Those who belonged to politically marginalized minority groups or disfavored clans became targets of this regime-sanctioned predation, and control over land became a focus for fighting in the 1990s. These people also had to rely on clans for protection, which had the overall effect of reinforcing clan identities. As a former Mogadishu lawyer and accountant wrote, clans became a tool for aggressive politicians to mobilize fighters. At the same time, clans provided protection from the disorder that they helped to create. This contradiction severely limited the hitherto positive role that clan authorities had played in the past in resolving conflicts and replaced it with a more violent and competitive version of Barre's politics of patronage.[63]

Barre's political strategy destroyed the political fields of leverage in which a unified armed opposition could develop. This was hard to do in Somalia, where lineage and local notables mattered a lot to most people. But like prewar leaders in West Africa, Barre's political networks dominated economic opportunities and incorporated networks of societal relations well beyond the formal bounds of the state. Labeling Somalia's conflicts as deep-rooted clan warfare confuses the outcome of the politics of the Barre years, which affected Somalis of all backgrounds, with its origins. It also understates the continuing popularity of the nationalist project born in the 1960s and 1970s of unifying all Somalis under a

---

61 African Rights, *Land Tenure, the Creation of Famine, and Prospects of Peace in Somalia* (London: Africa Watch, October 1993), 19.
62 Christine Besteman, *Land Tenure in the Middle Jubba: Customary Tenure and the Effect of Land Registration* (Madison: Land Tenure Center, Sept 1989), 39–40.
63 Mariam Arif Gassem, *Hostages: The People Who Kidnapped Themselves* (Nairobi: Central Graphics Services, 1994).

single flag; this goal continues to be shared by many Somalis in spite of internecine warfare and ambitious political actors who manipulate clan divides.

By the late 1980s, it seemed that Barre might face a unified rebellion. The United Somali Congress (USC) was established in 1989, albeit with factions based in Rome, Addis Ababa, and Mogadishu. But factions survived and proliferated as leaders used prewar political and business connections to pursue their own ambitions after Barre and about 200 of his kinsmen were chased out of Mogadishu. The USC was supposed to act as an umbrella organization for the Somali Salvation Democratic Front (SSDF), the Somali Patriotic Movement (SPM), and the Somali Democratic Movement (SDM), when in fact the leaders of each fought to seize state power and the resources and privileges of Barre's old political networks for themselves and their home communities.

Mohammed Farah Aidid, the chairman of the USC, thought that he should have become Somalia's next president.[64] Aidid had solid opposition credentials. He had been a military attaché for Barre's regime but also had been imprisoned due to suspicions that he was involved in a coup plot. Even so, the USC leadership endorsed Ali Mahdi as an interim president. A wealthy businessman, he supported the Manifesto Group, a pro-reform coalition made up of 144 moderate and well-respected intellectuals, community organizers, and merchants who called for the abolition of repressive laws, a national conference to prepare for multiparty elections, and the disarmament of militias and security forces. This group had a popular following in the wake of a July 1989 uprising to protest the arrest of leading Muslim clergymen that was violently crushed by the army. Barre's government responded to the Manifesto Group by arresting many of its members, including Aden Abdullah Osman Daar, Somalia's first president, distinguished for leaving office in 1967 after electoral defeat.[65]

Barre-era politics shaped the post-Barre opposition. Even though Ali Mahdi was an opposition leader, he grew wealthy during Barre's rule, "making a fortune especially through his wife's connections with

---

[64] He offers his own analysis of the situation in Mohammed Farah Aidid, *Somalia: From the Dawn of Civilization to the Modern Times* (New Delhi: Vikas Publishing House, 1994).

[65] Mohamed Sahnoun, *Somalia: The Missed Opportunities* (Washington, DC: United States Institute of Peace, 1994), 6–8.

the office of the president in the 1980s."[66] As Barre's regime was disintegrating, UN investigators reported that he sold off state assets to other businessmen and gained access to money that other officials had deposited overseas to purchase weapons from international arms dealers.[67] Figures such as Ali Mahdi were able to occupy more of the political stage as a result of the debilitating politicization of the country's education system. Barre was personally involved in university appointments, and his son-in-law, as minister of education, nominated deans of the faculty. Representatives of the ruling party were assigned to every faculty of the university, and informers were planted in classrooms to discourage antigovernment debate. Places in the university were reserved for ruling party cadres and relatives of government officials. Security services distributed antigovernment leaflets as a pretext to arrest those thought to be critics of the government. Corruption played a role in the political control of the university. A researcher's local contact explained:

> There is a whole network through the Ministry of Education, the Academy and the party who benefit from the grants given for research by donors. Corruption provides both an opportunity for personal enrichment as well as a tool for getting people to accept the government's political line. If you refuse to be incorporated into the system, life is made difficult for you.[68]

The Manifesto Group's political agenda faded amid the competition between Ali Mahdi and Aidid (both members of the same clan). This became apparent after the rivalry between these two ambitious men broke out into intense fighting in Mogadishu in November 1991. The Manifesto Group's subordination to kinship networks appeared even earlier, when its leader, Dr. Ismail Jumale Ossoble, a Mogadishu lawyer and former political prisoner, died in Rome in August 1990, and Ali Mahdi, a member of the activist's sub-clan, replaced him. Ali Mahdi could take on Aidid because of his business income and connections. Through an alliance with a local clan leader, he also controlled Mogadishu International Airport, itself a significant financial

[66] Daniel Compagnon, "Somali Armed Movements," in Christopher Clapham (ed.), *African Guerrillas* (Oxford: James Currey, 1998), 84. Mahdi's wife was Barre's legal advisor.

[67] United Nations Security Council, *Report of the Panel of Experts on Somalia Pursuant to Security Council Resolution 1425 (2002)* (New York: United Nations Security Council, 25 March 2003), 18.

[68] Africa Watch, *Academic Freedom and Human Rights Abuses in Africa* (New York: Africa Watch, 1991), 70–71.

asset, through the collection of landing fees and as a link to commerce with the outside world.

As during the 1980s, clan leaders supported and lent militias to politicians who promised the benefits of state power and who could offer protection. The Manifesto Group could not deliver these bene-fits, especially when it was not able to attract recognition by powerful outsiders as the appropriate vehicle for forming a new government. The ensuing scramble undermined efforts to discipline the young mili-tia members who had served as political muscle for politicians in the 1980s and who were in the habit of using their guns to loot other people's property.[69] The significant looting and abuses of civilians in Somalia's conflict were a direct result of how armed fighters were recruited and were serious enough to attract a US military–backed UN intervention force.

The failure to organize fighters and non-combatants around a broad political agenda was significant, given the wide popularity of nationalist and irredentist sentiments. This capacity to mobilize people around a popular political narrative did exist, and it appeared on occasion. On 3 October 1993, Aidid, now the head of the Somali National Alliance (SNA), was able to count on thousands of Somalis to confront the US military's elite soldiers sent to detain him and his associates. Eighteen American soldiers were killed, and the United States announced its withdrawal by the end of March 1994. This confrontation was a stark contrast to the destruction of Sierra Leone's West Side Boys faction in September 2000 at the hands of fewer than 200 British soldiers. This event highlights the difficulty of including Somalia's conflict squarely in the warlord category, even though elements of the pre-conflict state shaped fighting in ways that fit this label.

General Mohamed Said Hersi "Morgan" was a better fit for the warlord label. He appeared under the USC banner around Kismayo in southern Somalia as a "liberator" for his kinsmen, who in the late 1980s faced competition from the president's own kinsmen to control land. But Morgan, who was the son-in-law of the ousted dictator, the army commander responsible for leading the 1988 attack on Hargeisa in northern Somalia, and then briefly minister of defense in the old regime and army, sided with Barre. He served as the chairman of the Somali National Front (SNF), made up of remnants of the national

---

[69] Roland Marchal, "Les *mooryan* de Mogadisco: formes de la violence dans un espace urbain en guerre," *Cahiers d'Etudes Africaines* 33:130 (1993): 295–320.

FIGURE 9. Somali guys at Boroma. Photograph by L. J. M. Seymour.

army. He managed to capture Kismayo from Aidid's fighters in June 1993. Morgan also had to face Col. Ahmed Omar Jess, another army commander, who defied Barre in 1989, as the president's position began to weaken when foreign aid was withdrawn, and then sided with Aidid. As with many West African warlords, these rebel leaders benefited directly from their positions in Barre's army, their capacity to attract prewar militia fighters to their sides, and their access to the stockpiles of weapons that their country had accumulated.

Aidid's principal financial backer, Osman Hassan Ali Atto, also was well placed at the end of Barre's rule to play an important role in subsequent factional struggles. He built his fortune in construction and transport businesses and became a country manager for a Western oil company. He may have thought that he had enough resources to go it alone when he split from Aidid in 1994. Equipped with commercial contacts outside of Somalia, including a family-run transport business in Kenya, Atto shifted his alignments with various groups according to a logic that exhibited little ideological or programmatic consideration. UN investigators accused him of involvement in smuggling illicit drugs more than a decade after the collapse of Barre's regime.[70]

[70] United Nations Security Council, *Report of the Monitoring Group on Somalia Pursuant to Security Council Resolution 1519 (2003)* (New York: United Nations Security Council, 11 Aug 2004), 27.

Competition between Morgan's SNF and other armed groups in the south, their confrontation with Aidid's SNA, and Barre's effort to retake Mogadishu in 1991–92 played a key role in creating the famine that justified the creation of the multinational United Nations Operation in Somalia (UNOSOM) in April 1992. The US military's Operation Restore Hope joined this force in December 1992 under the umbrella of the multinational UN Unified Task Force (UNITAF). UNITAF brought more than 25,000 American soldiers as part of a 37,000-strong contingent under UN Security Council Resolution 794 orders to establish a secure environment for humanitarian relief operations in Somalia. Many American soldiers departed by mid-1993, but the 5,000 who remained joined UNOSOM II, charged by UN Security Council Resolution 837 to take "necessary measures" against those responsible for armed attacks against relief NGOs and to protect the international intervention force. The efforts of Aidid and the others to guard their own positions were seen as callous and cruel in foreign capitals and in UN councils. Such was the capacity of SNA to mobilize fighters that they attacked and killed twenty-five Pakistani peacekeepers on 5 June 1993. Fighting led to the 3 October 1993 spectacle of Aidid's support-ers killing eighteen American elite soldiers and wounding eighty-four others.

Whereas direct armed intervention provoked some rebel groups to rally supporters, more peaceful international engagement in Somalia tended to promote the fragmentation of rebel groups. International mediation efforts gave platforms to those who already controlled armed groups and disadvantaged other political groups. Even when negotiators pursued a bottom-up approach of wide representation, faction leaders who had access to money and guns were able to coerce or entice local clan notables to support them. But the prospect of a seat at a nego-tiating table also created incentives to split from one's group and loot communities to get the money needed to field one's own fighters. Thus of twelve major conferences from 1991 to 2002, the first conference seated representatives of seven major groups. By 1993, a meeting in Addis Ababa recognized fifteen groups. Twenty-eight signed the 1997 agreement negotiated in Cairo. The meeting in 2000 in Djibouti wel-comed well more than eighty factions. In an effort in 2002 in Kenya, about a thousand representatives showed up, but concerns about cost limited the meeting to 800. Such inclusiveness made sense to inter-national mediators, but not to authorities in Somaliland. As noted in the last chapter, authorities in Somaliland succeeded in imposing order

among many groups. These authorities feared that international negotiations would give some local leaders opportunities to turn their backs on
the agreements that limited their ambitions, which led these authorities
to ban participation in the meetings.

Developments in the 1990s pointed to the second way in which
the international community promoted rebel fragmentation in Somalia. Foreign NGOs needed protection, and "it was not long before the
Technical operators awoke to the fact that they could profit from the
vulnerability of NGOs... and sell protection to them too." Thus
the term "technical" entered the lexicon of wars in Africa, referring
to civilian pickup trucks armed with machine guns or light anti-aircraft
guns, because NGOs recorded their hire as "technical expenses."[71]
Thus although the intensely factionalized political landscape of Somalia owes much more to the prewar politics of state collapse under Barre's
rule, especially to his direct integration of clan networks within a system of violent patronage politics, international engagement shaped how
money was handed out. Factions appeared partly in response to new
sources of income and disappeared or merged as old sources dried
up. This was not the only logic that drove Somali politics, but it was
an important factor as new armed groups formed around sources of
income, replicating in miniature some of the features of patronage politics in the old prewar state.

Ultimately, many of Somalia's rebel leaders and even leaders of localized factions fit the definition of warlord in this book. That is, they failed
to offer a serious program or ideology to mobilize people to deal with the
larger problems of Somalia's situation or place in the world. Like West
African counterparts, these leaders of armed groups gained personal
power through using the benefits of their prewar political connections
and positions to control resources, and they sought to back this with
global recognition as sovereign rulers of Somalia, or lacking this, with
status as major players who were entitled to participate in internationally
mediated negotiations. This provided a slender and changeable basis for
mobilizing and disciplining fighters, which has remained a conspicuous
problem throughout Somalia's conflict.

Could Somalia's warlords have been otherwise under different circumstances? Aidid's triumph over the American military hints at the
possibility of a popular political narrative to organize a broader-based

---

[71] John Drysdale, *Whatever Happened to Somalia?* (London: HAAN Associates, 1994),
46–47.

rebellion. Somalia had a number of pre-1991 antigovernment, albeit factionalized, rebels. Some survived after 1991, but their formal political programs of anti-corruption and renewal did not weather the intervening years.[72] Somalia saw new groups driven by religious ideas that challenged the inherited contours of the Barre-era patronage system, a development that is considered in the next chapter. Their appearance alongside warlords highlights another theme of this book: that conflicts usually produce multiple possible trajectories, and leaders and fighters harbor diverse motives and agendas. Which ones triumph depends in large part on the global political context and on the nature of statecraft at that time. As shown by the conflict in Congo discussed in the following section, the context in the 1990s definitely tilted the odds in favor of warlords.

Warlords and Conflict in Congo

As in West Africa and Somalia, Congo's war from 1996 was very much about individuals repositioning themselves as an old presidential patronage network fragmented. The tendency for these patronage networks to be rooted in commerce, including in clandestine economies, and to shape how people rose in status and gained access to opportunities dragged all sorts of local struggles into the wider conflict. For example, President Mobutu's (1965–97) rule had favored people in the Banyamulenge ethnic group in eastern Congo, where he granted them land and local government positions. Mobutu saw that favoring people whom the majority saw as outsiders (as they traced kinship ties to Rwandan Tutsis) made these beneficiaries vulnerable and in need of presidential protection. To the extent that the president could manipulate and aggravate local tensions, this dependence grew, as did his role as arbiter when confronted with the complaints of "indigenes." Like politics in other warlord conflicts in the 1990s, this system of authority also produced the contours of its own fragmentation. Once central control waned, local notables found themselves in positions to raise their own militias, either as predators or protectors of contending communities, and were able to use their prewar influence in local economies and their control over armed young men to pursue their goals.

---

[72] Daniel Compagnon, "The Somali Opposition Fronts," *Horn of Africa* 15 (1990): 29–54.

In Congo, as in Côte d'Ivoire, democratic reform worsened the situation. Mobutu's April 1990 announcement of the advent of multiparty politics encouraged incumbent politicians and ambitious newcomers to mobilize the grievances of their communities to compete for office. Mobutu wanted as much competition of this sort as possible. The more that competition focused on personality and local tensions, the greater the fragmentation of the political opposition. The 1992 decision to appoint leaders of local majority communities to provincial governors' posts to replace the previously favored outsiders aggravated tensions over land disputes and local offices. These tensions provided a stage for "*le phénomène Hiboux*," the nocturnal and hence owl-like paramilitaries, and "*le phénomène Ampicilline*," the Groupe Spécial de la Sécurité Présidentielle, whose red berets and black clothes caused them to resemble the capsule of the powerful drug. Their aggression forced some – and gave opportunities to others – to form their own militias for protection and predation.[73] Mobutu sponsored "opposition" parties run by his ambitious clients to further fragment the political terrain and eclipse popular opposition movements; more than 200 parties were registered by 1991 and more than 380 by 1993.[74] The decline of Congo's universities also reduced the fields of leverage that elsewhere historically produced ideologically driven rebels. As in Somalia, security forces and networks of informants dominated university campuses. When students at the University of Lumbumbashi protested in 1990, security forces killed as many as 150 people.[75] Such events underlined the extent to which the seemingly "weak" Mobutu regime adroitly disrupted opposition from within, and with direct force when necessary.

The aftermath of Rwanda's genocide and the Rwandan Patriotic Front's (RPF) seizure of power in 1994 sent hundreds of thousands of refugees into Congo, including members of the Interahamwe militia, which took part in the genocide in Rwanda and then used the refugee camps as bases from which to launch attacks inside Rwanda. RPF agents then found supporters among the newly marginalized Banyamulenge population in Congo, who also faced threats from the radicals among the refugees. Tensions intensified in October 1996, when the

---

[73] Hubert Kabungulu Ngoy, *L'Insécurité à Kinshasa: une forme atypique de terrorisme urbain, 1990–2003* (Kinshasa: Imprimerie Cedi, 2004).

[74] Kabungulu Ngoy-Kangoy, *La transition démocratique au Zaire* (Kinshasa: Université de Kinshasa, 1995), Annexe, 27–54.

[75] Africa Watch, *Academic Freedom and Human Rights Abuses in Africa* (New York: Africa Watch, 1991), 121–26.

vice governor of North Kivu declared that the Banyamulenge, those whom Mobutu had favored, had to leave Congo, despite the fact that the great majority of them were born there. This act was part of the flawed "democratization" process in Congo in which ambitious local politicians vied to exploit conflicts over land, commerce, and political office to cultivate support among majority groups. From the perspective of the RPF government in Rwanda, these acts represented a new threat of persecution and steps toward the consolidation of anti-RPF rebels. Rwandan officials also criticized foreign humanitarian relief operations in eastern Congo for giving refugees resources and security that benefited the anti-RPF rebels.

Rwanda's RPF government thus helped to organize the Alliance des Forces Démocratiques pour la Libération du Congo (ADFL) under the leadership of Laurent-Désiré Kabila, the head of the failed insurgency in Congo in the 1960s noted earlier in this chapter. Since then, he had turned to business in Tanzania, exporting gold, ivory, and other rare animal products from the Congo region. Combining his leadership of a low-level rebellion and business, he was accused of directing more than 50 percent of the proceeds of his organization to his personal use.[76] The ADFL started as an alliance of four opposition groups in the image of the old anti-colonial rebels who enjoyed foreign backing, with Rwandan promotion of Kabila as leader. But given Kabila's lack of interest in ideological projects and the concern of his Rwandan backers to limit Congolese nationalism – Kabila's best shot at gaining a wider following – which they saw as threatening to their interests, there was little room for this rebel group to find an autonomous political voice. Kisasa Ngandu, one of the more outspoken members of the alliance, was "apparently assassinated by those who were uncomfortable with his Lumumbist sense of nationalism and patriotic duty."[77] Nonetheless, with Rwandan, and eventually also Ugandan, help, Kabila was swept into power in Kinshasa on 17 May 1997 to become Congo's next president.

Kabila's background as a lackluster rebel leader–turned–illicit businessman left him with few ideological credentials and little popular appeal. UN investigations into his post-1996 business dealings noted that Kabila "perpetuated many of the practices of his predecessors. He wielded a highly personalized control over State resources" that copied Mobutu's strategy of exercising political authority through control over

---

[76] Wilungula B. Cosma, *Fizi 1967–1986: le maquis Kabila* (Paris: L'Harmattan, 1997), 101.

[77] Nzongola-Ntalaja, *The Congo from Leopold to Kabila*, 226.

other people's access to economic opportunities.[78] Kabila was a true warlord in the sense of fighting to raise his own standing within the existing system of personal rule based on control over patronage networks and the resources on which they were based, much as Sankoh had done in Sierra Leone and Taylor in Liberia. This type of rule would have been difficult to justify to the wider population through a system of commissars similar to those who had provided discipline and focus for other rebels and their supporters.

Thus although his Rwandan and Ugandan backers may have appreciated Kabila's failure to effectively mobilize a wide segment of Congo's citizens, they eventually faced threats in Kabila's alternative political strategies. His efforts to build his own power base in the Mobutu fashion of cultivating local ethnic tensions presented both Rwanda and Uganda with the possibility that Kabila would use his growing condemnation of "foreigners" (including those whom the Rwandan government claimed they wanted to protect) to provide refuge to cross-border rebels. This threat loomed larger when Kabila kicked his Rwandan backer out of Kinshasa in July 1998 and turned to the governments of Angola, Zimbabwe, and Namibia to provide him with military and financial support. This led to a new round of fighting that lasted until 2002.

Rwandan and Ugandan officials cooperated to help support the Rassemblement Congolais pour la Démocratie (RCD), which appeared in August 1998 under the leadership of Professor Ernest Wamba dia Wamba. Following an academic career in the United States, Wamba dia Wamba became a professor of history at the University of Dar es Salaam, where he consolidated his credentials as a thoughtful critic of Mobutu. While at the university and as head of the Dakar–based Council for the Development of Social Science Research in Africa (CODESRIA), he developed an articulate analysis of Congo's politics that explained how Mobutu's system of rule undermined the capacity of social institutions as autonomous venues for political organizing and promoted a competitive scramble for position among individuals and narrow communities. Like the analysis here, he recognized this as a crisis of ideology that left in its place a violent politics that presented enormous obstacles to reformers.[79]

---

[78] United Nations Security Council, *Addendum to the Report of the Panel of Experts on the Illegal Exploitation of Natural Resources and Other Forms of Wealth of DR Congo* (New York: United Nations, 10 Nov 2001), 3.

[79] Ernest Wamba dia Wamba, "Mobutuism after Mobutu," *CODESRIA Bulletin* 3 and 4 (1998): 73–75.

The first obstacle to RCD unity lay in the violent local factionalism that Wamba dia Wamba had recognized as a legacy of Mobutu's rule. This meant that, although RCD captured up to a third of Congo's territory, many local RCD commanders built their own networks in the economy and contacts with outsiders to arm people loyal to them personally and to control resources. This led to general disorder and to parts of RCD becoming deeply involved in local politics. Commanders' pursuits of local agendas also led to their alliances with militias, some of which were hostile to the RCD's Rwandan and Ugandan backers' interests. Groups such as the Union des Patriotes Congolais (UPC) appeared as protectors of local ethnic communities and for the more partisan purposes of controlling land and commercial opportunities for a narrow group of people. The RCD coalition also drew on former ADFL leaders who fell out of favor with Kabila. In this context the ideas and programs of intellectuals, particularly ones like Wamba dia Wamba who had lived in exile, had little chance of serving as the dominant narrative for fighting.

The second major obstacle to insurgent unity involved the clashing interests of the RCD's Rwandan and Ugandan backers. This led to an RCD split, with Wamba dia Wamba leading the Ugandan-backed RCD-Mouvement de Libération (RCD-ML). These foreign backers also got drawn into the local ethnic and personal rivalries that were the preoccupations of their rebel proxies. For example, Ugandan officials countered Rwandan influence through support for the Parti de l'unité et la sauvegarde de l'intégrité du Congo (PUSIC) and the Forces Armées pour le Congo (FAPC), which included UPC dissidents who sought greater freedom to pursue their ambitions, at the same time that other Ugandan officials tried to cajole various factions to join a common front.[80] Thus Ugandan relations with rebels in Congo undermined the organizational discipline of the Ugandan People's Defense Force (UPDF) as some UPDF officers became wrapped up in their proxies' struggles to pillage local economies and recruit ethnic militias. The instrumental motives of these Congolese rebel commanders also made it fairly easy for them to switch backers, making them unreliable allies for foreigners and for each other. Moreover, Ugandan and Rwandan cooperation became difficult when PUSIC and FAPC rhetoric targeting "non-indigenes" was taken in Rwanda as a threat against co-ethnics and

---

[80] For example, "Agreement for Establishment of a Common Front for the Congolese Liberation Movements," mimeo, 21 Dec 1999 (in author's possession).

an indication that these groups would support Forces Démocratiques de la Libération du Rwanda (FDLR) insurgents who wanted to overthrow Rwanda's government.[81]

The warlord manner of war fighting was particularly corrosive to the UPDF. Because Uganda's army could not pay its own way in its intervention and because officers' collaboration with warlords or purely local militias offered numerous alternative opportunities to get resources, this had "massive consequences on the way the war is fought. Because civilians are the ones from whom the military can take its means of survival, armed violence is more often directed at civilians (including at times one's own camp) than at the enemy."[82] A UN investigation reported that "the Ugandan People's Defense Forces continue to provoke ethnic conflict" to continue to maintain "the control that Ugandans now exercise over trade flows and economic resources."[83] This involvement undermined Ugandan efforts to broker a unification of Wamba dia Wamba's RCD-ML with the Mouvement de Libération Congolais (MLC) under Jean-Pierre Bemba, a son of one of Mobutu's prominent business partners, and its threat to political control over the army was serious enough for officials back in Kampala to allow a commission of inquiry to investigate these activities.[84] Rwanda's military was more insulated from this divisive pressure, partly due to the highly centralized structure of the RPF, out of which it developed, and the direct threat that Rwandan officials saw in the activities of the FDLR, which aimed to cleanse Congo of ethnic Tutsis and invade Rwanda.

Zimbabwe's military intervention in 1998 to help Kabila's government battle the RCD and its foreign backers also reflected pre-conflict state politics that shaped how actors defined their motives and pursued their interests once they were engaged in Congo's conflict. Zimbabwe's President Mugabe justified intervention as necessary to help a fellow African leader to bring peace and order to his country. UN

---

[81] Koen Vlassenroot and Timothy Raeymaekers, "The Politics of Rebellion and Intervention in Ituri: The Emergence of a New Political Complex?" *African Affairs* 103:412 (2004): 385–412.

[82] Gérard Prunier, *From Genocide to Continental War: The "Congolese" Conflict and the Crisis of Contemporary Africa* (London: Hurst, 2009), 337. A good companion analysis of regional developments is found in Filip Reyntjens, *The Great African War: Congo and Regional Geopolitics, 1996–2006* (New York: Cambridge University Press, 2009).

[83] United Nations Security Council, *Final Report of the Panel of Experts on the Illegal Exploitation of Natural Resources and Other Forms of Wealth of the Democratic Republic of Congo* (New York: United Nations, 16 Oct 2002), 5.

[84] Justice David Porter, *Judicial Commission of Inquiry into Allegations of Illegal Exploitation in the DRC* (Kampala: Porter Commission, 2002).

investigators disagreed and noted that Zimbabwean military officers and civilian businessmen close to the president used the intervention to engage in commerce and sign favorable deals in Congo's mining industry. "The declining exchange rate, the failing Zimbabwean mining industry, and the critical energy shortage in Zimbabwe have left few sources for personal enrichment by Government officials. These officials started looking to the Democratic Republic of the Congo."[85] Congo had become an additional source of material wealth for Mugabe to sustain his patronage-based political network as Zimbabwe's economy shrank.

An additional factor promoting fragmentation may have been the international community's approach toward negotiations, which led to the 1999 Lusaka Agreement, which was the basis for the UN peacekeeping Mission de l'ONU en RD Congo (MONUC) and its recognition that "all the participants in the inter-Congolese political negotiations shall enjoy equal status."[86] Although this provision recognized the reality of fragmentation among armed groups in Congo, commanders found incentives to defy superiors to deal directly with the foreigners and use this autonomy to control resources on their own account. It took 1,800 primarily French soldiers in Operation Artemis in mid-2003 and the withdrawal of UPDF to finally bring a modicum of order to eastern Congo and fully deploy the UN peacekeepers. The French force showed its willingness to use force during its three-month deployment, which strengthened MONUC's position in the region and reduced levels of violence for the time being.

The Operation Artemis intervention revealed that a relatively small force trained in regular warfare could exploit the incapacity of the eastern Congo rebel groups and their local allies to resort to classic guerrilla warfare tactics. This was due to the fact that these rebels had very little popular support outside of their narrow communal bases and could not call on local people to take risks for them or hide them from the intervening foreigners. Even more revealing was the remarkable militarily effective intervention in Sierra Leone in 1995–96 of a

---

[85] United Nations Security Council, *Addendum to the Report of the Panel of Experts on the Illegal Exploitation of Natural Resources and Other Forms of Wealth of DR Congo* (New York: United Nations, 10 Nov 2001), 17. A comprehensive survey of intervention is found in John Clark (ed.), *The African States of the Congo War* (Kampala: Fountain, 2003).

[86] "Agreement for a Ceasefire in the Democratic Republic of Congo," *Foreign Affairs* [Kampala], July 1999, 15 [Annex A, ch. 5.2 (ii)].

force of about 200 men under the banner of Executive Outcomes, a South African private military ("mercenary") firm. Hired by Sierra Leone's government and allegedly paid in part with concessions to the firms' associates of mine diamonds in areas that they captured, the firm beat back RUF rebels and rogue Sierra Leone army units with a single helicopter gunship and two transport helicopters. One might have expected mercenaries who included ex-members of Koevoet and others who had fought for the apartheid regime to be unpopular in Sierra Leone. But refugees flowed back to areas that the firm captured, and its members could count on significant help from non-combatants who were eager to give information about rebel activities. This was because non-combatants trusted the foreign firm to protect them much more than they did the rebels or even their own government.[87] The firm left in 1996 under foreign pressure and difficulties in collecting its fees. But they showed that even a very small disciplined force could prevail over rebels who practiced irregular warfare through using violence against the non-combatant population to control and exploit their resources, which was a weakness that these rebels shared with the governments that they fought.

Conclusion: Warlords Trump Liberation Rebels

Congo's conflict, like those in West Africa and Somalia, reflected the nature of pre-conflict state politics and the collapse of political networks that were based on state rulers' personal control over resources rather than on "ancient ethnic hatreds" or immutable clans, or even on a simple scramble for resources. This kind of pre-conflict state politics had great bearing on how individual actors defined their motives and on which actors became prominent as conflict broke out. This politics drastically reduced the fields of leverage – identified in the first chapter as a critical element in organizing insurgencies in which leaders and commissars define and enforce a coherent ideology and political program – producing what Ernest Wamba dia Wamba called a "crisis of ideology," of which he and Congo's wider politics were casualties.

These warlord conflicts illustrate the difficulties of building viable liberation or reform rebel groups when the whole framework of

---

[87] Author's observations in Sierra Leone at that time; Eeban Barlow, *Executive Outcomes: Against All Odds* (Alberton: Galago, 2007), 353.

political life is subject to the interference of a regime that bases its authority on extreme versions of patronage networks well beyond the institutional limits of states. People and organizations that in other contexts would have participated in anti-colonial or reform rebellions instead became tools of domination through these networks. This remained true even after regimes collapsed. Those whose positions already provided access to resources and the capacity to wield violence continued to pursue politics in this mold. These political middlemen – businessmen who are also past or present government officials, heads of local NGOs, and leaders of ethnic militias, and who occupy positions of customary authority – appeared in all warlord conflicts and often found opportunities to elevate their own status and power once their own bosses' control weakened. The collapse of these centralized and often violent systems of patronage politics made way for a more fragmented and even more violent system of personal rule through patronage.

Eugéne Serufuli, governor of North Kivu from 2000 to 2007 and earlier an RCD official, was an exemplar of this kind of political middleman. He combined these roles with his influence in Tous pour la Paix et le Développement (TPD), an NGO organized to help Hutu refugees from Rwanda, Serufuli's co-ethnics, to resettle back in their home country. This NGO also served Rwanda's strategy of returning Hutu refugees to Rwanda so as to deny the antigovernment FDLR a base of support or recruitment in this cross-border ethnic community. Serufuli also was a senior member of Mutuelle Agricole des Virgunga, a cultural organization that raised its own militia amid the turmoil of the early 1990s.[88] This kind of position permitted middlemen to maintain their authority in multiple realms of social activity and to determine other people's mobility and become limited providers of protection. Meanwhile, external developments, such as the end of international support for ideologically driven rebel leaders, denied critics the old opportunities to recruit an outside power, whether foreign NGOs, citizen support groups, or even a Cold War superpower, to back a political idea. Especially as capital-based networks of political control infiltrated universities and declining economies convinced many aspiring professionals – historically the core of the anti-colonial, majority rule, and reform rebel leaderships – to leave, the political middlemen controlled

[88] Denis Tull, *The Reconfiguration of Political Order in Africa: A Case Study of North Kivu (DR Congo)* (Hamburg: Institut für Afrika-Kunde, 2005), 179–84.

the only realistic paths of upward mobility, and ideologues became lone wolves, hunted down before and during warlord conflicts.

The unsettling implication of this analysis is that African states in which similar kinds of centralized networks of patronage have not (yet) collapsed are candidates to see warlord rebels. The more important countries in this category include Nigeria, Kenya, and Sudan. Possible strategies to avoid the development of warlords include introducing accountability and transparency in government, which would limit the informal extension of political authority that is associated in many people's minds with cronyism and corruption. Such bold moves, actually undertaken in many places in the 1990s and later, generate serious threats to the privileges and security of members of the incumbent elite, so instead many regimes redouble efforts to undermine the organizational capabilities of others, even after they accept multiparty electoral reforms. Militias occupy a key position in these strategies. They also define the character of a parochial sort of warfare, which represents the next step in the evolution of warfare in Africa and is the subject of the chapter that follows.

CHAPTER 6

Parochial Rebels

The Oodua People's Congress (OPC) in southwestern Nigeria would seem to have been a good candidate to become a reform or a separatist rebel group. From about the mid-1990s, it had substantial grassroots support within the Yoruba ethnic community. It supported vigilante groups to protect this community against a terrible crime wave in which many people suspected police complicity. It worked alongside organizations that advanced political programs such as the Oodua Liberation Movement, the Oodua Youth Movement (OYM), and the Yoruba Revolutionary Movement. "Our primary objective," said OPC National Secretary Kayode "Sankara" Ogundamisi, "was to canvas a sovereign national conference that will lead us to an autonomous Yoruba nation," whereas the OYM called for an "Oodu'a Republic."[1] OPC organizers used alliances with cultural associations to promote the popular political narrative of self-determination and opposition to the corrupt state. OPC's capacity to control and administer neighborhoods and to fight the police suggested that it occupied new fields of leverage in congested urban areas to challenge the state and to chart a new political future.

A closer look at the OPC's activities revealed numerous links to incumbent politicians and showed how the OPC acted more as a tool of politicians' ambitions rather than as a new force in politics. This tendency became more pronounced with Nigeria's return to electoral politics in 1999, one year after the death of the dictator Sani Abacha. In

---

[1] Quote from Bolaji Tunji, "Why We Are Fighting OPC Secretary," *Guardian*, 22 July 2000, 15: Oodua Youth Movement, *Yoruba People's Charter of Self-Determination* (pamphlet, 1994).

206

December 2001, for example, Nigeria's Attorney General Bola Ige was shot in an unsolved murder. Ige's assassination followed his defection from the Pan-Yoruba group Afenifere and his decision to support the People's Democratic Party (PDP), Nigeria's dominant political party since the return to civilian rule in 1999, to pursue his ambitions in the 2003 elections. This contention earlier involved a gunfight at PDP headquarters and in the Osun State House of Assembly, each allegedly involving youths associated with OPC factions. The OPC spokesmen warned that their followers would help settle political scores.[2] Meanwhile, in northern Nigeria, *yandaba*, or gangs of impoverished youth, condemned modern Nigerian society as corrupt even while "some politicians have been reported to have been patronizing the group as the countdown to the 2002 local government elections begins" to use them as toughs to fight against their opponents' supporters.[3] In eastern Nigeria, a state governor in 2000 deputized the Bakassi Boys vigilantes as the official Anambra State Vigilante Services. The Bakassi Boys were originally popular dispensers of a rough-and-ready "jungle justice" as an alternative to the corrupt and inefficient state justice system. The governor then allegedly used the group to hunt down his political rivals and critics and provided protection for members who used their positions to loot and abuse citizens.

These actions showed the extent to which the OPC and other armed groups acted within the confines of Nigeria's existing political system rather than as rebels fighting to change it. Although these groups often organized in response to community grievances against the state, their actions often served the interests of a politician or clique, what some Nigerians call "godfathers." This behavior is still compatible with protecting a bounded community, usually defined in parochial ethnic or sectarian terms. Politicians who patronize these parochial rebels then take credit for this service, even if it appears to be provided in defiance of the corrupt state of which the politician is a part. Through manipulating ties of patronage, politicians can act in two political spheres. As insiders they benefit from their official office and position in the wider political network. This is what gives them the resources with which to provide for these parochial rebels. Then these politicians can portray themselves as local champions who really are concerned about providing their home communities with basic services like justice and

---

2 Vincent Obia, "Hate Thy Neighbour," *The Week*, 18 Feb 2002, 14.
3 Wola Adeyemo, "The Way Out," *Tell*, 8 Oct 2001, 20.

protection, and if necessary, they can depict themselves to domestic and international observers as the only alternative to anarchy. The irony that these "godfathers" are complicit in the problems that created injustice and insecurity in the first place is not lost on most people. Members of parochial rebel groups often recognize this contradiction too, and even complain that the long-term impact of their use of violence on behalf of their communities reinforces the existing oppressive system of authority rather than overthrowing it.

Those among parochial rebels who dream of rebellion suffer from the inability of ideologically minded leaders to find the social space – fields of leverage – to articulate new narratives and to recruit followers outside of a narrow ethnic or sectarian base. Political narratives are present in the discourses of individual parochial rebels, and they often shape their choices of popular music, their attire, and their discussions. But the ubiquity of patronage networks and their monopolization of economic opportunities and influence even in cultural organizations, NGOs, and other civic associations enable politicians to influence the range of choices available to the rank and filers of these subordinate rebel groups. This interference empowers new leaders who are more willing to subordinate other agendas to service to a politician "godfather." This type of leader acts as an intermediary between the politician's patronage and fighters' access to resources but may owe his (or occasionally her) position as much to the politician as to support among followers. As among the proxy rebels in the last chapter, these leaders are also hostages to the contingencies of their patron's support.

It is extraordinarily difficult to field political commissars under these conditions. This denies group leaders an important tool to maintain discipline, control recruits' access to resources, and focus on political goals. The loss of organizational capacity leaves the bonds of shared ethnicity or more local and contingent identities as the only real glue holding these groups together. This weakness suits the incumbent politicians who patronize these groups, as more radical political narratives might actually mobilize people who many politicians suspect really do not like them and the system that they represent. As the legislative head of a major political party in Nigeria confessed only one year after the return to electoral politics in 1999, the "majority of us cannot go home. You drive your NASS (National Assembly) car on the streets (and people) shout 'thief, thief.'"[4] References to corruption and the outrageous

---

[4] Godwin Onyeacholem, "This House Stinks," *Tell*, 4 Sept 2000, 18.

behavior of some politicians are ubiquitous in the popular culture of many countries. Whether people are angry enough to take up arms is another matter, but it would be reasonable to think that many citizens would welcome more radical political narratives and that some might join the sorts of leaders who produced anti-colonial, majority rule, and reform rebel groups. In this light, it is remarkable that this kind of warfare is so rare in contemporary Africa.

A key reason for this scarcity of broad-based rebel warfare organized around a shared political agenda in Africa lies in the capacity of incumbent political authorities to exploit the dichotomy between people's ideas about politics and their short-term interests in finding ways to survive in a political system that many dislike. Parochial rebels are products of this political system. They are subordinate actors, and unlike warlords, they do not fight to seize control of the state and set up their own regime. This has been true even when centralized patronage systems fragment, as in the last chapter, and key politicians became warlords who reconstructed their own versions of these patronage networks in their efforts to seize state power. At a local level, these systems of authority are surprisingly strong, at least in the sense of shrinking the fields of leverage available to critics, even if these systems do a poor job of sustaining state institutions or providing for the welfare of citizens. This kind of political authority is effective enough that two scholars who describe it particularly well gave their book the title *Africa Works*.[5]

The politics of parochial rebels (and warlords) helps to explain why societies with many angry people with access to political narratives and other information about rebels outside of Africa fail to stage similar rebellions at home. As with other rebels, parochial rebels reflect the nature of the states and regime politics in Africa. Many officials, as in the case of Sudan explored in the following, recognize that politician–parochial rebel alliances are effective tools for disrupting more threatening forms of organized violence. International pressure to change the rules of domestic politics in Africa reinforces trends that produce parochial rebels, even though it is clear that this is not the intention. The advent of democratic competitive elections has catalyzed parochial rebel violence in some countries, as competition for office weakens old mechanisms of control and causes politicians to rely more on armed

---

[5] Patrick Chabal and Jean-Pascal Daloz, *Africa Works: Disorder as Political Instrument* (Oxford: James Currey, 1999).

groups to entrench their authoritarian electoral regimes and to protect ethnically defined communities behind the multiparty façade, as is
shown in the cases of Kenya and Nigeria in the following discussion.
But first it is to the changing nature of states and regime politics, and
this change's impact on the character of warfare, that we now turn.

States, Regime Politics, and Youth Gangs

Most transitions from colonial rule, particularly in French and British
colonies, involved very brief periods of democratic reform prior to
actual independence. Colonial officials supported local leaders who
they believed would be amenable to the interests of the departing colonial power. The problem with this arrangement was that the politicians
who were most appealing to broad segments of society were those who
demanded redress for grievances associated with colonial rule. These
activists sought out alliances with communities much as anti-colonial
rebels did in their more contentious settings. They tried to build popular support through exploiting a backlash against practices of colonial rule that included the expropriation of land and other resources,
poor governance, support for local officials who used their offices to
exploit people, preexisting community conflicts, and unease at the disruptions of local cultures that came with economic development and
social change. Drawing strength from these grievances rather than for
obtuse academic ideas of "anti-imperialism" or folkloric notions of
national greatness was a promising strategy for shifting the entire political dynamic, but it also scared the departing colonial officials, who
feared radical influences. British officials investigating nearly constant
violence through the 1950s in Sierra Leone's mining areas were alert to
the threats of activists and noted that their concern about a "link with
the Soviet bloc is constant and ever before the committee."[6]

In Sierra Leone, populist activists took advantage of the advent of
party politics in the 1950s to campaign for the redistribution of revenues from diamond mining, the country's main source of wealth. Two
brothers, one a student in Liberia and the other at American University
in Beirut, organized the Kono Progressive Movement to tap popular concerns that a large foreign firm's concession agreement and the

[6] West African Archives [Kew Gardens], CO554/1509, "Disturbances in the Sierra
Leone Selection Trust Concession in the Kono Area of Sierra Leone," WAF 14/683/02,
October 1959.

migrant laborers who engaged in illicit diamond mining were robbing the region of its wealth. The brothers explained that the country suffered from "capitalist exploitation" and that the foreign mining firm's operation should be turned over to local communities. With this appeal, they built their organization beyond the narrow ethnic constituency in which they started. They even convinced local people to join forces with illicit diamond miners, who numbered about 50,000 at the time. In 1957, the party won seats in the first broad franchise election and merged a year later with a small party based in the capital that advocated an entire overhaul of the country's administrative system.[7]

The radical party's candidates faced serious obstacles by the time that Sierra Leone became independent in 1961. Five years earlier, British authorities tried to defuse local anger and manage the illicit mining problem by allowing small-scale miners to apply for licenses. Obtaining a license required assent from local authorities, most of whom supported the moderate ruling party as a condition for keeping their offices. Access to mining opportunities, whether legal or illicit, thus required one to maintain good relations with officials and politicians who supported the ruling party. This necessity turned many of the migrants into ready recruits for the violent "action groups" of local progovernment politicians instead of the party of the activists. Many of these local officials used their positions as intermediaries in this developing patronage system to field their own illicit mining gangs, providing miners with food and tools to dig and calling on them when needed during election time. This arrangement survived a military coup in 1967 and a change to a new ruling party in 1968. Ultimately, in this and in other authoritarian regimes, whether single party or multiparty, armed youth played significant roles wherever elections created opportunities for politicians to move up in the system of patronage. In Nigeria, for example, the 1964 election, only four years after independence, confirmed that "the use of violence, intimidation, and 'rigging'" meant that "popular faith in the integrity of the electoral process had been virtually eliminated. By this time the political class as a whole was not only popularly associated with electoral fraud and violence, but with corruption and incompetence as well."[8]

---

[7] Fred Hayward, "The Development of a Radical Political Organization in the Bush: A Case Study in Sierra Leone," *Canadian Journal of African Studies* 6:1 (1972): 9–13.

[8] Paul Beckett, "Elections and Democracy in Nigeria," in Fred Hayward (ed.), *Elections in Independent Africa* (Boulder, CO: Westview Press, 1987), 92.

The strength of this system of co-optation is visible in the fact that corrupt and deeply disliked politicians have weathered public anger for decades. One reason for this survival is that their recruitment of armed youths gives them roles as local patrons, even if their clients have qualms about their patron's politics. This patronage of youth gangs often has been cloaked in the form of cultural associations that reinforce local solidarities at the expense of narratives that permit wider recruitment. The violence associated with elections included intimidation of voters in Malawi's 1994 election by members of the Nyau secret society, for example. Reaching further back, some Sierra Leone gangs drew from Odelay societies, originally organized as fraternal organizations. Nigeria's Area Boys, who play a significant role in electoral violence, originated in Omo Eke (Lagos Boys) youth groups that started out as self-help associations for new urban migrants. In an illustration of this overlap of youth violence, community ties, and political patronage in northern Nigeria, an opposition party leader in the 1950s complained to the colonial government that local officials who served under British rule sent youths to attack schools aligned with the opposition party and to destroy party offices. The opposition party leader was committed to a "class struggle" and reform of "aristocratic political institutions" but found himself struggling against a "gangsterism now spread in all parts of the Region," with groups "set up by emirs' servants and NPC [Nigerian People's Congress, the dominant party] men."[9] These youth, who under other circumstances might have been recruited to oppose these incumbent politicians and officials, now found places in the patronage networks of NPC bosses who used their offices to divert state resources for the benefit of their clients. As in Sierra Leone, the would-be recruits in an ideological struggle instead relied on the favor of politicians whom most people thought were corrupt.

This bond between politicians who act as intermediaries in patronage networks and impoverished youth has provided regimes with an alternative to exclusive reliance on armies or paramilitary organizations to stay in power. These bureaucratic agencies are prone to participating in coups, but when used judiciously in combination with gangs of youth, that danger is reduced. Armed youth organized in decentralized and overlapping networks are more effective defenders of regime privilege than are youth organized in bureaucratic organizations and equipped

[9] Abdullahi Smith Centre for Historical Research, *Election Violence in Nigeria, the Terrible Experience, 1952–2002* (Kaduna: Vanguard Printers, 2002), 7.

with the latest weapons, at least when political authority is exercised through patronage and the manipulation of people's access to opportunities. Youth militias can be used to conduct irregular warfare against a country's own citizens whenever organized opposition appears. Disgruntled individuals often feel too intimidated to act against these youth militias. This increases the difficulty that ideologues face in recruiting others around what might already be popular political narratives and helps to explain why so many of Africa's most corrupt and predatory regimes have not had to face reform rebels, even when a significant portion of the population might welcome such an alternative.

Despite the development of these connections between youth violence and politicians, ideologues still tried to organize and recruit. Throughout the 1970s, Sierra Leone's university students vigorously resisted the ruling party's efforts to declare a one-party state and protested government corruption. Mirroring the activism of university students at Haile Selassie University and the University of Dar es Salaam who went on to become rebel leaders, these students articulated broad political critiques of government abuses of power that appealed to many Sierra Leoneans. In January 1977, the students protested to demand free multiparty elections and other reforms. Some of the students had significant ties to urban youth, and indeed thousands of citizens in the capital joined in. Protests spread to the countryside. But then youth gangs associated with politicians beat up the protestors and looted the university campus. Other urban youth joined in the mêlée, some of whom simply took advantage of the chaos to gather loot. This outcome was not surprising, given that youth gangs associated with politicians, including the country's vice president, already intimidated opponents and carried out political killings.[10]

This violence and the obvious association of government officials with thugs convinced many people that their government was unwilling to protect them, much less provide basic services. In other circumstances, this situation would have been ideal for organizing guerrilla warfare, as reform rebels should have had an easy time convincing citizens that they could out-govern the regime. But the regime's recruitment of youth gangs through channels that reached well beyond the formal institutions of the state crowded out these fields of leverage, as prime recruits to rebellions had the option of seeking their fortunes

---

[10] Ismael Rashid, "Subaltern Reactions: Lumpens, Students, and the Left," *Africa Development* 22:3 (1997): 20–24.

in the short term under the patronage of politicians. University ideologues discussed this situation, but there was little that they could do
about it. A university professor noted that "Fourah Bay College students
have annually and almost religiously commemorated January 29th as
All Thugs Day, with demonstrations, speeches, etc.,"[11] but students
were unable to organize the youthful thugs who attacked them. Even
though the students identified these youths as primary victims of the
mismanaged economy and government corruption, the isolated student
ideologues complained in a campus publication that they faced violence
from "a semi-illiterate bunch of trigger happy ghetto drug addicts"[12]
associated with the oppressive regime.

These youth did not need to like the regimes for which they fought.
A survey of Nigerian Area Boys who were implicated in attacks against
political opponents of the military government in the 1990s indicated
that their primary motivation was to receive material benefits from
politicians. Among the survey group, "81.25% admitted to being thugs
for one politician or the other." At the same time, an almost equal
percentage (78.12 percent) professed to support the opposition to the
dictatorship that they harried, and an even greater proportion (84.37
percent) reported that they were opposed to military rule, and many
said that they had participated in protests against the military's seizure
of power in 1993.[13] The compatibility of rebellious behavior and anti-
establishment attitudes with support for a regime shows the effectiveness with which Africa's most extreme patronage-based regimes had
disorganized public space.

The political use of violent gangs extended to universities when
gangs were used to strike at what historically had been a prime field of
leverage for organizing rebel groups. In Nigeria, violent "campus cults"
emerged in the 1980s, often out of previously peaceful fraternities, during a time when university staff unions and student groups criticized
the country's military. Students at the Obafemi Awolowo University,
one of Nigeria's most prestigious institutions of higher learning, alleged

[11] Cyril Foray, "The Road to the One-Party State: The Sierra Leone Experience,"
speech delivered at the Centre of African Studies, University of Edinburgh, 9 Nov
1988, 59.
[12] Thomas Cole, "Sierra Leone's Elections' 82 Post Mortem," *Awareness*, 5 Oct 1982,
32.
[13] Abubakar Momoh, "Area Boys and the Nigerian Political Crisis," Unpublished paper,
Department of Political Science, University of Lagos, no date [1998], 10–12.

that violent campus cults received support from the university's administration to attack and kill students who discussed political issues.[14] The authorities outlawed the National Association of Nigerian Students in 1986 and removed prominent professorial critics from their classrooms. Some of these professors took refuge abroad, while officials supported "peace movements" on campuses to undermine real student activism and to turn student organizations into vehicles to enter politics and access patronage. Some police sponsored vigilante groups to combat students who still insisted on protesting official corruption. The return to a civilian regime in 1999 after the death of the country's dictator – popularly thought to have been the result of an overdose of Viagra – did not end violence on university campuses. In 2004, after the violent deaths of six students on the campus of the University of Ibadan, an editorialist complained that "intra-campus groups are being infiltrated by politicians who perceive the members cheap sources for recruiting thugs for their selfish ends" and explained that the politicians supplied firearms to these groups.[15]

These events showed how the extension of violent forms of patronage politics into what ordinarily would have been the societal arenas in which to organize opposition instead crowded out ideologues and set groups against one another. Already in the 1960s and 1970s, there were numerous armed groups that used violence to protect their patron and to ensure their own access to benefits within that political system. Some of these groups later played more active roles in warfare as some of these political systems fractured. Like warlord rebels, how and why they fought reflected the nature of state authority. This pattern of fighting for a limited community such as co-ethnics or a patron's political network became prominent in violence in the 1990s and later in Kenya, Nigeria's Delta region, and Sudan's Darfur region, as detailed in the following. This increase in the violence associated with parochial rebels was related to the intensification of international pressures on African regimes to change how they dealt with their domestic critics, and in particular, to hold multiparty elections. This additional factor alongside the existing dynamics of patronage politics explains how parochial rebels emerged as a major category of rebels in the evolution of warfare in Africa.

---

[14] Lanre Adeleke, "The Attack Was Sponsored," *Tell*, 26 July 1999, 24.
[15] Editorial, "Resurgence of Campus Cults," *Daily Times* [Lagos], 29 June 2004.

Between Political Reform and Parochial Rebels

Most domestic and international advocates of democratic reform in African countries in the 1980s and 1990s thought that pressuring regimes to allow competitive multiparty elections and freedom for critics to form their own associations and to remove restrictions on public media would give voice to calls for change among citizens. Either this would force politicians to focus more on the welfare of citizens, or these politicians would be replaced through constitutional means. The early 1990s saw a huge wave of democratic reforms in Africa such that by 1994 only Libya's and Eritrea's governments refused to commit to at least the outward form of multiparty elections, even though multiparty elections in places like Togo, Chad, Burkina Faso, and others appeared to be little more than a façade behind which old regimes continued to hold onto power. Although there were numerous instances of hedging, sleights of hand, and restrictions on the operation of these electoral systems, the transformation was shockingly rapid, as only five years earlier, just seven African countries held multiparty elections. This development has tapped into deep popular desires for reform, even when regimes have tried to rig electoral processes in their favor.

Political reform was a popular agenda in many countries before the early 1990s. As shown by prewar activism in Liberia, discussed in the last chapter, and in Sierra Leone, discussed in the preceding section, the politics of these countries included substantial civic opposition to authoritarian rule. Between February 1990 and October 1991, the formation in ten countries of conferences to rewrite constitutions showed the domestic roots of the desire for political change; the organizers had no trouble mobilizing civic groups, religious institutions, and many other critics of authoritarian regimes to reform these political systems. The conferences led to genuine multiparty elections in some countries. Civic groups inside South Africa played a major role in the struggle against apartheid and were powerful forces by the time that real reform began in 1990. In almost all cases, domestic associations of lawyers, religious organizations, community development groups, and many other associations played active roles in this process. Moreover, public attention to these debates was considerable, which helped to generate great expectations for reform.

Africa's international creditors and foreign aid providers made it clear that African governments' willingness to conduct multiparty elections would play an important role in shaping their relations. The World

Bank's 1989 report on the poor economic conditions in Africa made a case for creditors to consider the willingness of debtor country governments to permit multiparty elections when deciding how to treat them.[16] The extreme dependence of Mozambique's government on foreign aid and credits in the late 1980s, equal to almost 70 percent of the country's entire domestic production, played a role in its adoption of reforms in 1990.[17] French president Francois Mitterand's warning in a speech on 22 June 1990 at the La Baule meeting of francophone African heads of state that French aid would be tied to democratization put pressure on governments to reform and encouraged reform-minded activists. Subsequent French support for dictators in Togo and Rwanda showed the limits of the willingness of French officials to sacrifice the pursuit of other interests to the promotion of democracy in Africa. But in the context of 1990, with the collapse of the Soviet bloc in progress, international pressures were real. The decision of Kenya's creditors in 1990–91 to refuse to reschedule Kenya's debt unless President Daniel arap Moi agreed to permit multiparty elections underlined the seriousness of this pressure. African government representatives in the Organization of African Unity (OAU) in July 1990 acknowledged that they had to consider reform as the price of normal relations with outsiders "in view of the real threat of marginalization of our continent" if they failed to do so.[18]

But not all regimes implemented reforms, and parochial rebels have played a crucial role in the survival of Africa's more extreme patronage-based political systems. In countries with stronger formal institutions and with more limited connections between politicians and youth gangs, such as Ghana and Tanzania, the introduction of multiparty systems was not so threatening to incumbent politicians. The prospect that those who were voted out of office could campaign to return later gave elites in general – government officials and their counterparts in business – some assurances that they could weather these reforms. But where state authority rested on the ruler's ability to manipulate access to resources

---

[16] World Bank, *Sub-Saharan Africa: From Crisis to Sustainable Growth* (Washington, DC: World Bank, 1989).

[17] David Plank, "Aid, Debt, and the End of Sovereignty: Mozambique and Its Donors," *Journal of Modern African Studies* 31:3 (Sept 1993): 408.

[18] Organization of African Unity, *Declaration on the Political and Socio-Economic Situation in Africa and the Fundamental Changes Taking Place in the World* (Addis Ababa: OAU, July 1990), art. 2.

in legal and clandestine channels to enhance his own power, losing an election was a recipe for permanent marginalization.

Parochial rebels also serve as tools of incumbent politicians to limit the tendency for electoral competition to raise the costs of patronage. Youth violence is an effective means of controlling subordinate politicians who might try to campaign with platforms that threaten the interests of their political patrons. Lower-level candidates can also use parochial rebels to hold down the costs of campaigns. This is important, because if voters are allowed a genuine choice of who represents them in a patronage-based system, voters are liable to sell their vote to the candidate who can offer them the most material rewards for their loyalty. Electoral violence helps to quell these demands through intimidation and denying recruits to activists and, in extreme cases, forces voters to rely on their local political brokers to use gangs to protect them from other candidates' militias. This dynamic turns voters into supplicants to whoever is the strongest local power broker or the politician-protector of their ethnic community, rather than demanding and critical individuals who are actually able to exercise a choice.

Incumbent politicians exhibit variable capacities to use violence to manage the threat of multiparty elections. Rival political strongmen in political systems that are already deeply divided face fewer obstacles in mobilizing rival youth gangs. Congo-Brazzaville is one such case. That country's turn to a multiparty system began in February 1991 at the start of a three-month-long national conference. The incumbent President Sassou-Nguesso faced serious criticism, and the conference gave executive power to André Milongo, a former member of the World Bank's board of governors. Student protestors and civic activists associated with Christian churches and labor unions asserted their agendas, but the real conflict emerged among faction leaders in the incumbent political establishment. Pascal Lissouba won the August 1992 election against Sassou-Nguesso and Bernard Kolélas, the mayor of the capital city, Brazzaville.

Milongo's effort to prevail over the incumbent political factions led him to set up his own paramilitary to counterbalance Sassou-Nguesso's influence in the military. With Lissouba's election, Milongo's paramilitary shifted to protect Kolélas and supplemented Kolélas's Matsuanisme militia, named after the anti-colonial hero André Matsoua. Together they became the core of Kolélas's Ninjas, as the professional soldiers trained newcomers from Kolélas's home region and from parts of the capital city. Lissouba pursued his bid to hold on to power through his Cocoye, Zulu, and Mamba militias, while the Cobras fought on former president Sassou-Nguesso's behalf. This militarization of factions took on a geopolitical dimension when Lissouba looked to members of Angola's political opposition for help, which then spurred Angola's government to give help to Sassou-Nguesso's forces.[19]

Fighting in 1993–94, mostly in the capital city, killed about 2,000 people and displaced between 100,000 and 300,000 people. Renewed fighting in 1997 killed another 10,000 to 15,000 people before Angolan help and access to oilfield revenues allowed Sassou-Nguesso's forces to prevail.[20] These militias, Congo-Brazzaville's parochial rebels, recruited among the political networks of the two contenders. Recruits included unemployed secondary school leavers and hometown youth who would have found government employment in earlier years. As combatants in factional conflicts, these militias took on an ethnic dimension to the extent that they reflected the hometown bases of their patrons, and members joined them for protection against other militias. But urban violence also reflected youth anger at the privilege of those who had done well out of their political connections. Targeting the homes of the well-connected for looting could be seen as a political statement as much as the looting itself.[21] But Sassou-Nguesso's receipt of 89.4 percent of the popular vote in the 2002 elections signaled his return to the role of arbiter in patronage politics, compared to his paltry 16.9 percent score in the 1992 elections, which reflected his declining control over patronage. Congo-Brazzaville's 2009 presidential elections also occurred on a multiparty basis. But the main opposition party joined Sassou-Nguesso's party, leaving ten independent candidates and two other parties' candidates to divide what was left after Sassou-Nguesso's 79 percent tally.

In Congo-Brazzaville and in other electoral authoritarian regimes in which a single head of the political establishment manages to maintain or reestablish control, those who do not join the "tame opposition" face government-instigated violence. This violence justifies politicians' claims that multiparty democracy cannot work in multiethnic societies. It also warns voters that rejection of their protectors may expose

---

[19] "Congo: Lissouba under Siege," *Africa Confidential* 34:25 (17 Dec 1993): 5–6.

[20] Rémy Bazenguissa-Ganga, "The Spread of Political Violence in Congo-Brazzaville," *African Affairs* 98:390 (1999): 37–54.

[21] Henri Ossebi, "De la galère à la guerre: jeunes et 'Cobras' dans les quartiers Nord de Brazzaville," *Politique Africaine* 72 (Dec 1998): 20–21.

them and their kinsmen to retribution from rival political factions' militias. This informal repression at the hands of neo-traditional parochial rebels armed with modern weapons along with arrows and machetes enables the security forces to stand aside and the government to deny to domestic and international observers that it violates human rights. The government conceals its involvement behind its claims that this "tribal violence" is really primarily over access to land or other deep-seated problems that are beyond any reasonable short-term solution. This strategy gives a new lease on life to the authoritarian practices of the single-party era and equips the political establishment to continue to dominate local public life and marginalize critics, including those who might have become leaders, and commissars, and fighters in ideological rebellions in other circumstances.

Election Violence in Kenya: Politicians and Parochial Rebels against Democracy

Responding to domestic and international pressure, in late 1991 President Daniel arap Moi's Kenya African National Union (KANU) government repealed the provision in the country's constitution that limited electoral contests to candidates of the incumbent ruling party. By the time that multiparty elections were held in December 1992, significant violence had broken out, a pattern that recurred with elections in 1997 and in 2002, and again in 2007. The violence associated with the 1992 election started as the political establishment turned against the prodemocracy movement. Ruling party youth wingers, Nairobi City Council *askaris* (police), and Provincial Administration demolition squads destroyed the homes of slum dwellers and others who had supported antigovernment protests. As one observer argued, "after the incidents of July 7th [1990], the government felt threatened by the existence of these shanties. It saw in slum dwellers a vulnerable and ready tool in the hands of crafty revolutionaries who might offer a better deal. . . . The government dreaded facing an organized people with common grievances."[22] Violence spread to rural areas, where "Kalenjin warriors" (ethnic kin of the president and many high officials) tried to force members of other ethnic groups out of these constituencies to

---

[22] Quoted in Mwangi Kagwanja, *Killing the Vote: State Sponsored Violence and Flawed Elections in Kenya* (Nairobi: Kenya Human Rights Commission, 1998), 10.

reinforce the ruling KANU party's electoral hold on these areas. The violent removal of other people left some KANU supporters in positions to take over the land of those who were pressured to leave. But those who benefited from violence or in whose name violence had been committed were left to wonder if a loss at the polls for the ruling party would mean retribution. These fears contributed to the ruling party's political control of these groups in this context of electoral competition.

Electoral violence and the expulsion of people from their land intensified the existing practice of the authoritarian regime's use of control over access to land as a political tool. An official inquiry directly connected land allocations to political support at election time. "Records examined by the Commission reveal that most illegal allocations of public land took place just before or soon after the multiparty elections of 1992, 1997 and 2002."[23] Politicians and business partners also used their connections to political networks to force titled owners off their land. This struggle over land gave the impression that violence sprang from deep-rooted ethnic tensions, but evidence from several official inquiries into electoral violence showed that this violence was of fairly recent vintage. Violence also took on an ethnic complexion in the efforts of some leaders of militias to appropriate land from those who were displaced (although it was doubtful that many individual fighters actually benefited in this way). Thus the real underlying cause of this "inter-ethnic" conflict included the desire to share in the benefits of political power among those who could mobilize armed youth to help others to acquire or hold onto the illicit power to allocate land and other resources.

Electoral violence also undermined the efforts of broad-based civic opposition groups. Three months before the 1992 elections, a parliamentary committee confirmed reports that high-ranking government officials were involved in training, equipping, paying for, and providing logistical support to violent progovernment militias.[24] This violence was geared toward intimidating opposition candidates and suppressing voter registration and turnout. "President Moi and his associates have not ceased their abuse of power, but merely have modified their tactics,"

---

[23] Republic of Kenya, *Report of the Commission of Inquiry into the Illegal / Irregular Allocation of Public Land* [The Ndungu Report] (Nairobi: Government Printer, 2004), 82.

[24] Republic of Kenya, *Report of the Parliamentary Select Committee to Investigate Ethnic Clashes in Western and Other Parts of Kenya* [The Kiliku Report] (Nairobi: National Assembly, 1992).

noted a report on human rights abuses. "Recently, the government has relied on different tactics, such as extra-legal intimidation and violence, to silence and disempower critics,"[25] such as church and community groups and professional associations like the Kenya Law Society. The use of parochial rebels who mobilized the short-term interests of fighters made violence look "tribal," as the government denied that it played a direct role in it. The origins of some of these groups in cultural associations and their use of spears and arrows (along with firearms) gave them a neo-traditional image that helped to conceal the real roots of the violence.

President Moi's 36 percent tally in the December 1992 poll exposed the limits of using violence to marshal support from an ethnic group and political stalwarts who represented a minority of the country's people, especially when voters were actually presented with choices. But sponsorship of parochial rebels helped to divide the opposition, too. Groups such as Taliban and Jeshi la Mzee (the Old Man's Army, a reference to the elderly Moi) appeared in advance of the next election. Neo-traditional in form and with names that were associated with distinct ethnic labels, these groups recruited fighters who operated as vigilantes to protect their home communities from the insecurity that groups like theirs were causing and those who sought the patronage of politicians. Jeshi la Mzee, for example, was formed with the sponsorship of senior members of KANU and elements of the KANU Youth Wing and was used to disrupt opposition activities.

Competitive elections in this context also pressed opposition politicians and communities to recruit parochial rebels to protect their interests. One of the more prominent groups of this sort, Mungiki, traces its origins to 1987, when a charismatic preacher led an ethnic Kikuyu neo-traditional alternative to the increasingly popular Pentecostal churches. A split in 1990 gave Mungiki a more distinct identity in the political realm, and the group registered as a political party in 1992 to compete in elections. Although Mungiki did not become a viable political party, the violent 1992 poll generated recruits for the group as displaced youth fled KANU-sponsored violence to take refuge in Nairobi's slums.[26] The spread of these crumbling and decaying slums registered the consequence of the government's tendency to spend revenues on patronage

---

[25] Binaifer Nowrojee, *Divide and Rule: State-Sponsored Ethnic Violence in Kenya* (New York: Africa Watch, 1993), 11.

[26] David Anderson, "Vigilantes, Violence and the Politics of Public Order in Kenya," *African Affairs* 101:405 (2002): 533–32.

rather than on maintaining infrastructure or providing services. This governmental failure prompted groups like Mungiki to provide protection and services such as the provision of water, signs of an effort to administer the people and areas that they controlled. Thus, at the outset, these groups might have appealed to some as more than short-term protectors, as also embodying resistance to the oppressive political establishment and an opportunity for hitherto marginalized people to have a voice in the country's politics.

Unlike anti-colonial, majority rule, or reform rebels, the leaders of groups like Mungiki neither encountered nor were inclined to search for the fields of leverage – the social autonomy – to mobilize followers around these alternative political narratives or to deploy commissars to maintain organizational discipline and enforce obedience to political objectives. Instead, the authors of yet another official inquiry into violence noted that the "gangs are devoid of ideology and operate on a willing seller basis. Given the hierarchical nature of gangs and the upward mobile hopes of their members to become as well off as their leaders, youth can be mobilized for a variety of reasons."[27] In fact, President Moi received "defecting" Mungiki leaders at his residence before the 2002 elections and secured declarations from its leadership that Mungiki would support the KANU party's presidential candidate, as two leaders tried to run for office on the KANU ticket.[28] This apparent aggrandizing behavior does not contradict the notion that Mungiki's fighters and supporters shared a sense of frustration with the political system. Moreover, it is not clear that the rank and filers of these groups endorsed the activities of their leaders or that these leaders shared their rewards with their followers, who continued to live in squalor and suffered from the shortcomings of their government in other ways. In this manner the organization of parochial rebels tends to reflect the hierarchies and compromises of the patronage-dominated political context.

Connections to politicians, whether aligned with ruling or opposition factions, gave some leaders of these groups good positions from which to launch protection rackets. Mungiki's opportunities included intimidating shop owners and operators of *matatus* (Kenya's ubiquitous minivan transportation) to pay protection fees. Involvement in micro-level disputes such as conflicts between renters and tenants tied even

---

[27] Republic of Kenya, *Commission of Inquiry into Post Election Violence* [The Waki Report] (Nairobi: Government Printer, 2008), 35.

[28] Mutuma Ruteere, "Dilemmas of Crime, Human Rights and the Politics of *Mungiki* Violence in Kenya" (Nairobi: Kenya Human Rights Institute, 2008), 17.

these intensely local interactions to the hierarchies of political networks as opposing groups took sides on the basis of the client's willingness and ability to pay or one side or the other's connections to political patrons. This practice made it very difficult for groups like Mungiki to present themselves to communities as reliable alternatives to the corrupt political system, because efforts to provide services or mediate conflicts in the communities that they control were liable to reflect the interests of a politician patron or a political faction.

This situation undermines ideologues connected to these groups or those trying to form new groups to recruit and mobilize followers from among an aggrieved population and frustrates efforts to out-govern the oppressive state. This crowded field also denies ideologues the opportunities that the rebels in earlier chapters in this book seized to dominate the communities and resources that they needed to co-opt and intimidate other groups that might otherwise seek ties to the government. These would-be rebels now contended with ethnic and sectarian groups that were able to find politician patrons and that limited options available to youth who joined with rebels for the usual reasons, such as protection, status, or fear or compulsion. "The power of these gangs should not be underrated," wrote concerned officials inquiring into the violence, "including their ability to force other poor unwilling youth to join them. . . . In this sense, youth are both being exploited and have become exploiters themselves."[29]

Electoral violence became especially widespread surrounding the December 2007 poll in which opposition candidate Raila Odinga's apparent lead disappeared and the incumbent president, Mwai Kabaki, was declared the winner. Kabaki had beaten Moi in the 2002 election, so the political establishment's ruling party faction now became the opposition faction as political patrons and their clients scrambled to preserve or to claim privileges. The nature of the violence associated with this turnaround illustrated the extent to which elections were about battles for position in a political hierarchy and not about contending policies or ideologies. In fact, the former opposition was at least as prolific in its use of parochial rebels as a political instrument. This violence led to the deaths of more than 1,000 people in the Rift Valley area and the displacement of up to half a million people, adding to the estimated 350,000 people still displaced from earlier violence.[30] These

---

[29] Waki Report, 2008, 37.

[30] United Nations Office for the Coordination of Humanitarian Affairs, *Displaced Populations Report* (New York: United Nations), issue 3 (Jan–June 2008), 2.

figures, along with the 1,500 thought to have been killed in violence in 1992–93,[31] and the prospect of violence in future elections put Kenya firmly into the category of states in conflict.

Given that Mungiki faced a violent state crackdown by 2007, it is not likely that it played a major role in the violence that followed. Other parochial rebels had become prominent, a sign of the factional fluidity of these groups. The crackdown and Mungiki's internal politics highlight how the shrunken fields of leverage left rebels like Mungiki's unable to exploit their prior actions and reputations to create their own political narrative. When Mungiki's leaders claimed that they opposed the government on whose behalf some of their followers committed violence, the group's public credibility was weakened. Moreover, some police officers believed that fighters acted without orders from Mungiki's highest commanders. This confusion points to suspicions that politician and businessman patronage encouraged factional splits within the organization.[32] This tendency of incumbent political authorities to use factional divisions to serve their own interests in the absence of rebel access to a foreign source of material or political support, such as anticolonial and other rebels had, destroys autonomous political projects. This difficulty is illustrated in the failed efforts of those who appear to have tried to chart a more autonomous political path. Attempts among some Mungiki leaders in 2000 to lead a mass conversion of members to Islam and threats to call for *jihad* against government efforts to ban the group may have been a cynical move. But conversion also could have helped with leadership efforts to assert control over its own membership and to insulate the organization from politician interference. The hostility of some Mungiki leaders to Christianity for engendering "mental slavery" suggested a search for a political narrative that would not be hostage to the vagaries of the country's existing political system.[33] The government's effort to ban this armed group and seventeen others, possibly out of concern for public safety and state control, also could have signaled that some politicians were alarmed that they were losing control over an instrument of violence.

---

[31] Nowrojee, *Divide and Rule*, 71.

[32] Human Rights Watch, *Ballots to Bullets: Organized Political Violence and Kenya's Crisis of Governance* (New York: Human Rights Watch, 2008), 44.

[33] Margaret Gecaga, "Religious Movements and Democratisation in Kenya: Between the Sacred and Profane," in Godwin Murunga and Shadrock Nasong'o (eds.), *Kenya: The Struggle for Democracy* (London: Zed Books, 2007), 80–81.

Attempts to rein in Mungiki and other groups featured yet more efforts on the part of officials to use non-state groups to apply violence to maintain political control. Reports indicate that death squads and the police targeted members of these groups in extra-judicial executions, killing as many as 500 in mid-2007.[34] State security forces acted as yet another faction, fighting for control in an environment in which parochial rebels still appealed to some politicians and provided some protection to communities. Ultimately, parochial rebels, like warlords, undermine the foundations of formal state institutions and authority, and they are part of the evolution of the political system outside of the framework of formal state institutions. But when parochial rebels begin to challenge their political patrons, these rebels have the capacity to disrupt the hierarchy of patronage politics even if they do not replace it with a new political paradigm. They can blackmail or switch patrons and threaten the interests of political factions, aggravating conflicts between these authorities. Meanwhile, the politicization of conflicts, even down to the level of disputes between tenants and landlords noted previously, deepens the societal impact of this contention as it denies political space to alternative organizations to recruit and discipline followers to change the political paradigm. This serious political dilemma, which is deeply rooted in the nature of state politics that produced warlord rebels and thus merits the inclusion of early twenty-first-century Kenya in a book about warfare, is not only a Kenyan problem, and so it is to the case of Nigeria that we now turn.

Parochial Rebels in the Niger Delta

The politics of violence in the Niger Delta region highlights the difficulty of organizing challenges to Nigeria's patronage-based system of political authority. At first glance, the Niger Delta provides an excellent venue for ideological cadres and their commissars to mobilize non-combatants for a rebellion. The Delta accounts for about 20 percent of Nigeria's population, but its oil resources supply about 40 percent of Nigeria's GDP, 75 percent of its government revenues, and more than 95 percent of its foreign exchange earnings, a situation that scholars

---

[34] Philip Alston, *Report of the Special Rapporteur on Extrajudicial, Summary or Arbitrary Executions, Addendum, Mission to Kenya* (New York: United Nations General Assembly, Human Rights Council, 26 May 2009), 8–11.

identify as ideal for encouraging separatist rebellions.[35] The region's people share a long-standing sense that the corrupt and distant political establishment is preoccupied with profiting from the region's wealth, often through violence, and has provided local people with little in return. Despite the great wealth that is extracted from the Delta, no significant part of the Delta benefits from a regular supply of potable water, the road system is practically nonexistent, and health and education facilities are in a deplorable condition.[36]

The serious lack of government capacity or political will to provide basic social services or to protect citizens from violence at the hands of politicians and their hired thugs after the 1999 transition to electoral politics, coupled with a deep shared sense of grievance across local ethnic communities, should cede the fields of leverage and provide the shared political narrative that rebel ideologues need to organize. Ideologues could draw from a rich historical legacy of rebellion, from the resistance to colonial rule by King William Koko of Nembe in the 1890s, Isaac Adaka Boro's leadership of an armed rebellion against Nigeria's government in 1966 to declare a Niger Delta Republic, and Ken Saro-Wiwa's defiance of the military dictatorship that hanged him and eight others in October 1995. Saro-Wiwa's Movement for the Survival of the Ogoni People (MOSOP) figured out how to tap the political and material resources associated with alliances with groups of foreign backers. Although it was not enough to save him from the hangman's noose, Saro-Wiwa attached his region's grievances to the human rights and environmental agendas of foreign NGOs, including Amnesty International, Human Rights Watch, Greenpeace, and Friends of the Earth, and to foreign officials, who pressured Nigeria's government on his behalf. Before his execution, Saro-Wiwa began to generate foreign support for MOSOP as a lever against the much more powerful Nigerian government. This environmental and human rights agenda gave MOSOP at least the possibility of breaking out of the narrow parochial agenda of self-determination

---

[35] Michael Ross, "Oil, Drugs and Diamonds: The Varying Role of Natural Resources and Civil War," in Karen Ballentine and Jake Sherman (eds.), *The Political Economy of Armed Conflict: Beyond Greed and Grievance* (Boulder, CO: Lynne Rienner, 2003), 47–70; Paul Collier and Anke Hoeffler, "The Political Economy of Secession," in Hurst Hannum and Eileen Babbit (eds.), *Negotiating Self-Determination* (Lanham, MD: Lexington Books, 2006), 37–59.

[36] United Nations Development Programme, *Niger Delta Human Development Report* (New York: UNDP, 2006), 40–42.

for the small ethnic Ogoni group and of mobilizing the broader Delta population.[37]

The Niger Delta's rebel groups that emerged after the 1999 transition to electoral politics are notable for their parochial focus on the interests of narrow ethnic communities and political factions, often in opposition to other Delta communities that share common grievances of violent exploitation and poor governance. Controlling the distribution of resources to fighters, the core task that all successful rebel groups to this point have had to master, appears to remain beyond the grasp of the Delta's rebels. These parochial rebel groups exhibit little capacity for or political interest in administering liberated zones against the very weak capacity of formal state institutions to provide social services or security. Instead, most of these parochial rebels contribute to the insecurity of the bulk of the non-combatant population. They show little concern for their reputations overseas (with the notable exception of the Movement for the Emancipation of the Niger Delta [MEND], explored in the following) and what support they gain from that quarter tends to reinforce their narrow ethnic or factional agendas. As in Kenya, these parochial rebels reflect the political system that many of them profess to fight. Their struggles are often geared toward gaining better positions within Nigeria's politics of patronage. This is not to argue that the very real popular grievances against corruption, officials who sponsor violence, government mismanagement, and foreign oil companies that exploit their resources and help produce environmental degradation are insignificant. The argument here and throughout this book is that the organization and behavior of rebel groups tend to reflect the fields of leverage, including their constriction or absence, that the domestic and international political environment shapes.

Political reform as it is implemented in Nigeria has tended to reinforce this parochialism among rebels. Nigeria's transition to a civilian electoral regime in 1999 occurred alongside a concerted effort to decentralize the distribution of government resources to the 36 states and 774 local government areas (LGAs) in which Nigeria's 150 million or so people live. In fact, this decentralization spread resources around to more local political networks rather than encouraging local administrative innovation. The global rise in oil prices in the early 2000s fueled this

---

[37] Clifford Bob, *The Marketing of Rebellion: Insurgents, Media, and International Activism* (New York: Cambridge University Press, 2005), 54–116.

expansion of patronage as oil exports generated a significant rise in revenues to Nigeria's federal government. This led to a fourfold increase in federal allocations to state and local governments between 1999 and 2005. In 2004, four states in the Niger Delta, which contained 11 percent of Nigeria's population, received about a third of these allocations, or $2 billion.[38] Monthly allocations to Rivers state LGAs, for example, grew from less than $2 million in 1999 to more than $14 million in 2006. Over the same period, monthly federal allocations to Rivers state rose from about $5 million to almost $100 million. A former state government official noted:

> When allocations are made, it is at the local government level that . . . they now see this money as money that has come just gratis to be shared out among political friends and members of the ruling party. The result is that after paying salaries they scarcely have enough to do anything else. . . . When you go to remote areas and see what is there you wonder if government even considers that they exist.[39]

This very real increase in state revenues, ostensibly part of the federal government's response to popular demands that the Delta region receive a greater share of the benefits of its oil resources, fueled patronage politics. With the end of military rule, elections beckoned as routes to power and wealth, but also as something that incumbents needed to manage, lest voters actually be allowed to punish them for corruption and poor services. Nigeria's civilian electoral regime thus reinforces the role of the political godfathers, the senior politicians who finance elections and organize violence through their personal control of resources and connections. In return, those who win elections to governorships and other offices serve as proxies for godfathers, channeling a share of these resources back to their godfathers through using their offices to divert state assets, exempting others from the enforcement of laws, and through the allocation of state contracts. As they pay back their godfathers and allow them to play a role in subordinate officials' appointments, these officeholders become godfathers to other people, whether in the realms of government, business, or criminal activities, while reinforcing the ruling party's grip on power. The stakes involved in contesting elections grow as victory is about much more than just

---

[38] Human Rights Watch, *Chop Fine: The Human Rights Impact of Local Government Corruption and Mismanagement in Rivers State, Nigeria* (New York: Human Rights Watch, Jan 2007), 21–22.

[39] Human Rights Watch, *Chop Fine*, 42; on allocation figures, 25, 76.

serving in an official capacity, and thus elections become very violent affairs.

This violent politics of patronage can be unstable. The case of the godfather Chris Uba in Anambra state, bordering the Delta region, illustrates some of the problems of this post-1999 link between electoral violence and patronage politics. Uba, a member of the PDP (the ruling People's Democratic Party) Board of Trustees, sponsored Chris Ngige's candidacy for governor in the 2003 election. This sponsorship entailed a written contract that spelled out Ngige's obligation to allow Uba to control the governor's appointments and awards of contracts. In return, Uba helped to rig the election, but afterward, Ngige reneged on his agreement with his godfather. Police took Ngige away, and he was forced to sign a resignation letter. Ngige petitioned in courts to have his resignation under duress invalidated. Thugs then attacked Anambra's seat of government and burned it down. A band of assassins waylaid his convoy, but the governor's forces were able to return fire.[40] This episode was just a sequel to Anambra's legacy of factional violence. Anambra's previous governor, Chinwoke Mbadinuju, also fell out with his godfather, but at that time the police force was divided between the two camps. Equipped with his own "official" vigilante service, that governor proclaimed that he would "deal ruthlessly" with his opponents: "I'll definitely react," he declared, "people will die."[41]

The situation in Anambra shows how, as in Kenya, youth recruitment into the factional battles of politicians disrupts the fields of leverage needed for organizing other kinds of rebellions. Delta state politicians recruited members of the violent cults noted previously to prevent people from voting in the 2003 and 2007 elections. One cult member said of the 2007 election, "The PDP has ruled for eight years and so they have the money and they have the power.... Other parties say when we are in government you will enjoy money... but the PDP will pay you immediately, so people prefer this. What the PDP is, is guns and money."[42] Some politicians allegedly recruit armed supporters from the university campus gangs, with recruits expecting a role in the winner's political network as muscle and beneficiaries.[43]

---

[40] Daniel Smith, *A Culture of Corruption: Everyday Deception and Popular Discontent in Nigeria* (Princeton, NJ: Princeton University Press, 2008), 125–34.

[41] Anayochukwu Agbo, "Wartime in Anambra," *Tell*, 4 Feb 2002, 37.

[42] Human Rights Watch, *Criminal Politics: Violence, "Godfathers" and Corruption in Nigeria* (New York: Human Rights Watch, Oct 2007), 37.

[43] Dayo Thomas, "Killer Cultists," *The Week*, 4 Feb 2002, 12–14.

Against this tendency for fighters to serve the interests of political factions, the December 1998 Kaiama Declaration of the Ijaw Youth Council (IYC) articulated a clear set of political demands that fit well with popular narratives of government exploitation and other misdeeds. Against the backdrop of attacks on oil pipelines and production facilities, this declaration asserted community ownership over oil in ethnic Ijaw areas, asked oil companies to leave pending resolution of resource ownership issues, and signaled support for other self-determination movements in Nigeria.[44] The IYC's declaration represented an effort to assert greater direction on the agendas of parochial rebels. But many of these groups in Ijaw and other communities took neo-traditional names that reflected local identities and cultural practices, such as Egi Youth Federation, Egbesu Boys of Africa, and Feibagha Ogbo, and were not inclined to recruit and mobilize people who did not belong to these communities.

At first, it seemed that violence in the Delta region signaled a clear demarcation between the forces of the state and a growing rebellion. State security forces had already killed about 2,000 people in the Delta between 1994 and 1998.[45] Security forces destroyed the town of Odi in November 1999 and killed an estimated 2,000 people there in reprisal for allegedly harboring rebel fighters. A February 2005 attack on Odioma killed "scores" of people.[46] These and other assaults were met with more community attacks on oil pipelines and installations. Although often depicted as local efforts to profit from the sale of stolen oil, it is also reasonable to consider the attacks as a political act in the re-appropriation of local resources. April 2002 saw the first armed seizure of an offshore oil facility, with the taking of hostages and kidnappings of oilfield workers throughout the year. These rebels, regardless of their parochial character, asserted a capacity to disrupt the main source of state revenue and threaten the security of politicians' positions.

Although they exercised a capacity to confront state forces by the early 2000s, the Delta's parochial rebels did little to challenge the incumbent state's political authority to govern. From the perspective of anti-colonial and other rebels, they had a great opportunity to set up their

---

[44] Kaiama Declaration, http://www.unitedijawstates.com/kaiama.html, accessed 20 Dec 2009.

[45] Akanimo Sampson, "Blood from the Pipelines," *Punch*, 19 July 2000, 20.

[46] Elias Courson, "Odi Revisited? Oil and State Violence in Odioma, Brass LGA, Bayelsa State" (Berkeley: Institute of International Studies, University of California, Berkeley, 2006), 2.

own governance structures across the clans and ethnic communities of
the Delta to show local people the contrast of their ideas and capabilities with the government's poor performance. Delta rebels also did not
appear to field commissars to discipline fighters, organize the numerous armed groups around a single political narrative, and coordinate
tactics. A key reason for this was that fighters and their commanders
often sided with various political factions that competed for office in
the Delta's state and LGA administrations. This is not to presume that
fighters and their commanders did not harbor political grievances that,
if satisfied, really would have led to a radical change in how Nigeria was governed. But the nature of local factional competition within
the incumbent government tapped into the competing interests among
fighters and commanders to jockey for position in this political network. The pursuit of these more immediate interests involved the use
of tactics calculated to gain access to the resources that state officials and
foreign oil companies controlled, as well as the use of criminal activities.
These pursuits were still compatible with the parochial rebels' personal
resentment toward the predations of government officials and the sense
of marginalization by the political system that many of these fighters
and commanders helped to reinforce.

The political evolution of Mujahid Asari Dokubo, an individual who
in many respects fits well in the category of ideologue and political
activist, illustrates the interplay of ideological and instrumental agendas
in a parochial rebellion. Previously known as Melford Dokubo Good-
head, Jr., Asari (as he is popularly known) is the son of a judge. He
attended the University of Calabar law school and then the Rivers State
University of Science and Technology in the 1980s but left both programs before receiving his degrees. He participated in a born-again
congregation before converting to Islam "because Islam is a revolutionary religion."[47] He visited Libya, where he received military and
political training, but doubted the relevance of Libyan ideas to the
Delta's situation.[48] He contested the 1993 House of Assembly elections
but failed to gain a seat. In 2001, Asari was declared the winner of elections to the IYC's presidency, but the validity of the vote was contested,
and a rival claimed the office. Asari then focused on establishing the

[47] Ibim Semenitari and Anayochukwu Agbo, "'Nigeria is a Dubious Entity'" [interview
with Dokubo Asari], *Tell*, 18 Oct 2004, 16–18.
[48] International Crisis Group, *Fuelling the Niger Delta Crisis* (Brussels: ICG, 28 Sept
2006), 4.

Niger Delta People's Volunteer Force (NDPVF) in an effort to force the government to heed the demands in the Kaiama Declaration.

The NDPVF acquired resources through "bunkering," or the siphoning of oil from pipelines for sale to illicit dealers, a defensible activity to many from the point of view of the struggle to gain control over local resources. Extortion rackets and other illicit activities contributed to the group's resources, pursuits that involved collaboration with existing youth gangs. Because fighters collected resources through their own efforts, the NDPVF's main role was to act as a protector. These activities and affiliations brought the NDPVF into competition with local politicians who used these gangs for personal protection, to help rig elections, and to assist their own illicit business operations. As a new force, the NDPVF came into conflict with the incumbent Rivers state governor in a competition to patronize armed groups. The governor allegedly turned to the rival Niger Delta Vigilante Service (NDVS) under the leadership of Ateke Tom. Tom, like Asari, identified himself as a defender of Ijaw community interests. Tom completed primary school before he emerged as a local vigilante leader and then garnered security contracts in the early 1990s from a foreign firm to protect its installation.

Members of each group and their affiliates allegedly received offers of political protection, including license to carry out profitable bunkering operations, if they would help drive out opposition party campaigners and candidates. Rivers state government officials reportedly backed Asari's election to the IYC presidency to exploit divisions in the Ijaw community and to extend patronage to fighters who were under Asari's and Tom's protection. This brought the NDPVF and NDVS and their affiliates into conflict with one another.[49] Intervening in what was now armed conflict between PDP factions in September 2004, Nigeria's President Obasanjo mediated a truce between Asari and Tom. This situation of politician patronage took issues like self-determination and resource control for specific ethnic communities and merged them with struggles against other communities to claim the right to host an LGA headquarters or other portals to connect to the patronage networks of the Delta's political establishment.

The Federated Niger Delta Ijaw Communities (FNDIC), another umbrella group representing militants, appeared poised to articulate

---

[49] Human Rights Watch, *Rivers and Blood: Guns, Oil and Power in Nigeria's Rivers State* (New York: Human Rights Watch, Feb 2005), 4–6.

broader community grievances. Originally called the Niger Delta Volunteer Force, evoking the historical memory of a rebellion in 1966,
fighters associated with FNDIC attacked Itsekeri rivals in the late 1990s
in a conflict over the relocation of an LGA headquarters. The FNDIC's
top leadership, however, began to break away from this narrow agenda
in 2003, relying on the Internet and contacts with foreigners to cir-
culate their critiques of the Delta's political system and the role that
violence played in it. But the FNDIC soon fell prey to the allures of
security contracts with oil companies and the offers of official positions and the opportunity to become a link between government and
militants. Predictably, this shift produced tensions within the group
between those with more radical aims and those who compromised
with the forces against which they supposedly fought.[50] This process
of FNDIC co-optation reached to the highest levels of Nigeria's government, as President Obasanjo reportedly allocated the lease of an oil
block to people linked to FNDIC officials.[51]

Ideologues faced repeated, serious difficulties in asserting alternative
political agendas when politicians and oil companies controlled fighters'
access to resources and when very small gangs of fighters could conduct their own bids for patronage. One activist reported that aggressive
fighters disrupted efforts to meet with community leaders to discuss
the problems of factional conflict and created an environment that was
hostile to the kinds of ideologues and activist organizers seen in other
rebellions, so that now "an educated person will fear to meet with the
grass roots."[52] Several female activists reported that they tried to deal
with the problem of factionalism through organizing in social networks,
such as religious associations and tightly knit business contacts, that
were more exclusive to women and that were relatively insulated from
the allures of patronage from politicians. But they also reported that
young women were joining violent gangs.[53]

Isaac Boro's experiences in 1966 highlighted the extent to which
the nature of warfare had evolved in this parochial direction in the
Niger Delta. Like contemporaries in other African universities, Boro,

---

[50] Ukoha Ukiwo, "From 'Pirates' to 'Militants': A Historical Perspective on Anti-State
and Anti-Oil Company Mobilization among the Ijaw of Warri, Western Niger Delta,"
African Affairs 106 (2007): 602–05.
[51] "Nigeria: All Come to the Aid of the Party – and Fight It Out," *Africa Confidential*
48:23 (16 Nov 2007): 7:7.
[52] Interview with a MOSOP leader, Port Harcourt, 25 May 2005.
[53] Interview with activists, Port Harcourt, 31 May 2005.

a student of chemistry at the University of Nigeria's Nsukka campus, discussed politics with his classmates. After deciding that the Delta region's problems lay in the corruption of Nigeria's government and the exploitation of its oil resources by foreign firms, Boro and his class-mates declared that "we were to break the Niger Delta Area away into a nation and strive to maintain it."[54] Quite unlike leaders of parochial rebel groups, they decided that they needed to try to replace Nigeria's government in the Delta with a rebel liberated zone. Boro and another activist traveled to Ghana to seek help for their enterprise from offi-cials there. To their consternation, they found that Kwame Nkrumah's government already supported an Ijaw league. After a failed attempt to visit the Cuban embassy, the two returned to Nigeria. Soon after Nigeria's January 1966 military coup, Boro and his associates began to recruit volunteers for their Niger Delta Volunteer Service – NDVS, the inspiration for the names of Tom's Niger Delta Vigilante Service and the FNDIC – and put considerable thought into how to sustain their operation. Many of their recruits were fleeing government tax collec-tors. The rebels concluded that attacks on tax agents would be a good way to announce their presence to the Delta population. They issued proclamations to foreign oil firms demanding that local communities be given greater compensation for extracted resources. Their "revolution" lasted just under two weeks in February 1966 and was no match for the Nigerian military. Nonetheless, the contrast between Boro's effort and later organizations shows how rebel warfare has changed in the Delta, even as admirers appropriated the acronym from Boro's widely remembered and popular rebellion.

MEND appeared in late 2005 as yet another umbrella group. This group demanded the payment of a $1.5 billion court judgment against foreign oil firms for environmental damage and the release of Asari and other Ijaw political figures. MEND also demonstrated the capacity to launch attacks on oil production installations, including a 2008 attack on an offshore platform 120 kilometers from the Delta's coast. These attacks contributed to a decline in Nigeria's oil production from about 2.7 million barrels per day in 2006 to about 2.0 million barrels per day in mid-2009.[55] Even though MEND was able to coordinate attacks on oil installations, its coalitional character, lack of apparent interest in setting up liberated zones, and lack of direct control over fighter's access to

[54] Major Isaac Boro, *The Twelve Day Revolution* (Benin City: Idodo Umeh, 1982), 96.
[55] "Nigeria: Why the Banks Stay Optimistic," *Africa Confidential* 50:19 (25 Sept 2009): 2.

resources seem to indicate that it suffered from the same problems that faced other ideologues. Indeed, the head of Nigeria's state oil company said that his firm paid $12 million in protection money to fighters associated with MEND. MEND spokesmen denied this allegation, but given the legacy of other umbrella groups in the Delta like NDPVF and FNDIC, it is reasonable to assume that MEND could not control the behavior of its affiliated fighters.[56]

MEND has shown signs of an alternative strategy for overcoming the constraints of Nigeria's political context and its negative consequences for rebels' fields of leverage. Like the other umbrella groups in this region, MEND has not appeared to possess the capacity to fight for or run liberated zones. MEND instead has focused on the propaganda and practical consequences of disrupting oil production instead of fighting to control non-combatant populations. Posing as the coordinator of a threat to Nigeria's contribution to the global supply of oil, MEND may play a role in provoking officials from the United States and other countries to pressure Nigeria to solve its domestic political problems with counterinsurgency strategies that emphasize better government services to populations and control over official corruption. Foreigners may figure that Nigeria is a better ally and a more reliable source of a critical commodity if Nigerians view their government as effective, which therefore increases its basis for legitimacy. The United States and other customers of Nigeria's oil thus can become levers in the strategies of savvy ideologues. Avoidance of alliances with rebels in other parts of the world, which the United States or other governments would find threatening, is especially important for keeping international and domestic pressures focused on changing the behavior of Nigeria's government rather than on eliminating MEND's personnel.

The activities of rebels, whether or not they are parochial, enable MEND's spokesmen to maintain an image of inexorable pressure on the industry and on government revenues, regardless of the immediate personal motivations of fighters or the connections of their commanders to incumbent politicians. Moreover, the mysterious nature of MEND's leadership – its spokespeople Jomo Gbomo and Cynthia Whyte appear to be pseudonyms for several people – and its use of e-mail and Web sites to communicate make MEND a difficult target for violent government reprisals. Such rebel ideologues could as easily write dispatches from a

[56] "The Niger Delta: Wasteful Wars, Foreign Friends," *Africa Confidential* 49:17 (22 Aug 2008): 6–7.

British or American university and thus mitigate the ideologue's problem of finding the social space in which to devise a rebel challenge to state power. This seemingly relentless action of others does not require that MEND's ideologues engineer attacks and hold territory. Provided that the Delta's parochial rebels do not prey on non-combatants, or at least provided that any violence can be blamed on politician godfathers, MEND is somewhat insulated from the problems associated with factional divisions that have plagued other rebel ideologues.

MEND's vulnerability lies in its nature as a propaganda hub. Its success rests on the willingness of the consumers of its propaganda to see the only solution as lying in the radical reform of Nigeria's government, more local control over how natural resources are exploited, and allocation of a larger share of profits to local inhabitants. Concerned foreign officials and reformers inside Nigeria must see Nigeria's government officials as the actors who are both most threatening in this conflict and most amenable to a change in behavior. These are perspectives that other global events such as, for example, a sudden and severe drop in oil production in another part of the world or a spectacular terrorist attack on the scale of the September 11th attacks on Washington, DC, and New York could upset. MEND's failure (or unwillingness) to challenge Nigeria's government through setting up liberated zones also limits the degree to which it can challenge Nigeria's incumbent political establishment. Although attacks on oil installations are a serious business, the response also can be that this is just a matter for the police and other security services and does not require a coordinated effort to out-govern rebels. But given the severe constraints that rebel ideologues face in contexts found in Kenya and Nigeria that produce parochial rebels, MEND's strategy represents an intriguing sign of evolution in a new direction for warfare in sub-Saharan Africa, an issue taken up in the concluding chapter of this book.

Parochial Rebels through a Historical Lens

The earlier chapters in this book explain how anti-colonial and other rebellions in retrospect appear as part of a project that extended beyond the seizure of power to include efforts to reshape and build up the capabilities and legitimacy of states. Although each conflict had distinct characteristics, the conflicts as a whole contributed to a common pattern in which rebels, shaped as they were by the politics of the states in which they fought, experimented and pursued strategies that shifted political paradigms toward their goals. Some were more successful than others, whether they sought to end colonial rule, minority domination, or violent and predatory regimes. But successful or not, the shared purpose was significant. Although parochial rebel wars are very much fixtures of the present, it is useful to imagine what these more contemporary wars would look like if one were endowed with the capacity to travel far into the future and then view them with the benefits of a similar degree of hindsight. How might a retrospective historical view of parochial rebels look?

First, one might see these wars as contributing to a process of state collapse, or at least a severe testing of the capacity of central governments to rein in violence when it served their interests to do so. Political changes such as the introduction of competitive multiparty elections, largely forced on many regimes through domestic and international pressures, tested the capacities of these regimes to manage their own members and to control factional scrambles among those eager to improve their status within the existing political hierarchy. All of these conflicts included regime politics that incorporated non-state violent actors and global and domestic changes that disadvantaged the ideologues who appeared in these societies, as in every society. These drivers promoted factional division, among the politicians who used rebels as proxies to fight one another for position, and among the rebel fighters and commanders who learned how to exploit the political anxieties and weaknesses of their patrons to assert their personal interests. This dynamic created a considerable collective action problem. How could all of this tit-for-tat violence, the pursuit of deeply personal and narrow community interests, and the associated reciprocal anxieties of attack from others be overcome? Such would be the core necessity if Africa were to return to the kinds of rebel warfare that featured liberation and reform rebels with their liberated zones, their commissars, and therefore their capacity to organize and socialize their fighters to battle for a shared purpose.

The second element of a retrospective view might focus on the conflicts hidden inside parochial rebel warfare. Although this history of the evolution of warfare has shown that every rebel group contains members who harbor a predictably diverse range of motives and grievances, the very limited ambitions of parochial rebels will be seen to have been mismatched with the broader political concerns of most people. Parochial rebels will be seen as having done a poor job of addressing the experiences of people who lived for many years with governments that neither represented them nor played very positive roles in their daily lives. Borrowing a comparison with a case for which we really do have greater hindsight, the experiences of citizens in countries like Kenya and Nigeria in the early twenty-first century can be compared to the conditions facing people in China at the beginning of the twentieth century. In both, several generations suffered through insecurity and worsening material conditions (or at least the perception that things were getting worse) and had integrated deep disdain for their government into elements of their popular culture, attitudes, and expectations. Reflecting this generational aspect, the former head of Nigeria's Economic and Financial Crimes Commission, Nuhu Ribadu, after leaving Nigeria in the wake of an assassination attempt, noted that corruption had cost Nigeria more than $380 billion since independence. This problem in Nigeria and elsewhere "is the reason why Africa is Africa today. Not long ago, we were at par with several other parts of the world. Today we are really decades away, and it is certainly because of corruption. We are desperate for change. We want change," he said.[57]

At this juncture it is necessary to repeat the caveat that many countries in Africa do not have parochial rebels and that real electoral choices for voters have brought significant change in places like Ghana, South Africa, and Tanzania. These countries also tend to have stronger formal state institutions; reforms tend to deliver real benefits to people and help to make them better off. But these also are countries that did not see the extensive development of regimes that used informal networks of patronage to crowd out social action through choking off historic fields of leverage.

The experiences of other countries illustrate this relationship between weak institutions, patronage politics, the proliferation of violent factional conflicts, and the rise of parochial rebels. Sudan's rulers, for example, have long been wary of building strong state institutions, particularly to keep regimes in power, even though previous rulers were removed in coups in 1969, 1985, and 1989, with failed attempts at coups in 1970, 1971, and 2003, and an armed raid of the capital city in 2008. But these coup plots really were manifestations of factional struggles. Thus it has been safer for those in power to take care to limit the capabilities of security services and balance this with

[57] John Pomfret, "A Conversation with Nuhu Ribadu, Anti-Corruption Crusader," *Washington Post*, 24 May 2009, http://www.washingtonpost.com/wp-dyn/content/article/2009/05/22/AR2009052202025.html, accessed 12 April 2011.

reliance on parochial rebels to balance and divide competing factions. Although the conflict in Darfur has been fought over a number of other issues, Sudanese officials play a significant role in dividing rebel groups there. A UN panel of experts investigating the conduct of government and violent non-state actors in the conflict in Darfur "found evidence of continued support by the Government of the Sudan for armed militia groups operating in Darfur,"[58] and other investigators identified government efforts to co-opt and divide rebel leaderships as some high-profile rebel leaders joined government ranks.[59]

This government strategy (and, as noted in the last chapter, the tendency of those convening international conferences to welcome growing numbers of factions) changed the situation in 2004, when the Sudan Liberation Army (SLA) and the Justice and Equality Movement (JEM) dominated the rebel scene. By May 2006, JEM and SLA each had split into two groups. By October 2007, negotiation organizers were able to invite JEM–Collective Leadership and JEM-Azraq, while other JEM factions stayed away. By 2008, conveners could now chose between SLA/M, SLA/AW, SLA–M/Unity, SLA–Front for Liberation, SLA/Khamees, SLM–Classic, SLA–Free Will, and even the Mother of All SLAs.[60] This is the sort of situation that tends to become even more fragmented as rebels become ever more parochial in their pursuits, in the context of international pressure on Sudan's government to hold multiparty elections. As in Nigeria and Kenya, incumbent politicians struggle to manage these elections, which become more expensive and violent affairs once real choice at least becomes a possibility. Moreover, the interests of foreigners and domestic activists who press these regimes become hostage to regime strategies if the failure to manage contending factions risks leading to the collapse of the central government and its replacement with many contending parochial rebel groups. The preceding example of MEND is all the more intriguing for its possibility of breaking out of this mold of rebel–state politics.

---

[58] United Nations Security Council, *Report of the Panel of Experts Established Pursuant to Resolution 1591 (2005) Concerning the Sudan Prepared in Accordance with Paragraph 2 of Resolution 1713 (2006)* (New York: United Nations, 3 Oct 2007), 56.

[59] Victor Tanner and Jérôme Tubiana, "Divided They Fall: The Fragmentation of Darfur's Rebel Groups" (Geneva: Small Arms Survey, 2007), 46.

[60] Reuters, "Who Is Attending Darfur Talks, Who Is Not," *Sudan Tribune*, 27 Oct 2007, http://www.sudantribune.com/spip.php?article24453, accessed 14 April 2011. Gerard Prunier, "Armed Movements in Sudan, Chad, CAR, Somalia, Eritrea and Ethiopia" (Addis Ababa: Center for International Peace Operations [Berlin], 2008), 2–5.

The general dearth of rebel organizational options is surprising and unusual in the context of considerable community grievances, the presence and proliferation of viable political narratives, and new technologies that help like-minded people communicate and get their message to intended audiences. One can imagine that it would not be terribly difficult to convince people that their oppressive government and its failure to undertake real reform that improves their situations are a result of Western support for corrupt regimes, or that corruption and violence are signs of deviation from an idealized version of a culture under assault from the corrosive effects of foreign ideas and behaviors. One thing is certain; the evolution of warfare in independent Africa will continue. What form these changes are likely to take and what will have to happen to bring them into being are the subjects of the next – and concluding – chapter.

Conclusion: The Past and Future of Warfare in Africa

Violent encounters between states and rebels and the international community's assumptions about how Africa's states should be governed underscore the last half-century of warfare on the African continent. The founding compact of the Organization of African Unity (OAU) in 1963 that forbade countries from conquering their neighbors' territories had a very real impact in nearly eliminating conventional wars between African states. Much of this had to do with the mutual recognition of vulnerabilities. But the wider global decision that international borders would be sacrosanct no matter how illogical or inconvenient they may appear has turned attempts at conquest such as Iraqi leader Saddam Hussein's bid in 1990 to annex Kuwait into futile projects that generate almost total condemnation by other states and in this case reversal by a military invasion. This compact has largely held in Africa, as it has in much of the rest of the world. The Tanzanian invasion of Uganda in 1978–79 forced from power Uganda's President Idi Amin after he had violated this compact with his occupation of a chunk of Tanzanian territory. Ethiopia's and Eritrea's war, which broke out in May 1998, was about the exact location of an international border, not its revision. The Ethiopian army's 2006–09 intervention in Somalia came at the invitation of the weak, UN-backed transitional government. Morocco's war to annex Western Sahara on Spain's withdrawal from its colony in 1976 really was an irredentist exception, although some argued that Morocco made no claim against the territory of an existing sovereign state.

Thus the history of warfare in Africa over the past half-century is largely a history of rebel wars within an existing system of states. At first it seemed that the rejection of conquest, along with the international acceptance of the idea that every colony was to be accorded the right to sovereign majority rule, was to the overwhelming benefit of anti-colonial rebels. In a rare Cold War consensus, officials in the United States and the Soviet Union agreed, albeit for different reasons, that colonial rule had no place in the international system. Anti-colonial rebels satisfied their African supporters that they were intent on creating indigenous states that would join with the others in a regional system of sovereign statehood. The majority rule rebels completed this realization of African state sovereignty. The goals of these rebels and the results of their struggles were easy to incorporate into the international system, and this was formalized in these rebels' acceptance of the established international order.

Regardless of the penchant among anti-colonial rebels for Marxist-Leninist projects of internal transformation, these rebels and the states that the winners then ran were hardly radical in their designs. This underlying conservatism has been consistent even when, as in the Angolan government's interference in wars in both Congos, regimes have tried to influence developments in the domestic politics of neighbors. These interventions took place through aid to factions in neighboring states and through selective support for rebel groups. But cross-border intervention in this fashion does not end the mutual recognition of international boundaries, even if this behavior signals the interference in another state's domestic affairs that the mutual recognition of sovereignty is supposed to block. Even so, powerful armies such as Angola's or Ethiopia's have not been deployed against neighbors in conventional invasions, even when the actions of neighbors have threatened the security of these regimes. Non-African countries, including the United States and the Soviet Union, readily pursued their interests though local clients. But their interference in regional or domestic affairs did not challenge the configuration of states in Africa. This was a fortunate outcome during the Cold War, as it removed fears that a rival's client state would use conquest as a way to extend its own and its patron's power. Thus African rulers have been denied the historic state-building tool of mass mobilization for war with neighboring countries, with the benefit that African populations have been spared one of history's greater scourges.

Reform rebels did not challenge this consensus in their refashioning of the domestic politics of existing states. Their goal was to govern these countries better than their predecessors had done and to make their states more capable in economic terms; in effect, to become better members of the existing international system. Reform rebels also engaged in conflicts with neighbors, but they accepted that this kind of conflict was best pursued through the support of proxy rebel groups, even if this occasionally involved members of their militaries crossing international borders in support of their clients. But warnings of deeper change in this domestic and regional order started to appear. The appearance of armed factions associated with past and present regimes, conceived in part as instruments to bolster these regimes, came to be the principal threat to their security and a basis for the rise of warlord and parochial rebels.

The broad international consensus against international war and conquest survived the end of the Cold War and the decay of domestic political order in a significant number of African states. The real shift in the evolution of Africa's wars came with the growing difficulties that the leaders of regimes faced in policing their own political associates. In many countries, leaders' loss of control over the allocation of patronage resources, coupled with the weakening of state institutions needed to generate revenues, gave license to heads of rival factions to appropriate resources and build their own patronage networks. International pressures to hold competitive elections further weakened centralized control over this politics of patronage. These developments encouraged ambitious politicians to tap into the ruling party youth wings, paramilitaries, and militias to pursue their fortunes. But even as these political actors became warlords, they still accepted the international consensus. Liberia's Charles Taylor, for example, remained focused on becoming the president of Liberia and convincing outsiders to support this goal, rather than trying to remake the map of West Africa. Most dramatically, the collapse of the central government in Somalia in early 1991 and the absence of a viable replacement since have not resulted in international moves to extinguish Somalia's sovereign status, no matter what happens inside its borders. This turmoil has not led any other state or rebel group to question Somalia's sovereign status outright.

The real change with this development came with the constriction of the fields of leverage that rebels with ideological and broad political agendas needed to build up their organizations, develop their ideas, and recruit and discipline their followers. The age of the committed guerrilla fighters in the countryside, battling state forces to control and administer populations, appears to have largely disappeared from the African scene. One of the core messages of this book is that the passions and grievances of individuals, and the resources and tools with which Africa's wars of the past fifty years have been fought, even the ubiquitous AK-47, have remained fairly constant. Change has come in the politics that shapes rebellions' fields of leverage, and in the reception given to rebels in the region and the rest of the world. Therefore, the pursuit of the question of the shape of warfare in Africa's future involves an investigation into the changes that are most likely to affect the fields of leverage that rebels need to figure out what they are really fighting for and to organize and execute their strategies.

The Future of Warfare in Africa

Some officials in the United States, Europe, and elsewhere worry that warlord and parochial rebels might create the conditions of anarchy, and that this could become a new field of leverage that would encourage a new kind of much more radical rebel who rejects Africa's division into sovereign states and who could even launch threats to the world's most powerful states. US president George W. Bush declared that the 11 September 2001 attacks on Washington, DC, and New York "taught us that weak states, like Afghanistan, can pose as great a danger to our national interests as strong states . . . poverty, weak institutions, and corruption can make weak states vulnerable to terrorist networks and drug cartels within their borders."[1] US civilian and military policy makers have labeled the areas where warlords and parochial rebels are most often found as "ungoverned spaces" in which armed terrorists can seek refuge and organize for attacks on other states in defiance of the intentions of the weak local sovereign. Their fear is that violent religious extremists could become the new ideological rebel leaders and commissars and go on to convince their parochial rebel associates and fighters to interpret their local grievances and aspirations in light of a new narrative of anti-Western religious extremism. Unlike the Marxist-Leninist internationalists of the anti-colonial struggles and the majority

---

[1] George W. Bush, *The National Security Strategy of the United States of America* (Washington, DC: White House, 2002), http://georgewbush-whitehouse.archives.gov/nsc/nss/2002, accessed 22 Feb 2011.

rule rebels who fought against apartheid, this new narrative's inter-
nationalist vision of uniting a global community of the faithful would
be truly revolutionary in questioning the existence of contemporary
sovereign states.[2]

One of the core messages of this book is that warlords and parochial
rebels actually do not fit easily into a simple schema of state collapse and
ungoverned spaces. The argument in the preceding pages is that the
regimes in Africa base their authority most thoroughly on the manipulation of access to patronage opportunities, have been very effective
in disrupting the organizing strategies of ideologues, and have made
deployment of rebel commissars considerably more difficult than under
colonial or apartheid regimes. Although warlords and parochial rebels
signal the fragmentation of these regimes, these regimes' instruments
of domination and control survive, as warlords and parochial rebels
continue to occupy the social spaces – the fields of leverage – that historically harbored the rebel ideologues and commissars who organized
to fight for alternative political programs.

The ironic "success" of the warlord and parochial rebels and the
state politics that produce them is that each stands as an obstacle to
ideologically driven armed rebellion in African societies. It is as if the
politics of rebellion has reached a cul-de-sac in the worst-off parts of
the continent, with a surplus of armed conflict and a dearth of political
transformation. This is not to declare that reform does not take place
in Africa. The rule of law and growing prosperity of some countries
such as Ghana, Tanzania, and others chart a different course. Democratic reforms result in real positive changes in people's lives in some
countries, usually in the places where politicians historically were more
reluctant to collaborate with armed gangs to assert their authority. But
for those countries that have seen the bulk of warfare in recent decades,
their politics resembles the impasse of Chinese politics by the beginning of the twentieth century. Like the generations of Chinese peasants
through the nineteenth century, citizens of these countries have seen
their countries become less stable and slip further behind the rest of the
world in economic terms. Like most Chinese people who endured the
scourge of warlords in the 1920s, most Africans have been mortified by

---

[2] The White House, *National Security Strategy of the United States of America* (Washington, DC: Government Printing Office, March 2006), 20; RAND International Security
and Defense Policy Center, *Dealing with Failed States and Ungoverned Spaces* (Santa
Monica, CA: RAND, 2005).

FIGURE 10. American military culture. Photograph by William Reno.

the conduct of the warlords and frightened by the insecurity and violence that accompanied their presence. In both contexts, warlords were
also prisoners of the politics out of which they emerged and obstacles
to reformers. With hindsight, the warlords of China are seen as part of
an interregnum, a period in which the seeds of change away from the
stagnation of the old regime were laid.[3] Transformative rebels found
their fields of leverage in rural areas away from state power and in close
contact with the people whom they were able to mobilize for the struggle
against Japan's occupation of China's coastal provinces from the 1930s.
Does the disruptive localism of warlord and parochial rebel warfare in
parts of contemporary Africa show similar signs of development away
from its impasse?

Some scholars raise the possibility that warfare in contemporary Africa actually contains elements of the violent construction of
new kinds of elite groups that are suited to building more capable
and effective states. In a landmark study, Christopher Cramer notes
that

[3] Lucian Pye, *Warlord Politics: Conflict and Coalition in the Modernization of Republican
China* (New York: Praeger, 1971), 3–12.

modern societies, in part, may be the unintended consequences of the business of war. . . . Characteristics of contemporary violent conflicts that are often regarded as signs of the pathological meaninglessness or the undoing of development are in fact dramatic examples of processes that have been, historically and logically, at the very heart of modernization, development and the transition to capitalism.[4]

As in this book, Cramer replaces the narrow confines of the method-ological individualism of much of economics and political science to look at motivations for fighting in the contexts of actual conflicts. Rather than searching for statistical regularities or game theoretic models, he considers how social coalitions and the presence or absence of certain kinds of actors shape how fighters and commanders translate their per-sonal motivations into action. That violence may lay the groundwork for long-term positive change is an old idea. Karl Marx argues in the first volume of *Capital*: "Force is the midwife of every old society pregnant with a new one."[5] Rather than "development in reverse," war might mark a new stage in the process of violent accumulation of resources with which to finance a stronger state, settle longstanding political con-flicts, and free new social actors to undertake a transformation of the economy.

It is conceivable that such a process might occur in Angola – Cramer's main African case – or in Ethiopia and Rwanda, where rulers are heirs to an enduring state with a long historical experience with bureaucratic institutions. It is much harder, however, to see where the core of stronger state institutions can be found in the context of con-tending warlord rebels and parochial rebels. There are a number of points about politics in these states and about contemporary statehood in Africa more generally that show a different direction for the evolu-tion of warfare in Africa's future. The first is that international pressure is likely to continue to limit the options available to political actors in Africa. As noted in the last chapter, pressure to hold elections may improve political conditions in some countries. But it also may block an authoritarian reformer in a country with weak institutions and that is exposed to the risks of internal disorder. Authoritarian rule, in both its populist and its elitist guises, has served as a bridge for constructing viable political and economic institutions in such notable examples as

---

[4] Christopher Cramer, *Violence in Developing Countries: War, Memory, Progress* (Bloom-ington: Indiana University Press, 2007), 172.

[5] Karl Marx, *Capital*, vol. 1, ch. 31, http://www.marxists.org/archive/marx/works/1867-c1/ch31.htm, accessed 12 April 2011.

Japan, Turkey, Iran, and China. At best one hopes that this authoritarian interlude is just that: a temporary condition. But also there is the tendency for authoritarian rulers and their foreign backers to justify their projects with references to dangers that are no longer present or did not exist in the first place. Even so, there is as yet a poor record of impoverished, war-torn countries turning into self-sustaining examples of democratic and economically prosperous polities. Where democratic processes are sustained with extensive international tutelage, such as in Congo, Liberia, and Sierra Leone, it is not clear that the international community is willing to commit the political will, resources, and attention necessary to see through these closely supervised democratic transformations.

Would-be authoritarian modernizers also face the international constriction of domestic political options, which for Africa now includes prohibitions against military coups, at least in principle. This is a bit like the 1815 Congress of Vienna's efforts to stuff the genie of violent nationalism back into the bottle and restore monarchial order in Europe after the disruptions of the Napoleonic wars. The decision of the African Union (AU) to suspend Mauritania after the 3 August 2005 coup until elections were held in 2007 reflected the AU's support for constitutional principles in member states and for the sanctioning of leaders of coups d'états. Mauritania was suspended again after the 6 August 2008 coup. Guinea was suspended from the body after its 22 December 2008 coup; it now faces the added sanction of a UN panel, which recommended the criminal prosecution of the country's leader after his army killed and abused opposition protestors.[6] This defense of human rights is laudable, and these incidents reveal the genuine popularity in Guinea of this principle. The point here is that the intensification of international intervention further constrains the political options available to political actors in Africa.

From the perspectives of state houses (or army barracks), the possible outcome of conceding to international pressure to hold elections may be to stimulate the factional competition that leads to warlords and parochial rebels and will thus result in the further dissolution of state order. Some international actors may appreciate this tradeoff, and that contributes to the relative ease with which some incumbent political establishments are able to manipulate the electoral process and reforms

---

[6] "Guinea Junta Should Be Tried – UN," *BBC News*, 21 Dec 2009, http://news.bbc.co .uk/2/hi/africa/8425384.stm, accessed 27 May 2010.

in general. In the countries where the politics of patronage has crowded out the fields of leverage that civic groups and rebels alike need to organize their followers, the likely successors to these regimes will be warlords and parochial rebels.

What if regimes that manipulate militias and gang violence undertake real administrative and political reforms and actually manage to survive? The establishment of new limits on politics in these states may mean that fields of leverage for ideological rebels will emerge at a time when populations still have to struggle with the legacies of political violence and wrecked economies. US and European assistance to some African states stresses a sort of counterinsurgency approach in which these foreign governments provide material assistance and training to strengthen the security services of states and to help these governments establish a more durable administrative presence among their own citizens. This is to help reformers build stronger state institutions and to provide more services to hitherto neglected communities. Just as the old counterinsurgency strategy against the rebels who built liberation zones required that the state out-govern the rebels to gain control over populations, the fight against violent patronage politics and corruption requires the construction of well-run formal institutions that can conduct surveillance and provide services to the people in these hitherto ungoverned spaces. Then the social spaces that withering patronage networks and politician-affiliated gangs vacate are supposed to become arenas for the civic groups and businesses that will become the engines of economic prosperity and the forces to focus citizen pressure on governments to ensure accountability and responsive policies. Thus many officials in the security establishments in Europe and the United States assert that they need to help African governments establish state institutional authority as quickly as possible.

If the analysis in this book is correct, instead of civil groups, ideological rebels may appear to take advantage of the social space that real reform of this kind of violent patronage system would vacate. One can find some examples of ideological rebels who have tried to do this. Kenya, for example, has occasionally harbored fighters associated with al-Qaeda who have taken refuge in the anonymity of Nairobi's urban neighborhoods. But it is hard to organize a broad-based radical social movement or to set up "liberated zones" in competition with parochial rebels and their politician patrons for the same social space. As shown in the previous chapter, militias that are tied to politicians can employ young fighters who reject the aims of their patrons yet remain bound within these narrow political confines. Real reform in Kenya just might succeed in limiting the interference from these political networks and lending more autonomy to social networks and organizations. Then the would-be parochial rebel recruits might instead encounter commissars who could begin organizing in these social spaces to create alliances with like-minded people, co-opt local authorities, attack state and foreign forces, and then exploit the popular backlash against this disruption in terms that fit a broader global narrative. A less violent and less corrupt Kenya would still contain marginalized communities and frustrated unemployed school leavers who will readily blame even the improved political situation for their problems. It is not hard to imagine that messages that, for example, blame Western support for the country's corrupt and violent political class for people's everyday hardships would find a lot of resonance. These ideologues could capitalize on Kenya's history of resistance to colonial rule in the Mau Mau rebellion of the 1950s. Their message might include references to the forces of economic globalization and might link them to the discomfort that many people feel about rapidly changing customs and the breakdown of old social certitudes that were previously the provenance of parochial rebels.

Africa has had a dearth of ideological rebellion in recent decades. The massive graft surrounding Nigeria's oil wealth, the poor state of its public services, and the inability or unwillingness of the country's government to ensure citizens' security might suggest that this country has reached a revolutionary threshold. Considerable sectarian tensions in the middle of the country, the presence of violent groups with names such as Taliban (al Sunna wa Jamma, or Followers of the Prophet), and moves by northern governors to appease more radical segments of public opinion with more extensive applications of sharia law would seem to make this place an attractive recruiting ground for ideological groups with broad political narratives like al-Qaeda. But many of these *hisbah* groups and others supporting more extensive applications of sharia law are sponsored by state governments in the manner of the parochial rebels in the Niger Delta. The governor of Zamfara state was a driving force for the organization of the Zamfara State Vigilante Service, charged with enforcing sharia law. These and other organizations provide employment for desperate youth and played instrumental roles in the 2003 and 2007 elections. This has left more autonomous groups like al Sunna wa Jamma, led by former university students, more exposed to the security services after it attacked several police stations. Chances are, however, that it is the efficiency of the political system's co-optive tendencies rather than the efficiency of Nigeria's security services that explains this dearth of radical organizing.

The suggestion here is that a thorough reform of Nigeria's political system could contribute to the rise of violent radical alternatives to the current political paradigm. Yet writing off reform dooms people to insecurity and predatory rule, the perpetuation of a sort of political slum that destabilizes more successful neighbors and leaves people materially worse off and more insecure. But somehow relying on the continuation of this situation to protect foreigners from the perceived threat of a new and radical form of religious extremist internationalism would be a cynical and short-sighted policy indeed. That stance would likely lead to the dominance of warlord and parochial rebels in the event that these patronage-based regimes collapse. And as the history of these regimes in Africa shows, the risk of failure is significant, and once it collapses, it is very hard to restore a central authority.

Alternative Fields of Leverage

Another potential field of leverage may lurk in the societies in which centralized patronage-based authorities and their states disappeared some time ago. A generation of people in Congo, or at least those outside of Kinshasa, has come of age without much personal experience of living under the authority of a central government. Somalia, or at least the southern two-thirds of that country, now hosts a second generation of youths who have had to contend with a range of warlords, parochial rebels, and more ideologically driven alternatives. The mortality of an aging political establishment inherited from the old Somali state – or their decisions to retire in the United States, South Africa, or elsewhere – makes a restoration of the old political network unlikely. Meanwhile, the new leaders who replace these politicians appear to remain trapped in the paradigm of competition between rival warlords and the difficulty of coordinating parochial rebels who arm to protect themselves and their home communities from one another.

The competition among new generations of these rebels may push some leaders to search for a way to gain a decisive advantage over rivals. The dynamic of this kind of competition would resemble that which some scholars observe among radical nationalists outside of Africa. In places such as Yugoslavia in the 1980s, local politicians with very narrow political bases of support sought to widen their appeal through adopting more radical political narratives to differentiate themselves from their more run-of-the-mill rivals. Their rivals recognized the value of this strategy and began to launch their own extreme appeals. A sort of bidding war began in which each leader tried to out-radicalize the other in an effort to rise above the field of competition.[7] Although this bidding war did not appeal to many Yugoslav citizens, it offered new opportunities for marginalized youth to improve their social status, gain access to income, and protect themselves and their families. It also interjected the radical nationalist political narrative into the conflict and became a vehicle to recruit affiliated groups to fight under a single leadership.

Somalia's long-running conflict would be a good place to search for this kind of competition among armed groups. Even if ideologues were very successful in advancing their political narrative, elements of the conflict would continue to be about internal feuding and competition among groups for local power and resources. But this kind of politics creates new openings for the true believers. The ideologues finally would be received as serious actors who are relevant to otherwise parochial concerns. Ideologues again would define the goals of armed groups, and their commissars would shape how fighters would be recruited and disciplined. Existing leaders would have to concede to this new ideological discipline or risk being accused of betrayal of the group's newfound aims. Efforts to make instrumental use of such appeals, a reasonable step for a desperate and ambitious warlord or parochial rebel, could initiate a new process of change. Like the anticolonial rebels, this "post-collapsed state" kind of organization would succeed through its control over the recruitment of fighters and the resources needed to field an armed force. The capacity to field commissars would go a long way to mastering the mechanisms needed to control factionalism. This kind of rebel would be able to eliminate rivals and administer communities under his or her control, a critical step toward convincing the fence-sitters and intimidating opponents into cooperating.

Somalia shows some signs of rebel innovation. Its Harakat al-Shabaab Mujahideen (Movement of Warrior Youth) pays attention to mass media technology to convey its message of rebellion to wider

---

[7] Jack Snyder, *From Voting to Violence: Democratization and Nationalist Conflict* (New York: W.W. Norton, 2000), 68–69.

audiences. YouTube offers an excellent platform for propagandizing accomplishments for groups like HAMAS and Hezbollah[8] but has generally been ignored as a medium among rebels in Africa. The use of propaganda videos among Somali rebels reflects the extent to which these groups try to pursue a population-centric strategy that bypasses their competitors and is accessible to overseas supporters. This would have to be matched with political commissars to aid in recruitment, orientation, and discipline of fighters. These videos at least try to convey that the rebels can protect the people (and also try to intimidate them). Somali rebels stand out among contemporary African rebels for their attention to this organizing strategy.[9] The absence of similar efforts among rebels in an increasingly wired continent reveals the extent to which these counterparts do not try to appropriate popular narratives or contend directly for the devotion and support of non-combatant populations.

Rebel videos, mobile phones, and other decentralized forms of communication suggest another set of future rebel strategies and fields of leverage. Perhaps rebellions and other wars of Africa's future will not be conducted over territories with clearly defined populations typical of the heyday of the anti-colonial and majority rule rebels. A more political approach, as opposed to open warfare, would be the key to finding an appropriate population to convert to the rebel cause. Popular culture that is shared across parochial divides would be an important vehicle for this kind of change. These connections tend to be segmented by generation rather than ethnic group or political faction and could be used to exploit youth anger at the failures of their leaders to protect them or to provide them with the rewards that they see, or at least think they see, in representations of other societies.

This kind of rebel strategy would open up urban areas to revolt and rebel organizing. As the factory floor was to the Marxist of a century ago, the urban slum, coupled with advances in information technologies, would link together individuals to promote a shared consciousness of oppression and grievance. Social networking sites, already popular in many parts of Africa and well suited to linking politically a geographically fragmented population, would provide a new field of leverage that would be independent of the old patronage networks of government

---

[8] A good HAMAS YouTube video is found at http://www.youtube.com/watch?v=3WYH9fwAz4w, accessed 23 Feb 2011.

[9] "Al Shabaab" and "nasheed" as search terms on YouTube produce http://www.youtube.com/watch?v=2-i6sMYkEVE, accessed 23 Feb 2011.

officials, parochial rebels, and warlords. The potential is already on us, as by 2010, Nigeria had 43 million Internet users, about 29 percent of the country's population.[10] The Movement for the Emancipation of the Niger Delta, noted in the previous chapter, also stands out as a group of rebels that make use of this medium, exploiting with limited success the propaganda value of their attacks on oil installations to try to energize a loose coalition of activists and fighters.

The drawback for rebels of this potential new strategy is that it would be difficult for ideological leaders to build hierarchical organizations and discipline fighters. Ideologues would need to find a new key to mobilizing and coordinating populations around a focal cause. They would benefit from the self-recruitment of people who see images or hear news of their deeds, but with this they would have to weather the fragmenting tendencies of this more collaborative network, as individuals react to their local circumstances. This decentralization, however, would provide rebels with protection from counterinsurgents and other rival organizations, as it is much harder to identify this kind of network than it is to map a 1960s or 1970s rebel group's liberated zone. Battling it would require that governments cede considerable degrees of autonomy to their local officials and community groups, a prospect that would frighten many of the continent's more unpopular and insecure regimes. In an even more radical prospect, governments would have to engage their own citizens more deeply.

In any event, there is ample evidence that warfare in Africa is evolving in new directions, and it is likely that elements of these changes are already on us. As the survey of the different categories of African rebels has shown, conflicts in Africa tend to contain elements of multiple types of rebels, even as one type wins out. The task for the observer in the present is to peer at this tapestry of warfare, looking at it as if possessing the hindsight of someone from the future. The hope of this author is that this survey of the history of warfare in Africa goes at least partway to detecting the elements of the present that will write the history of the future.

[10] "Internet World Stats," http://www.internetworldstats.com/stats1.htm, accessed 22 Feb 2011.

Suggested Readings

Chapter 1

Clapham, Christopher. *Africa and the International System: The Politics of State Survival.* New York: Cambridge University Press, 1996.

Dube, Emmanuel. "Relations between Liberation Movements and the OAU," in N. M. Shamuyarira, ed., *Essays on the Liberation of Southern Africa.* Dar es Salaam: Tanzania Publishing House, 1975, 25–68.

McGowan, Patrick. "African Military Coups d'État: 1956–2001." *Journal of Modern African Studies* 41:3 (2003), 339–70.

Scott, James. "Revolution in the Revolution: Peasants and Commissars." *Theory and Society* 7:1 & 2 (1979), 97–134.

Chapter 2

Guinea-Bissau

Cabral, Amilcar. "Brief Analysis of the Social Structure in Guinea," in his *Revolution in Guinea.* New York: Monthly Review Press, 1969.

Chabal, Patrick. *Amilcar Cabral: Revolutionary Leadership and People's War.* New York: Cambridge University Press, 1983.

Chaliand, Gérard. *Armed Struggle in Africa: With the Guerrillas in "Portuguese" Guinea.* New York: Monthly Review Press, 1969.

Davidson, Basil. *The Liberation of Guiné: Aspects of an African Revolution.* Hammondsworth: Penguin, 1968.

Mozambique

Cabrita, João. *Mozambique: The Torturous Road to Democracy.* New York: Palgrave Macmillan, 2001.

257

Finnegan, William. *A Complicated War: The Harrowing of Mozambique*. Berkeley: University of California Press, 1992.

Gersony, Robert. *Summary of Mozambican Refugee Accounts of Principally Conflict Related Experience in Mozambique*. Washington, DC: US Department of State, 1988.

Henriksen, Thomas. *Revolution and Counterrevolution: Mozambique's War of Independence 1964–1974*. Westport, CT: Greenwood, 1983.

Kitchen, Helen. "Conversation with Eduardo Mondlane." *Africa Report* (Nov 1967): 31–51.

Minter, William. *The Mozambican National Resistance (Renamo) as Described by Ex-Participants*. Washington, DC: Georgetown University and African European Institute, 1989.

Mondlane, Eduardo. *The Struggle for Mozambique*. London: Zed, 1969.

Angola

Bridgland, Fred. *Jonas Savimbi: A Key to Africa*. Edinburgh: Mainstream, 1986.

Davidson, Basil. *In the Eye of the Storm*. Garden City, NY: Doubleday, 1972.

Guimarães, Fernando Andresen. *The Origins of the Angolan Civil War*. New York: St. Martin's Press, 2001.

Marcum, John. *The Angolan Revolution, Volume I: The Anatomy of an Explosion (1950–1962)*. Cambridge, MA: MIT Press, 1969.

Marcum, John. *The Angolan Revolution, Volume II: Exile Politics and Guerrilla Warfare, 1962–1976*. Cambridge, MA: MIT Press, 1978.

Chapter 3

Zimbabwe

Cilliers, Jakkie. *Counter-Insurgency in Rhodesia*. London: Croom Helm, 1985.

Lan, David. *Guns and Rain: Guerrillas and Spirit Mediums in Zimbabwe*. London: James Currey, 1985.

Nkomo, Joshua. *The Story of My Life*. London: Methuen, 1984.

Ranger, Terence. *Peasant Consciousness and Guerrilla War in Zimbabwe: A Comparative Study*. Berkeley: University of California Press, 1985.

Reed, William Cyrus. "International Politics and National Liberation: ZANU and the Politics of Contested Sovereignty in Zimbabwe." *African Studies Review* 36:2 (1993): 31–59.

Namibia

Leys, Colin and John Saul. *Namibia's Liberation Struggle: The Two-Edged Sword*. London: James Currey, 1995.

Soggot, David. *Namibia, the Violent Heritage*. New York: St. Martin's Press, 1986.

Stiff, Peter. *The Covert War: Koevoet Operations in Namibia 1979–1989*. Alberton: Galago, 2004.

South Africa

Ellis, Stephen and Tsepo Sechaba. *Comrades against Apartheid: The ANC and the South African Communist Party in Exile*. London: James Currey, 1992.

Gerhart, Gail. *Black Power in South Africa: The Evolution of an Ideology*. Berkeley: University of California Press, 1978.

Johnson, Phyllis and David Martin, eds., *Apartheid Terrorism: The Destruction Report*. London: James Currey, 1989.

Mabaringalala, Nicholas Haysom. *The Rise of Right-Wing Vigilantes in South Africa*. Johannesburg: University of Witwatersrand, 1986.

Chapter 4

de Waal, Alex. "The Politics of Destabilisation in the Horn, 1989–2001," in A. de Waal, ed., *Islamism and Its Enemies in the Horn of Africa*. Addis Ababa: Shama Books, 2004, 182–230.

Lischer, Sarah Kenyon. "Collateral Damage: Humanitarian Assistance as a Cause of Conflict." *International Security* 28:1 (2003): 79–109.

Uganda

Kasfir, Nelson. "Guerrillas and Civilian Participation: The National Resistance Army in Uganda." *Journal of Modern African Studies* 43:2 (2005): 271–96.

Museveni, Yoweri. *Sowing the Mustard Seed*. London: Macmillan, 1997.

Ngoga, Pascal. "Uganda: The National Resistance Army," in Christopher Clapham, ed., *African Guerrillas*. Oxford: James Currey, 1998.

Rwanda

Mushemeza, Elijah Dickens. *The Politics and Empowerment of Banyarwanda Refugees in Uganda, 1959–2001*. Kampala: Fountain, 2007.

Prunier, Gerard. *The Rwanda Crisis*. New York: Columbia University Press, 1995.

Eritrea and Tigray

Berhe, Aregawi. "The Origins of the Tigray People's Liberation Front." *African Affairs* 103:413 (2004): 569–92.

DeMars, William. "Helping People in a People's War: Humanitarian Organizations and the Ethiopian Conflict, 1980–1988," PhD dissertation, University of Notre Dame, 1993.

Pool, David. *From Guerrillas to Government: The Eritrean People's Liberation Front*. Athens: Ohio University Press, 2001.

Young, John. *Peasant Revolution in Ethiopia, the Tigray People's Liberation Front, 1975–1991*. New York: Cambridge University Press, 1997.

Sudan and Somalia

Metelits, Claire. "Reformed Rebels? Democratization, Global Norms and the Sudan People's Liberation Army." *Africa Today* 51:1 (2004): 65–82.

Nyaba, Peter. *The Politics of Liberation in South Sudan: An Insider's View*. Kampala: Fountain, 1997.

Prunier, Gerard. "A Candid View of the Somali National Movement." *Horn of Africa* 14:1–4 (1991): 107–20.

Chapter 5

Blok, Anton. "The Peasant and the Brigand: Social Banditry Reconsidered." *Comparative Studies in Society and History* 14:4 (Sept 1972), 494–503.

West African Conflicts

Abdullah, Ibrahim. "Bush Path to Destruction: The Origin and Character of the Revolutionary United Front (RUF/SL)." *Africa Development* 22:3 (1997): 45–76.

Abraham, Arthur. "War and Transition to Peace: A Study of State Conspiracy in Perpetuating Armed Conflict." *Africa Development* 22:3 (1997): 101–16.

Ellis, Stephen. *The Mask of Anarchy: The Destruction of Liberia and the Religious Dimensions of an African Civil War*. New York: New York University Press, 1999.

Gberie, Lansana. *A Dirty War in West Africa: The RUF and the Destruction of Sierra Leone*. London: Hurst, 2005.

Konate, Yacouba. "Les enfants de la balle: de la FESCI aux mouvements des patriots." *Politique Africaine* 89 (2003): 49–70.

Ogunleye, Bayo. *Behind Rebel Line: Anatomy of Charles Taylor's Hostage Camps*. Enugu: Delta, 1995.

United Nations Security Council. *Report of the Panel of Experts Appointed Pursuant to United Nations Security Council Resolution 1306 (2000), Paragraph 19 in Relation to Sierra Leone*. New York: United Nations, Dec 2000.

Somalia

Compagnon, Daniel. "Somali Armed Movements," in Christopher Clapham, ed., *African Guerrillas*. Oxford: James Currey, 1998, 73–90.

Drysdale, John. *Whatever Happened to Somalia?* London: HAAN Associates, 1994.

Dualeh, Hussein Ali. *From Barre to Aideed: Somalia, Agony of a Nation*. Nairobi: Stellagraphics, 1994.

Gassem, Mariam Arif. *Hostages: The People Who Kidnapped Themselves*. Nairobi: Central Graphics Services, 1994.

Marchal, Roland. "Les *mooryan* de Mogadisco: formes de la violence dans un espace urbain en guerre." *Cahiers d'Etudes Africaines* 33:130 (1993): 295–320.

Congo

Clark, John, ed., *The African States of the Congo War*. Kampala: Fountain, 2003.

Nzongola-Ntalaja, Georges. *The Congo from Leopold to Kabila*. New York: Zed Books, 2002.

Prunier, Gérard. *From Genocide to Continental War: The "Congolese" Conflict and the Crisis of Contemporary Africa*. London: Hurst, 2009.

Reyntjens, Filip. *The Great African War: Congo and Regional Geopolitics, 1996–2006*. New York: Cambridge University Press, 2009.

United Nations Security Council. *Addendum to the Report of the Panel of Experts on the Illegal Exploitation of Natural Resources and Other Forms of Wealth of DR Congo*. New York: United Nations, 10 Nov 2001.

Vlassenroot, Koen and Timothy Raeymaekers. "The Politics of Rebellion and Intervention in Ituri: The Emergence of a New Political Complex?" *African Affairs* 103:412 (2004): 385–412.

Chapter 6

Bazenguissa-Ganga, Rémy. "The Spread of Political Violence in Congo-Brazzaville." *African Affairs* 98:390 (1999): 37–54.

Chabal, Patrick and Jean-Pascal Daloz. *Africa Works: Disorder as Political Instrument*. Oxford: James Currey, 1999.

Rashid, Ismael. "Subaltern Reactions: Lumpens, Students, and the Left." *Africa Development* 22:3 (1997): 19–43.

Kenya

Anderson, David. "Vigilantes, Violence and the Politics of Public Order in Kenya." *African Affairs* 101 (2002): 531–55.

Human Rights Watch. *Ballots to Bullets: Organized Political Violence and Kenya's Crisis of Governance*. New York: Human Rights Watch, 2008.

Kagwanja, Mwangi. *Killing the Vote: State Sponsored Violence and Flawed Elections in Kenya*. Nairobi: Kenya Human Rights Commission, 1998.

Nowrojee, Binaifer. *Divide and Rule: State-Sponsored Ethnic Violence in Kenya*. New York: Africa Watch, 1993.

Republic of Kenya. *Commission of Inquiry into Post Election Violence* [The Waki Report]. Nairobi: Government Printer, 2008.

Nigeria

Abdullahi Smith Centre for Historical Research. *Election Violence in Nigeria, the Terrible Experience, 1952–2002*. Kaduna: Vanguard Printers, 2002.

Bob, Clifford. *The Marketing of Rebellion: Insurgents, Media, and International Activism*. New York: Cambridge University Press, 2005.

Human Rights Watch. *Criminal Politics: Violence, "Godfathers" and Corruption in Nigeria*. New York: Human Rights Watch, Oct 2007.

Momoh, Abubakar. "Area Boys and the Nigerian Political Crisis." Unpublished paper, Department of Political Science, University of Lagos, no date [1998].

Ukiwo, Ukoha. "From 'Pirates' to 'Militants': A Historical Perspective on Anti-State and Anti-Oil Company Mobilization among the Ijaw of Warri, Western Niger Delta." *African Affairs* 106 (2007): 587–610.

Index

CPSIA information can be obtained at www.ICGtesting.com
Printed in the USA
LVOW12s0946210813

348845LV00004B/275/P